Creative Expression and the Law

Nancy J. Whitmore
Eugene S. Pulliam
School of Journalism and
Creative Media at Butler University

ROWMAN & LITTLEFIELD
Lanham • Boulder • New York • London

Acquisition Editor: Natalie Mandziuk
Acquisition Assistant: Sylvia Landis
Sales and Marketing Inquiries: textbooks@rowman.com

Credits and acknowledgments for material borrowed from other sources, and reproduced with permission, appear on the appropriate page within the text.

Published by Rowman & Littlefield
An imprint of The Rowman & Littlefield Publishing Group, Inc.
4501 Forbes Boulevard, Suite 200, Lanham, Maryland 20706
www.rowman.com

86-90 Paul Street, London EC2A 4NE, United Kingdom

British Library Cataloguing in Publication Information Available

Library of Congress Cataloging-in-Publication Data Available

ISBN: 978-1-5381-2706-3 (coth)
ISBN: 978-1-5381-2707-0 (paperback)
ISBN: 978-1-5381-2708-7 (ebook)

♾™ The paper used in this publication meets the minimum requirements of American National Standard for Information Sciences—Permanence of Paper for Printed Library Materials, ANSI/NISO Z39.48-1992.

Contents

Introduction

More now than ever, we live in a world awash in individual expression and user-generated content. The ability to engage, copy, share, and recreate that expression has never been easier, and the impulse to create has never been stronger and more widespread. As a highly valued and encouraged human attribute, expressive creativity brings with it a need to understand the legal protections and constraints that most often arise from the production of creative works of communication. This book is devoted to that understanding.

Creative Expression and the Law is written for students who are preparing for and individuals who are engaged in careers as professional content creators. The book's aim is to help students, creative entrepreneurs, and professionals better comprehend the areas of communication law most closely connected to creative endeavors. Accordingly, much of the book is devoted to those areas of law that can be applied in practice when communicators are generating ideas, producing content, and protecting their creative work.

To foster a comprehensive understanding of communication law, this book also explores the purpose behind each legal area and draws connections among them in an attempt to show how each area of law fits together in an overall framework. In doing so, the development of legal thinking is explored as an evolving story shaped by the US Constitution and its commitment to freedom of speech. As new avenues of expression emerge, it is important for professional communicators to be conscious of the constitutional through line that fuses together what are often viewed as disparate legal areas. To accomplish this goal, the book uses cases and case outcomes to explain and illustrate overarching legal thought rather than engage in a lengthy and detailed case analysis. Infographics and visual examples of creative work found at the center of legal disputes are also used to aid in the explanation of legal principles and standards. These images are an important part of this text given the role that visual cues play in helping us—as content creators—learn, retain, and utilize information.

The book begins where modern legal thought on freedom of speech began, with an exploration of the vital role ideas play in American society. Even ideas we loathe and that challenge traditional ways of thinking have great value in our democratic system. The open debate conflicting viewpoints provoke allows us to develop new cultural attitudes and move society forward. Given this valued outcome, we learn that the First Amendment is designed to err on the side of allowing viewpoints into the marketplace of ideas rather than restricting them.

Based on the marketplace framework, chapter 1 explains how free speech claims are analyzed and decided by courts. This discussion includes an examination of the role, development, and application of legal standards to case facts, and the various activities that fall under the "speech" protection of the First Amendment. This chapter also fosters an appreciation for the breadth of protection the First Amendment provides for expressive activities and lays the groundwork for the discussion that follows.

With the constitutional groundwork clearly established, the text introduces the story of commercial and corporate speech and explores their place within this structure. In doing so, chapter 2 compares the function and characteristics of commercial expression with the purpose upon which free speech law rests. This chapter includes detailed information regarding the test that courts have adopted to adjudicate restrictions on commercial speech as well as the issues surrounding the definition of commercial speech. This chapter aims to provide a firm understanding of the law governing commercial and corporate speech and the constraints and freedoms under which these speakers work.

Beginning with chapter 3, the book shifts its focus from disputes directed at government restrictions on speech to cases between content creators. Throughout history, authors and artists have borrowed ideas from the past and reimagined and reinvented them into works of the present. This expressive process has been fueled by both the freedom to create and right to protect that creation through copyright law. Viewed as an "engine of free expression," copyright law was enacted to stimulate the production of creative works by granting an intellectual property right in products of the mind. In doing so, the law sets up an inherent tension between the First Amendment's free speech guarantees and the restriction on expression that occurs with the ownership of a copyright. Chapter 3 explores this tension and the central elements of copyright law. It also provides a general understanding of the law's purpose and placement within a First Amendment framework.

Central to the placement of copyright law within a First Amendment framework is the protection transformative works receive from the affirmative defense of fair use. Chapter 4 focuses on fair use and explains what transformation means in law and to the marketplace and why—from a theoretical perspective—a transformative use is less likely to interfere with the economic interest of a copyright owner. In its exploration of the role transformation has played in the outcome of lawsuits involving intellectual property and creative expression, this chapter spotlights works that were found to be transformative and those that were not. The intent in doing so is to show how fair use is applied to new creative endeavors that are constructed from copyrighted works.

The concept of transformation is also an important consideration in the unauthorized use of a celebrity's name or likeness in a commercial context. Through a patchwork of state right of publicity laws, celebrities have an intellectual property right in their name and likeness that allows them to reap the economic benefits of their fame as well as to control the type of commercial exposure they receive. As in copyright law, this right has First Amendment implications in that it restricts the use of a celebrity's identity in a commercial context. Chapter 5 provides a general overview of the the-oretical underpinnings and central prongs of right of publicity law. As with chapters 3 and 4, the intent is to identify common characteristics among creative endeavors that resulted in right of publicity lawsuits and to tie those characteristics to the concept of transformation. The goal is to provide a more detailed understanding of the uses held to be transformative and a fair use of a celebrity's likeness.

The likelihood of consumer confusion is a central component in trademark, trade dress, and false association law. Chapter 6 examines this concept and looks at creative works that were likely to cause consumer confusion to the marketplace and works that were not. In doing so, the chapter explains these areas of trademark law and uses case law to analyze creative endeavors from a legal perspective in an effort to better understand how to create works that are less likely to confuse the marketplace and run afoul of trademark law.

Chapters 7 and 8 examine two specific areas of trademark law: trademark dilution and false advertising. Chapter 7 explores dilution, a fairly new area of trademark law and one that does not involve the concept of consumer confusion in its adjudication. This chapter examines dilution law and creative works that were held to dilute famous marks and works that did not. Chapter 8 examines marketing techniques that have triggered claims of false advertising. Special emphasis in this chapter is placed on advertising that constituted either an implied false message or a literally true but misleading advertisement. Both types of false messages can occur from highly creative advertising.

The book ends where it begins with the American idea of freedom of speech. Only this time, it focuses on false statements of fact that harm the reputations of public and private figures. In this realm, the First Amendment provides a level of free speech protection that is virtually unmatched throughout the world. As a result of the stunning unanimous Supreme Court decision in *New York Times v. Sullivan*, state-based libel law has developed into a complex area of law that sharply favors the public interest in robust debate at the expense of reputational interests. Chapter 9 explores that complexity as well as the extension of First Amendment protection into the disclosure of private facts and intrusion upon seclusion.

Because much of the information contained in this book is based on case law, detailed citations are included at the end of each chapter along with the definitions of key terms used in the chapter. I encourage readers to explore the endnotes and the cases and other material cited. The cases used in the book have much to teach us not only about communication law but about the expressive spirit that resides in all of us. To that point, I want to express my profound gratitude to the artists and small business owners who so graciously permitted me to share their creative expression with you. The inclusion of their works is key to helping visual communicators develop a more comprehensive understanding of creative expression and the law. It is an honor to include their works and their stories in this book.

1

Freedom of Expression

In law, there is no better friend to a communication professional than the First Amendment to the US Constitution. Ratified in 1791, the First Amendment places strong limits on government power and in so doing guarantees certain rights and freedoms to the people of the United States. Chief among these limitations is the amendment's restriction on the government's power to abridge the freedom of the American people to engage in expressive activities.

Amendment I

Congress shall make no law respecting an establishment of religion, or prohibiting the free exercise thereof; or abridging the freedom of speech, or of the press; or the right of the people peaceably to assemble, and to petition the government for a redress of grievances.

Today's broad-based protection against government interference with speech activities did not come easily. It developed over the centuries, one **case** and one **opinion** at a time. The body of law from which we draw our understanding of the free speech clause of the First Amendment continues to evolve as the **judicial system** repeatedly grapples with important and controversial free speech questions, many of which have arisen through changes in communication technology and culture.

As new questions of law arise, it is important for professional communicators to understand the ideas and distinctions that shape the constitutional protection afforded expressive activities. These general principles and legal framework give free speech law its stability and set the ground rules against which every law enacted to regulate expression plays. This means that regardless of whether creative expression is embroiled in an intellectual property dispute, a libel claim, or an outright infringement battle with the government, it rests on a legal foundation built by the rules, principles, and concepts established in First Amendment case law.

ORIGIN OF THE MODERN FIRST AMENDMENT

While the First Amendment was ratified in 1791, it was largely uncontested until the twentieth century. The origin of what some call the modern First Amendment can largely be traced to the early 1900s and US involvement in World War I. Prior to World War I, courts usually ignored free speech claims and exhibited widespread hostility to the value of free expression to a democratic society.[1] As a result, the scope of the government's constitutional power to restrict free speech rights was largely unknown as the United States entered the twentieth century and found itself embroiled in a world war.

In an effort to suppress opposition to or interference with the war effort, Congress passed the Espionage Act in 1917. The act prohibited any attempt to promote insubordination in the military or interfere with military recruitment or military operations. A year later the Espionage Act was amended to allow for the criminalization of "any disloyal, profane, scurrilous or abusive language" about the US government or the nation's Constitution, flag, or military forces. Violations of the Espionage Act were punishable by a fine of $10,000 and/or prison sentences of up to twenty years. Some two thousand arrests were made that resulted in nearly nine hundred convictions.

On **appeal** to the **US Supreme Court**, several **defendants** challenged their convictions on First Amendment grounds. The majority of the justices were largely unsympathetic to these claims and refused to engage any broad philosophical questions regarding the purpose and scope of the free speech clause. It wasn't until the fall of 1919 that two justices began to tackle the question of why—as a nation—we should value and protect expression that we oppose or find objectionable.

In his **dissenting opinion** in *Abrams v. United States*, Justice Oliver Wendell Holmes Jr., joined by Justice Louis D. Brandeis, introduced the **marketplace of ideas** concept to affirm free speech protection of wartime dissent. In time, the marketplace of ideas theory became embedded in First Amendment law. Today, it is the central organizing principle upon which free speech law rests.

Dissenting Opinion

Though a dissenting opinion—even from the US Supreme Court—is not binding as **precedent**, it has the ability to spur a dialogue within the legal community that can lead to modifications and changes in legal thought and subsequent opinions.

Marketplace of Ideas Theory

The marketplace of ideas theory begins with the vital role ideas play in an open, free, and democratic society. Even those ideas that we vehemently oppose and will eventually discard have great value in a democratic system because they challenge traditional ways of thinking and help us develop new cultural attitudes and progressive approaches. The collision of a wide variation of ideas produced by a properly functioning marketplace also allows us to refine and strengthen core beliefs that have withstood the stress of scrutiny over time.

Throughout its history, the marketplace of ideas theory has helped to define the purpose of the free speech clause and the degree of protection the clause provides against government interference with expressive activities. Today, the First Amendment is used as the primary legal tool to secure a wide variation of viewpoints in the marketplace. In doing so, the amendment has provided broad-based protection for individual expression against the expectations and attitudes of the majority. This protection extends even to ideas society finds offensive and forms a bedrock principle upon which First Amendment law is built.

For more than a century, the amendment has been called upon to provide a shield against government regulation of the street-corner speaker espousing unpopular ideas. Because ideas are so important to the proper functioning of our free speech system, First Amendment law operates from the belief that the more speech in the marketplace, the better it will function. This means that the remedy for bad speech and harmful ideas is more good speech, not restriction of offensive speech. First Amendment law is designed, therefore, to err on the side of allowing ideas and viewpoints into the marketplace rather than in restricting or punishing them. In doing so, the law recognizes government's power and strong desire to manipulate public information to achieve its political aims. It also recognizes that the marketplace of ideas must be free from such control. For only an unregulated marketplace has the ability to effectively expose, vet, and filter the persistent supply of ideas it receives so that a small percentage can withstand public scrutiny and ultimately survive.

> **Distrust of Government**
>
> Free speech law is built largely on a distrust of government power. In his dissent in *Abrams*, Justice Holmes acknowledged the strong desire by those in power to "sweep away all opposition" in order to achieve their political aims.[2]

Viewpoint Restrictions

In 1919, Jacob Abrams faced twenty years in prison for distributing leaflets that called on American workers to unite against the government and its military mission. While Abrams was not arrested for committing the unlawful action he advocated, he was eventually imprisoned for urging others to revolt and strike. In his dissent in *Abrams v. United States*, Justice Holmes articulated the **clear and present danger test** in an attempt to determine when the US government could constitutionally punish a speaker for advocating illegal conduct. While the government has broad powers to punish lawless behavior, the First Amendment impedes the use of that power to punish speech activities, such as advocacy. In factual situations where a speaker is urging others to violate the law, the clear and present danger test provides judges with guidance in determining where the line lies between protected speech and unprotected speech. While no bright lines exist in First Amendment law, the test allows government to constitutionally restrict speech *if the speech is intended and likely to cause imminent violence*. Situations where grave and serious danger is likely to occur before there is time to reason or talk through the situation would rise to a level of "imminent" lawlessness. In these circumstances, government can constitutionally restrict the advocacy that is fueling the emergency situation.

The imminent lawless standard illustrates the degree to which speech is protected under the First Amendment. This concept instructs the nation that suppression of an expressive activity based on its message is constitutionally justified only as a last resort—when various other forms of control have failed to address the situation. The purpose of this last resort approach is to preserve as many viewpoints as possible in the marketplace. It accomplishes this task by drawing the line between advocacy and incitement as close to violent conduct as possible. In this way only a small sliver of speech is removed from marketplace of ideas. This last resort approach also reduces the **chilling effect** that occurs when speakers are afraid to engage in protected speech activities because they fear they will be arrested and creates the **breathing space** speakers need to feel safe when they are expressing their views.

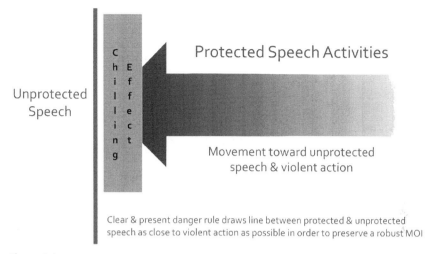

Figure 1.1.

Chilling effect and breathing space are two important concepts in free speech law. Another related concept is a **distrust of government**. Free speech law is built on the idea that government has the power and the incentive to manipulate public debate by suppressing ideas or information it doesn't like and favoring ideas and information it does like. We see this concept play out during election season when officials who are currently in power and want to remain in power are motivated to suppress any viewpoints that are critical of their performance. Free speech law recognizes this motivation and has been structured to curtail it as well as to ensure that as many viewpoints as possible are able to enter the marketplace.

LIMITING GOVERNMENT POWER

Courts have the power of **judicial review**. This means that they have the power to review and determine whether a law or government action violates the Constitution. The doctrine of judicial review gives judges the authority to strike down a law—to declare it null and void—if they determine the law is unconstitutional. Armed with this authority, judges are left to determine how intensely a case needs to be examined. When cases involve government action that restricts or compels speech based on its viewpoint, message, or idea, judges strictly scrutinize case facts. In this way, courts make government officials prove that their actions were not intended to favor or disfavor some viewpoints over others. This level of review—known as **strict scrutiny**—is very difficult for government officials to pass, and is, therefore, reserved for claims involving the curtailment of certain fundamental rights.

Strict Scrutiny Review

Under strict scrutiny review, a heavy burden falls on government to show that its regulation is *narrowly tailored to advance a compelling government interest*. In the application of this review standard to a set of facts, government will need to demonstrate that the regulation is

1. Attempting to further a **compelling government interest**
2. Is necessary to advance the compelling interest
3. Is narrowly crafted to restrict only those expressive activities that allow government to achieve the compelling interest

Prong 1: The Compelling Government Interest

Federal, state, and local governments enact laws, make decisions, and take actions to further a public interest or concern. For example, laws that regulate the size, placement, and condition of billboards along state highways are often enacted to

1. Advance traffic safety by decreasing the visual clutter such signage produces and
2. Maintain the natural beauty of the environment through which the highway runs.

Traffic safety and the attractiveness of an area are the interests government is trying to advance through regulation. While both are legitimate government interests, traffic safety would most likely be viewed as a highly important and overriding objective for the government to achieve. Courts have labeled such interests as compelling. While no definitive set of criteria exists that defines a compelling interest, courts have held interests such as protecting the public's health, safety, and security; maintaining a stable political and election system; safeguarding the physical and psychological well-being of minors; protecting children from indecent speech; and preventing racial discrimination to be compelling.

Compelling interests come into play when laws that restrict content based on its message are constitutionally challenged. In such cases, the government is required to show that it is furthering a compelling interest through its regulation of speech. In relation to the hypothetical above, this would mean that a billboard signage law that restricted a specific viewpoint, say opinions critical of the state's governor, would not pass strict scrutiny review if the law was enacted solely to maintain an aesthetically pleasing roadside area. Instead, the government would be called upon to show that the regulation is intended to advance a compelling interest, such as traffic safety.

Prong 2: Advancing the Compelling Interest

If a court concludes that the interest is compelling, the next step in the review process is to determine whether the restriction actually advances the interest. A regulation advances the interest when the harms the government seeks to alleviate are real, not merely speculative, and the restriction diminishes those harms in a direct and substantial way.

Let's go back to the hypothetical situation. Here we have a law that bans content on billboards that is critical of the governor. The ban is necessary, according to the law, to achieve a substantial decrease in traffic accidents. Under prong two of strict scrutiny review, the government would need to show that traffic accidents do occur on this stretch of highway and that prohibiting a message critical of the governor would reduce those accidents to a material degree. To successfully pass this prong, the government would need to rely on a sufficiently persuasive common-sense argument or some empirical evidence to support its rationale. Because all sorts of signage distract drivers, it would be extremely difficult to convince a court that the elimination of just one particular message would actually decrease driver distraction and improve traffic safety. If the government failed to satisfy this prong, the court would strike down the regulation as unconstitutional. To pass strict scrutiny, the government must demonstrate that its regulation fulfills all three prongs.

Prong 3: Narrowly Tailoring the Regulation

While prong 2 examines whether the action government wants to take will actually further the compelling interest it is trying to achieve, prong 3 examines the fit between the amount of speech restricted and the advancement of the objective. In the application of the narrowly tailored prong, courts examine how precisely the regulation has been crafted. Evidence of one or more of the following three elements will most likely render the regulation unconstitutional.

Over-inclusiveness: A regulation will not pass strict scrutiny review if it restricts a significant amount of speech that *is not* applicable to the interest. This requires the government to demonstrate that the amount of speech restricted is necessary and relevant to advance the compelling interest. While perfect tailoring is largely impossible, regulations that burden speech that is unrelated to the goals government is pursuing are susceptible to a finding of over-inclusiveness.

Under-inclusiveness: The flip side of over-inclusive is under-inclusive or laws that fail to restrict a significant amount of speech that *is* applicable to the interest. For example, a law that restricts minors from purchasing violent video games in an effort to curb aggressive behavior may be viewed as under-inclusive given that the regulation does not include other applicable media that minors are likely to access. A regulation that is under-inclusive is viewed with skepticism. In the example, government is not actually alleviating the harm it associates with violent video games when it allows minors to actively engage with other forms of aggression-inducing media. This suggests that the stated objective is not legitimate but rather a disguise for government's desire to favor one form of speech and suppress another.

Least restrictive alternative: The narrowly tailored prong also requires an examination of whether a nonspeech alternative would work essentially as well as the speech restriction at furthering government's stated objective. In the example, a court may find that a public service campaign or other educational materials directed at parents would work equally as well as or better than a prohibition on video-game purchases. In this case, the regulation would fail the narrowly tailored requirement as government has additional tools that do not affect protected First Amendment activities that it could use to alleviate the harm of consuming violent media.

The least restrictive alternative requirement is also applied in situations where options exist that secure the interest but are less restrictive to speech. These situations differ from the over-inclusive inquiry in that the amount of speech restricted is associated with achieving the interest, but alternatives exist that allow government to restrict less speech and still realize its objective.

The difficulty of successfully meeting the strict scrutiny standard reinforces the value the US Constitution places on public participation in the ideas market. It also applies pressure on public officials to craft laws and take actions that achieve the government's objective without diminishing or skewing the debate that takes place in the marketplace.

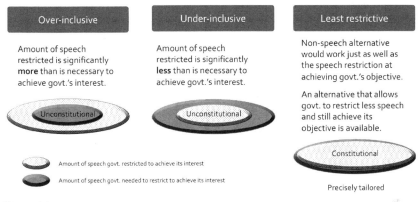

Figure 1.2.

Scrutiny Standards

- Provide a common starting point for reasoning in a case
- Mandate order that a series of legal questions must be answered
- Help retain a consistency in law
- Provide guidance to the judiciary and help prevent judicial bias

---

Expressive Conduct

While the ultimate goal of free speech law is to foster debate on public issues, the word "speech" in the amendment's free speech clause has been held to cover much more than oral and written communication. Over the years, courts have provided First Amendment protection to a variety of activities that implicate both speech and nonspeech conduct. The distinction between speech and conduct is important given the lower level of scrutiny courts generally give to constitutional challenges of laws that do not involve fundamental rights. Most laws that regulate everyday conduct as well as those that regulate unprotected speech fall into that class and are routinely upheld as constitutional if they are *logically related to a legitimate government objective*. This form of scrutiny is known as **rational basis review**. It is the most relaxed level of judicial scrutiny applied by the courts and differs from strict scrutiny review in a number of ways.

First is the high regard courts display toward the government's position. Under the rational basis review, courts generally presume that government's action is constitutional. This runs counter to strict scrutiny review which presumes the opposite—that the government's action is unconstitutional. Additionally, under rational basis review, the burden of proof is placed on the party challenging the law—rather than the government. This essentially requires the **plaintiff** to show that the law at issue is *not* rationally related to every single conceivable interest that might support the government's action. Lastly and perhaps most importantly, courts do not question how significant the interest is, insist on proof that the regulation is an effective means of advancing the interest, or seriously examine any alternative means by which government could have achieved its objectives. A regulation may even be based on a reasonable speculation unsupported by evidence.[3] Instead, all that is needed is a legitimate government purpose that is rationally related to the regulation. Moreover, the motivation for the regulation does not need to be asserted by the government. The court may even provide its own justification for the law. Given its lax requirements, it is quite easy for government to enact laws that satisfy rational basis review.

Many times throughout our nation's history, illegal conduct, such as burning draft cards and flags, blocking entrances, erecting tents, and occupying public spaces, has been used to express a message. These actions raise an interesting constitutional question given that the prohibited conduct used to send the message can be constitutionally curtailed under the rational basis standard. However, if this low level of review was applied to **expressive conduct**, the lack of judicial scrutiny that would result would effectively allow the government to suppress unfavorable viewpoints through restrictions on the conduct used to convey those views. Understanding that expressive conduct implicates both the strict scrutiny and rational basis review standards, the court developed a mid or intermediate level of examination that is not as protective of free speech rights as strict scrutiny but also not as favorable to government action as rational basis review. Intermediate scrutiny review is used to decide cases where prohibited conduct is employed to communicate a message. This level of review was designed to

1. Preserve government's power to restrict illegal conduct and advance nonspeech objectives and
2. Prevent government from using that power to regulate behavior in order to manipulate the ideas market or silence critics.

Today, protesters charged with violating a statute that prohibits the burning of the national flag or erecting tents in public places may challenge the arrest on First Amendment grounds. In these cases, a court must first determine whether the conduct at issue qualifies for free speech protection. While a limitless variety of activities can be labeled as speech, the actions that actually receive free speech protection must exhibit the following two qualities:

1. The speaker intended to convey a particular message and
2. The likelihood is great that those who view it will understand the message.[4]

Once an individual's conduct satisfies these two prongs, it is considered expressive conduct. At that point, the speaker can raise a First Amendment challenge to a restriction on the nonspeech conduct used to send the message. By applying intermediate scrutiny to such a challenge, courts recognize both the speech and nonspeech elements in expressive conduct and provide a level of review that respects the valuable role ideas play in the marketplace and the essential responsibility government has to control illegal conduct independent of its potential to convey a message.

Activities that have received First Amendment protection as expressive conduct:

- Tattoos and tattooing
- Liking on Facebook
- Playing video games
- Wearing of armbands
- Raising one's fist in the air
- Parades and marches
- Flag burning and burning a draft card
- Picketing, solicitation, and begging
- Honking a car horn
- A wedding ceremony
- Artistic expression and nude dancing

Time, Place and Manner Regulations

The intermediate scrutiny standard is also employed in factual situations where government attempts to merely reroute a speech activity. Examples include regulations that restrict the placement and size of billboards or the location and time of parades or marches. These restrictions differ from regulations that target a nonspeech activity that is totally unconnected from any potential for speech. With **time, place, and manner regulations**, the restriction on speech is not unintended. Instead these restrictions are designed to redirect speech within the marketplace but not remove it, and are, therefore, viewed as less restrictive of First Amendment rights.

Nevertheless, time, place, and manner regulations can severely curb the impact and reach of certain expressive activities and with that may be motivated by a desire by government officials to discriminate among ideas while appearing as if they are pursuing nonspeech objectives. For example, cities hosting national political conventions may attempt to limit the visibility of protesters by locating free speech zones and parade routes miles away from the site of the convention. In 2016, Cleveland prohibited free speech activities within a 3.3-square-mile radius around the convention site. Within this "event zone," such activities as marches and large gatherings without a permit and electronically amplified speeches were banned. The event zone, the largest for a national political convention at the time, was reduced to 1.7 square miles after a federal judge struck down the city's original plan on First Amendment grounds. Additionally, the designated parade route, which took participants over a bridge and out of sight and earshot of the city center, was altered to increase the visibility of demonstrators.

Levels of Judicial Review

Rational Basis Review	Intermediate Scrutiny Review	Strict Scrutiny Review
Applied to laws that do **not** limit speech in any way & laws that regulate unprotected speech.	**Applied** in situations where: 1. prohibited conduct was used to communicate a message or 2. govt. imposed a time, place or manner regulation on speech activities.	**Applied** in situations where govt. has restricted or compelled speech based on its content. This includes the message, idea, viewpoint or subject matter of the speech or the identity of the speaker.
1. Regulation is presumed to be constitutional if restriction is rationally related to a legitimate govt. interest. 2. Court largely defers to govt.'s judgment and does not seriously examine whether other ways of achieving the objective would be more effective.	Burden of proof is on the government to show: 1. Regulation actually furthers an important govt interest. 2. Regulation does **not** restrict expression on basis of viewpoint or impact of the message on an audience. 3. Any incidental restriction on free speech does **not** burden **substantially** more speech than is necessary to advance govt.'s interest, i.e. the regulation is not **overinclusive**. 4. Ample alternative forums exist for communicating the message to its intended audience.	Burden of proof is on the government to show: 1. Compelling interest is present. 2. Restriction is necessary to advance the compelling interest. 3. Means used to achieve compelling interest is least restrictive of expression, i.e. no non-speech alternatives will work or no alternatives that restrict less speech will work. 4. Means used to achieve the objective is **not** underinclusive or overinclusive.

Figure 1.3.

Intermediate Scrutiny

Intermediate scrutiny consists of four prongs that are applied to First Amendment challenges of conduct-based and time, place, and manner regulations. (See figure 1.3). Prong 1: To pass prong one of this standard, the government must show that the law at issue advances an important—rather than compelling—interest. This means that a restriction that furthers a legitimate nonspeech interest, such as limiting visual clutter or reducing the wear and tear on a public park, is sufficient enough to pass the first prong of the standard. Prong one will most likely not present much of a hurdle for government in cases where the regulation is clearly content neutral and the restriction on the speech activity is negligible. In such cases, the judiciary is less likely to seriously examine the degree to which the nonspeech objective is furthered.

Clark v. Community of Non-Violence illustrates this point. In *Clark*, a group of demonstrators received a permit from the National Park Service (NPS) to erect two symbolic tent cities on parkland in Washington, DC. The purpose of the demonstration was to draw attention to the plight of homelessness in the United States. To accomplish this goal, the group intended to actually sleep in the symbolic tents, but the Park Service denied their application for a permit to do so while allowing them to stage a twenty-four-hour vigil at the site. Because the sleep activity was an intended element of the group's overall message, the permit denial triggered a constitutional challenge.

The Park Service based their denial on an NPS regulation that permitted sleeping activities only in designated campgrounds in order to limit the wear and tear on park property. In their scrutiny of prong one, the justices split into two camps. The dissenting camp maintained that the actual sleep function would not damage park property in any meaningful manner and thus no substantial government interest was served by the restriction. The majority countered that the sleeping prohibition avoided some actual or threatened wear and tear on parklands. In this case where the restricted sleep activity is not central to the overall message, and the overall message is still allowed to effectively enter the marketplace, the majority was willing to accept the regulation. The *Clark* opinion is important in that it exposes how intermediate scrutiny review can be used to uphold a content-neutral regulation on expressive conduct even though the regulation is ineffective at furthering the government's objectives.[5]

Content Neutral versus Content Based

The primary purpose of the intermediate scrutiny standard is to restrain government's strong incentive and power to censor particular viewpoints and messages. The standard accomplishes this by requiring government to treat all speech in a similar fashion regardless of its message. Referred to as the content-neutral distinction, the second prong of the intermediate scrutiny standard examines whether the government's action can be justified without reference to the content of the regulated speech. Regulations that single out a particular viewpoint or message for differential treatment will fail the content-neutral prong and may be subject to strict scrutiny review.

As an organizing framework, the content-based/content-neutral distinction provides judges with an effective way to review the facts of a case and categorize the First Amendment issues that the facts raise. Cases where the facts indicate that the government is regulating expression out of a concern for the ideas expressed are viewed as **content based** and reviewed under strict scrutiny. On the other hand, factual situations where the government regulates expression without any regard for the ideas expressed are viewed as content neutral and reviewed under intermediate scrutiny. This distinction is important given that under strict scrutiny review, government restrictions are rarely permissible.

While the content-based/content-neutral distinction allows the judiciary to respond to a variety of free speech issues in a fairly predictable and structured manner, the determination of what exactly constitutes a "content-based" regulation is not necessarily a clear-cut decision.

Courts agree that viewpoint or message-based regulations are content based given their ability to distort public debate and exclude particular points of view from the marketplace. But court opinions have differed on whether restrictions that discriminate based on the subject matter of the speech should be considered content based. Some regulations, such as those that target sexually explicit speech for strict zoning restrictions or prohibit a public schoolteacher from presenting material unrelated to the class subject, are viewed as less threatening to core First Amendment values than restrictions on a particular idea or message. For this reason, in certain circumstances, courts have concluded that subject-matter restrictions are content based only when the regulation also discriminates on the basis of the speaker's message.

Keep in mind that First Amendment freedoms are in the most danger when the government's desire for restriction comes from a disagreement with the actual ideas being conveyed. Ideologically driven actions that are directed at an entire subcategory of speech will most likely be seen as content based and subjected to strict scrutiny review. Government actions less directed at manipulating the marketplace of ideas and more directed at achieving legitimate, nonideological goals are more likely to be viewed as content neutral and subjected to only intermediate scrutiny.

While content-neutral laws are viewed as less threatening to overall First Amendment values, they do limit speech activities in ways often intended to disadvantage or otherwise impair the dissemination of certain messages. A case in point is the statute at issue in *McCullen v. Coakley*, which made it a crime to stand within thirty-five feet of the entrance to a clinic that provides

Content-Based v. Content-Neutral	
Content-Based	**Content-Neutral**
A regulation is content based if the law regulates speech because of the topic discussed; idea, viewpoint or message expressed; or the identity of the speaker.	Content neutral regulations must be justified w/out reference to content of speech. A neutral regulation may have an incidental effect on some speakers or messages but not others, but their purpose cannot be content-related.

Key questions to answer when examining the facts
 	
1. *Is govt. regulating speech b/c it disagrees with message speech conveys or favors some ideas over others?*
 	
    Example: A city ordinance that prohibited the flying of all flags except the U.S. flag.
 	
2. *Are govt's justifications for regulating speech related to content of speech?*
 	
    Example – Texas flag burning law – underlying purpose of the law was to preserve the flag a symbol of national unity.
 	
3. *Does govt need to examine what is actually being communicated to determine whether a violation of law has occurred?*
 	
    Example – A law that prohibits all but 10 categories of signs.
 	
4. *Does govt need to examine who is actually communicating the message to determine whether a violation of law has occurred?*
 	
    Example – A law limiting the content of newspapers, but only newspapers.
	Key elements to examine when analyzing case facts
	
	Govt.'s underlying purpose or motivation for:
	
	  • enacting law, policy, regulation
	  • making decision
	  • taking action
	
	Focus on:
	
	  • Language of statute or policy
	  • Activities law or legal action actually regulates
	  • Amount of discretion given to govt. official
	  • How evenhandedly law was/can be applied to all speakers.
	
	Examples of a content neutral regulation: A law that prohibits anyone from blocking the entrance to a health care facility to ensure unimpeded access to health care facilities.

Figure 1.4.

abortion services. The thirty-five-foot buffer zone was intended to increase public safety by relieving congestion and obstruction around reproductive healthcare facilities. In practice, however, it prevented antiabortion activists from counseling women as they entered the facility, but did not restrict clinic employees from escorting patients into the building. Despite the restriction imposed on sidewalk counselors, the court held that the law was content neutral because it regulated *where* the activists stood, not *what* they said.[6]

The *McCullen* ruling contrasts with the viewpoint-based regulation of *Texas v. Johnson*, a case that stemmed from a staged demonstration in front of Dallas City Hall where Gregory Johnson "unfurled the American flag, doused it with kerosene, and set it on fire."[7] Johnson was arrested for violating a state statute that criminalized burning or otherwise physically mistreating the US flag in a way that would offend others. Because Johnson burned the flag as an expression of political discontent, the court concluded that the conduct was expressive in that its message was both intentional and overwhelmingly apparent.[8]

In cases involving speech and nonspeech conduct, intermediate scrutiny applies if the state's objective is unrelated to the expressive component of the conduct. Here Texas enacted the statute to preserve the flag as a symbol of national unity. Given this interest, Johnson would not have been punished for burning the flag as a respectful means to retire it. Instead, he was arrested because the state found the idea he expressed offensive. Finding that the statute was content based, the court ruled that Johnson's conviction was unconstitutional. Here, the court said that the constitutional remedy for Johnson's actions is education and a renewed respect for the flag by those who disagree with his message.[9] In the end, the *Texas* case teaches us that restricting an idea *simply* to avoid offense is an unconstitutional objective that will fail strict scrutiny review.

Narrowly Tailored

Intermediate scrutiny review also includes an examination of whether the objective could be achieved with a more limited restriction on speech. Referred to broadly as **narrow tailoring**, this requirement is concerned with the scope of the restriction in relation to its stated objectives. In intermediate scrutiny cases, the government will satisfy the narrow tailoring prong if the regulation does not "burden substantially more speech than is necessary" to advance government's interest.[10]

Let's revisit *McCullen v. Coakley*, the case that concerned a Massachusetts statute that created a thirty-five-foot buffer zone around facilities that provide abortions. In *McCullen*, the state of Massachusetts was attempting to ensure public safety, prevent harassment and intimidation, and combat the obstruction of clinic entrances with the enactment of the buffer zone.[11] While the state chose a buffer zone, it could have accomplished these objectives through the more limited means of arresting and prosecuting those individuals who obstruct, threaten, harass, or otherwise impede a patient's entry into the healthcare facility. The state said it chose the buffer zone in part because it made policing the entrance to these facilities much easier.

The court took issue with the state's efficiency argument and said that the government needed to show that measures that burden substantially less speech would fail to achieve the stated objectives, and "not simply that the chosen route is easier."[12] Here the court found that the buffer zone deprived the activists of their two primary methods of communication—the ability to communicate face to face and distribute literature into the hands of arriving patients. By impeding these means of communication, the statute effectively stifled the message of the activists.

In the end, the court recognized the significance of the state's interest in ensuring public safety and access to healthcare facilities but held that the state took the extreme measure of closing a substantial portion of a public forum to all speakers to achieve those interests. Moreover, it did so without seriously considering alternatives far less burdensome to free speech activities.[13] Given the serious burden the buffer zone placed on speech and the numerous alternatives open to the government to achieve its interests, the state failed to satisfy the narrowly tailored prong of the intermediate scrutiny standard and, thus, violated the First Amendment rights of the activists.

Overbreadth and Vagueness

Laws that restrict free speech activities must be reasonably clear in terms of their scope and application. Imprecisely worded or overly broad statutes are especially onerous from a First Amendment standpoint because they often discourage individuals from speaking out at all. Given the chilling effect such laws can have, plaintiffs may **facially challenge** the law's constitutional legitimacy on the grounds of vagueness or overbreadth. If the challenge is successful, the law will be invalidated.

Vagueness as a legal principle rests on the idea that fair treatment through the justice system depends on clear notification of what behavior is acceptable and unacceptable. This principle allows courts to invalidate laws that are written so unclearly that persons of common intelligence can only guess at what conduct is prohibited and will differ in their conclusions. Vague statutes can entrap innocent individuals and punish people for speech they could not have known was illegal. This system is also ripe for arbitrary enforcement as it gives law officers broad discretion to decide what speech will not be permitted in the marketplace.

A lack of clarity and threat of discriminatory implementation was evident in a Massachusetts law that made it a crime to treat the US flag "contemptuously"[14] and a Cincinnati city ordinance that prohibited three or more people from assembling on any sidewalk and conducting themselves in a "manner annoying to persons passing by."[15] The statutes were struck down for vagueness based on the imprecision of the words "contemptuously" and "annoying." The words lacked a common, verifiable meaning, providing that what one person would consider contemptuous or annoying another person may not. This ambiguity compels citizens to tread cautiously with regard to expressive activities and makes it difficult for law officers to determine exactly what conduct violates the statutes.

The threat of a chilling effect and discriminatory enforcement also extends to laws found to be unconstitutional under the **overbreadth** doctrine. With overbreadth, the clarity of the statute is not at issue. Instead this doctrine is concerned with the amount of expression targeted by the law. In overbroad cases, a plaintiff will argue that some applications of the law are permissible under the First Amendment while others are impermissible. A statute will be invalidated if it punishes too great an amount of constitutionally protected speech. A case in point involved a policy that prohibited "all First Amendment activities" in an airport.[16] The court noted that the policy effectively prohibited even protected expression, including talking, reading, and wearing campaign buttons and symbolic clothing. Here the policy needed to be narrowed to restrict only those speech activities that would hinder airport activities.

Vague and overbroad regulations make speakers unnecessarily cautious when engaging in expressive activities. In the late 1980s, public universities ran into trouble when they began restricting speech that "stigmatize[d]" or "victimize[d]" an individual based upon race, ethnicity, sex, and the like. Although these restrictions were intended to maintain a nonhostile learning environment, they were struck down as unconstitutional on both the vagueness and overbreadth principles.

Here the court found that the terms "stigmatize" and "victimize" elude a precise definition and made it impossible to distinguish between protected and unprotected conduct.[17] Even the university's counsel could not articulate a definition of these terms that would distinguish them from protected speech that was merely offensive. Given that the imprecise language left students guessing at whether their comments would later be sanctioned, the policy was struck down as vague. The policy was declared overbroad as well. While the university argued that the policy was not applied to protected speech, the court found that it was applied to serious, nonhostile comments made in the context of classroom discussion and that the university "failed to consider whether a comment was protected by the First Amendment" before proceeding with the sanction.[18]

More recently, the court struck down a Minnesota statute that prohibited the wearing of "political" badges, buttons, or other such political insignias within a polling place to protect voters from undue influence and preserve the integrity, order, and decorum of the election process.[19] A nonprofit election reform group and individuals who were sanctioned for wearing such apparel as a Tea Party t-shirt and "Please I.D. me" button challenged the statute's undefined use of the term "political." The court noted that the word denotes anything relating to government or dealing with the structure and affairs of the government, politics, or the state and that under literal dictionary definitions, a t-shirt or button that merely implored people to "Vote!" would be forbidden.[20]

Public Forum Doctrine

Governments at all levels own and manage vast expanses of property where communication occurs. From the millions of acres of public lands to the immense array of facilities that house the agencies, branches, and sectors of government, the sheer amount and type of property under government control presents distinct First Amendment challenges. These issues involve decisions that control which speakers will be able to use government property for what types of expressive activities.

To resolve these challenges, the court has fashioned a framework that determines the degree of First Amendment protection expressive activities will receive in a particular forum. Under this framework, government property is divided into two broad forums: public and nonpublic. **Public forums** are generally open to all speakers and topics of discussion whereas **nonpublic forums** are restricted to specified speakers and topics. The determination of what designation a particular piece of property will receive is based on the characteristics of the property, its use and purpose, and the policies and practices long associated with it.

Public Forums

In the free speech marketplace, public forums stand out as places historically and traditionally devoted to uninhibited debate and public assembly. Public streets, sidewalks, and parks have provided the background for some of the most powerful and important political demonstrations in our nation's history and continue to be the chosen sites to air grievances with present-day conditions. The long and venerated role these places have played in the advancement of public issues can be attributed to the heightened degree of protection speech receives in a public forum. In these forums, content-based restrictions on speech, including regulations that exclude speakers based on their identity, are subjected to strict scrutiny review, and content-neutral time, place, and manner regulations receive intermediate scrutiny review.

The power to impose reasonable time, place, and manner regulations on where, when, and how speech activities may occur in a public forum recognizes a government's role in maintaining the property for its intended purpose and use. Streets and sidewalks are primarily intended to move traffic and are not readily available for large demonstrations or parades. To manage competing uses of the property, governments have the authority to impose fee-based permit requirements on speakers who are seeking access to the forum for expressive activities. Permit schemes raise serious constitutional issues because they require citizens to first inform the government of the desire to speak and then obtain a permit to do so. This type of regulation is considered a **prior restraint** on speech and is presumed unconstitutional given the ease at which it allows government to prevent disfavored ideas from entering the marketplace and the significant burden it places on potential speakers who must fill out submit an application, and then wait for a decision. Courts have noted that the process alone has the ability to discourage potential speakers.[21]

For the application process to pass constitutional review, the decision to grant or deny a permit must not be based on the content of the expression or an opposition toward any speaker. Instead, standards for awarding permits must be justified by objective factors that take into account the nature of the place and the pattern of normal activities. This means that public officials are prohibited from using their own discretion as a basis to award or deny a permit and must provide an explanation for denial and allow for a process of review. Constitutional challenges to permit denials are subjected to interme-diate scrutiny. These cases will succeed if the regulation is content based or written in such a way that allows the administrator to consider the message or conceivable reactions to the speaker in the granting of the permit.

While public forums expose all of us to ideas and messages we might not otherwise experience, they represent just a small fraction of the public prop-erty on which communication occurs. The majority of property controlled by the government is designated a nonpublic forum and governed by a different standard. In a nonpublic forum, government may restrict access to or limit expressive activity as long as the regulation is (1) reasonable in light of the purpose of the forum and the surrounding circumstances and (2) not an effort to suppress a viewpoint officials dislike. To more fully understand nonpublic forums, it is helpful to break them down into three categories—designated unlimited, designated limited, and nonpublic.

Designated Unlimited Public Forum

Unless a piece of property qualifies as a traditional public forum, citizens have no general right to access it for open-ended expressive purposes without permission from the government. However, government may decide to inten-tionally open an otherwise nonpublic forum for indiscriminate access and expressive activities. When it does so, it creates an open public forum in which expressive activities receive the same protections as if they occurred in a traditional public forum. Once government creates a designated public forum it is not obligated to keep it open, but as long as it remains open, expressive activity is not restricted to a particular subject or speaker. In practice, however, government rarely creates such a forum. Instead, it is more likely to create a limited public forum.

Designated Limited Public Forum

Limited public forums are created when government intentionally opens a space for speech on a particular topic or grants access to the property for a certain group of speakers. Limited public forums are quite common. They include advertising space on buses, a municipal auditorium dedicated to musical, and theatrical productions and a student newspaper.

Perhaps the most notable of the limited public forums is an open comment period at a public meeting. The purpose of such a forum would most likely be to conduct public business and hear the views of citizens. Given this purpose, the public comment period may be confined to the particular issue the government body is considering. The government can also impose time limits on the comments and prohibit speakers from making personal attacks, speaking when another person has the floor, and other such narrowly defined, content-neutral restrictions to preserve civility and decorum and further the forum's purpose.

Topic- and speaker-based restrictions are constitutional in a limited public forum if they are reasonable in light of the purpose of the forum and the surrounding circumstances and not an effort to suppress viewpoints. Unconstitutional viewpoint discrimination occurs when the government excludes a perspective on a subject otherwise permitted by the forum. Let's say that a public library has opened a meeting room to citizens for discussion on education, specifically kindergarten through twelfth grade, but prohibited discussion on vouchers and charter schools. Because vouchers and charter schools represent a perspective on childhood education, the exclusion would be viewpoint based. In short, exclusions cannot be based on the ideology, opinion, or perspective of the speaker.

Nonpublic or Closed Forums

Nonpublic forums are sometimes referred to as closed forums because they are not compatible with or intended for general access and unrestricted expressive activity. They are created to conduct the business of government or for some other nonexpressive purpose. Nonpublic forums include such property as courtrooms, prisons, military bases, public hospitals and morgues,

Open Public Forum (General Access)	Designated Unlimited PF (General Access)	Designated Limited Public Forum (Selective Access)	Nonpublic Forum (Selective Access)
Historically devoted to public assembly & debate.	Intentionally opened by govt. for unlimited public expression.	Intentionally opened by govt. for speech of a particular type/topic and/or to a particular group of speakers.	Intent & nature of nonpublic forum is incompatible w/ free speech activity.
Examples: Parks, sidewalks, court house steps, city squares, public streets.	Examples: University mall, free speech zones, open townhall meeting (not many like this).	Examples: Ad space on transit terminals/buses; convention centers; student media; spaces open to particular groups for discussion of specific issues.	Examples: Courthouses, govt. offices, public schools, morgues, public hospitals, military bases, airports, polling places.
Govt.'s ability to restrict speech is sharply curtailed.	Once open - receives same protections as traditional PF.	Functions as open PF for groups & topics included. But functions as nonpublic forum for groups & topics excluded.	Dedicated and used for business, education and other dedicated govt. purposes.
Speech regs are constitutional if:		Speech regs are constitutional if:	
• Valid TPM restrictions, includes permits. • Content-based regulations must pass strict scrutiny.		• Reasonable in light of purpose of forum & surrounding circumstances. • Not an effort to suppress viewpoint.	
		• TPM & strict scrutiny can be applied to speakers/ topics included.	• More freedom to exclude certain perspectives when primary function is adm. or content selectivity is essential to purpose, e.g. library.

Figure 1.5.

government offices, public schools, airports, public transit terminals, internal mail systems, and polling places. The primary function of these forums is administrative rather than to facilitate discussion. In these settings, government may impose reasonable restrictions on speech to preserve the forum for its intended use and purpose. This includes selective access and subject matter and speaker-identity-based distinctions. As with all forums, government is not permitted to engage in viewpoint discrimination.

Government Speech

It is important to note that the forum analysis applies to government's power to restrict *purely private* speech occurring on government property.[22] When government uses public property to convey its own message, it is not restrained by the public forum framework. In such circumstances, the property used to communicate the message is not considered a forum at all but rather a place for government speech. A case in point is *Walker v. Texas Division, Sons of Confederate Veterans*. In *Walker*, the Texas Department of Motor Vehicles rejected the Sons of Confederate Veterans' proposal for a specialty license plate featuring a Confederate battle flag. Here the court held that license plate designs constitute government speech. When government speaks, the forum analysis does not apply. This leaves government free to embrace some viewpoints and exclude others.[23]

Forum Analysis and the Internet

In deciding matters that implicate the public forum doctrine, a court must first decide which type of forum is involved in the case. Once the forum is identified, the appropriate First Amendment standard is applied. Because government's authority to control access and expression varies among the forum categories, the specific category selected is a significant factor in the outcome of the case. This is especially true in factual situations involving online communication and the government's use of social media and other internet-based platforms. Given that the relationship between the First Amendment and the internet is not well developed, courts must first grapple with the appropriateness of extending the forum analysis to various governmental uses of cyberspace.

Under the forum analysis, informational websites that do not provide a mechanism for public comment would be viewed differently from sites that solicit public feedback. Given its one-way communication, the former is likely to be viewed as government speech unrestrained by the forum analysis while the latter with its interactive feature closely resembles a limited or unlimited public forum. The exact designation of the latter would depend on the site's purpose, structure, and intended use. Regardless of which designation was chosen, government would still retain the authority to delete the website should the forum become unworkable.

A more contentious area of online communication is government's use of social media. In *Packingham v. North Carolina*, the court identified online platforms in general and social media in particular as the most important places for the exchange of views today.[24] Few would dispute the vital role social media plays in public communication among government officials and citizens. It provides virtually unprecedented access for constituents who want to express their opinions directly to their representative as part of a very public interactive feed. And for a citizen who has a disapproving opinion that the representative doesn't want to hear, it may be the most effective way to convey it. That is, until the individual is blocked from viewing and replying to the public official's posts.

Lawsuits from constituents who have been blocked by a public official have begun to bubble up in state and federal courts.[25] In these cases,
individuals were blocked after they posted comments critical of the official.
One of the first questions raised by such actions is whether the social media
account constitutes a place owned or controlled by the government. While
social media platforms are not owned by the government, courts have reasoned that an account operated by a government official, maintained in part
by the official's staff, and used as a channel for official government communication is a place controlled by the government.[26]

When government controls property that is opened to the public, it creates
a designated public forum. In the realm of social media, this means that the
interactive space associated with each post qualifies as a forum. Blocking
members of the public from accessing this space solely because the official disagrees with the viewpoint posted would constitute an impermissible
content-based restriction. Under this analysis, the official would be required
to provide access to the interactive space by unblocking the user. Government
officials have countered this line of reasoning and argue that their social
media accounts represent personal, private speech unconstrained by First
Amendment considerations. While public officials do retain their rights to
engage in private speech while serving in office, the legal line that delineates
their private views from their official communication is far from clear.

A recent case on point involves President Donald Trump's use of the
blocking function on Twitter. The case was brought by individuals who were

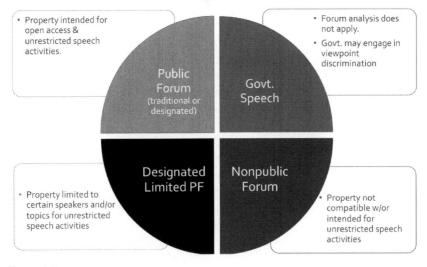

Figure 1.6.

blocked after posting replies critical of the president and his policies. Because they were blocked, they could no longer view the president's tweets, directly reply to those tweets, or use the @realDonaldTrump webpage to view the comment threads associated with the president's tweets. These restrictions also prevented them from interacting with others in the comment threads. At issue in this case was whether the interactive space associated with each tweet constituted a public forum.

The Second Circuit ruled that "yes"—the space is a public forum. The court based its conclusion on the fact that the president's tweets are used as a channel of communication for

1. Interacting with the public about his administration;
2. Announcing matters related to official government business; and
3. Gauging and evaluating the public's reaction to his actions and policies.[27]

In addition, the court noted that the president's tweets are considered official records that must be preserved under the Presidential Records Act. Given the manner in which the account is used, the court concluded that the interactive space created a public forum that is sufficiently controlled by government and as such, Trump was "not entitled to censor selected users because they express views with which he disagrees."[28] By blocking these individuals, the president is excluding them from a public forum based on the ideas they express. Because government may not deny access to a public forum based on the viewpoint of the speaker, the president's actions were ruled unconstitutional.

CHAPTER SUMMARY

The story of the right to free expression in the United States begins with a belief in the value of ideas and the struggle to create a self-functioning marketplace that would fuel their continual production. The importance of a robust marketplace of ideas and its ability to foster an environment rich in discussion and debate cannot be understated in free speech law. It is the instrument that sustains a self-governing, democratic system, and in doing so constitutes the central organizing principle upon which free speech law is built.

If you stand back and think about chapter 1 from a marketplace perspective, you will notice a framework developing that is highly committed to the creation and preservation of ideas and viewpoints. This framework begins

How free speech law fits together

Marketplace of Ideas Theory
- Need unrestricted MOI that fosters open debate
- Debate produces ideas that are wiser

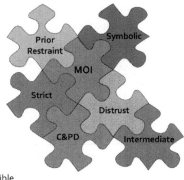

Distrust of Government
- Govt. has strong desire & power to manipulate MOI
- Free speech law needs to curb that desire & power

Clear & Present Danger
- Line between protected & unprotected speech drawn as close to incitement as possible
- Reduces chilling effect that results from fear of punishment for speech

Prior Restraint
- Govt. censorship of speech before it is published
- Presumed unconstitutional because it prevents ideas from entering the MOI

Strict Scrutiny
- Level of review applied to restrictions of speech based on its idea
- Extremely difficult for government to overcome

Intermediate Scrutiny
- Level of review applied to restrictions on expressive conduct & TPM regulations
- Curtails govt. ability to use conduct-based regulations to suppress ideas

Symbolic Speech
- Extends free speech protection to expressive conduct
- Creates a more robust marketplace by increasing amount and type of protected ideas

Figure 1.7.

with the application of strict scrutiny review to any government action that seeks to manipulate the flow of ideas into the marketplace and follows with the same heightened protection of free speech activities occurring in a traditional public forum. At this stage, courts exhibit a strong distrust of government activities. When government actions are driven by a viewpoint-neutral objective, courts are less distrustful and apply a lower level of scrutiny that provides more constitutional leeway for the state to achieve its objectives. But even viewpoint-neutral statutes that regulate speech in a nonpublic forum must be written with clarity and precision to provide protection against vague and overbroad laws that chill expression and diminish the supply of ideas entering the marketplace. These organizing principles are central to the legal framework surrounding communication law.

KEY TERMS

Appeal   A judicial process that allows a legal decision to be reconsidered by a higher court. This means that a party that is unhappy with the decision of the trial court may ask an appellate court to review the lower court's reasoning. However, appeal to the US Supreme Court is rarely granted. The High Court considers approximately eighty cases a year out of seven thousand to eight thousand petitions.

Breathing Space   Courts have recognized the need to curb sanctions on questionable speech in order to encourage widespread participation in the marketplace of ideas. The concept has been used to safeguard false and erroneous speech in public debate.

Case   In the legal sense, a case is a fact-based dispute between parties. Courts are responsible for resolving these disputes through a process that typically involves the interpretation and application of law.

Chilling Effect   Instances where the mere existence of sanctions on expressive activities causes speakers to suppress their participation in the speech market out of fear of punishment.

Clear and Present Danger Test   This test determines when speech is an incitement to violence and can be constitutionally removed from the marketplace. To pass the clear and present danger test, speech must be intended and likely to cause imminent, serious lawless action. Violence is imminent when it is likely to occur before there is time to reason or talk through the situation.

Content-Based Distinction   Cases where the facts indicate that the government is regulating speech because of the topics discussed; the ideas, viewpoints or messages expressed; or the identity of the speaker. These cases are subject to strict scrutiny review.

Content-Neutral Distinction   Factual situations where the government regulates expression without any regard for or reference to the ideas expressed. A content-neutral regulation may have an incidental effect on some speakers or messages but not others, but its purpose cannot be content related. These cases are subject to intermediate scrutiny review.

Defendant   A case is brought against a defendant. This means that the defendant is the person or party that is defending against a criminal charge or denying a wrongdoing in a civil case.

Dissenting Opinion   A dissenting opinion is written by a judge who disagrees with the majority. Dissenting opinions are an important legal tool that not only point out problems with the majority's reasoning but also provide a vehicle that allows judges to express their frustration with the court's decision.

Expressive Conduct   Expressive conduct refers to a speech activity that uses behavior to send a message. Also referred to as symbolic speech, expressive conduct involves nonverbal, nonwritten forms of expression, such as burning draft cards and flags. In expressive conduct cases, government is prevented from using its power to regulate behavior as a means to suppress speech.

Facial Challenge   The ability to challenge a law as written is called a facial challenge. Facial challenges differ from as-applied challenges. In a facial challenge, you are arguing that the law is always unconstitutional and thus needs to be struck down for the benefit of society. This differs from an as-applied challenge where the plaintiffs are arguing that the law as applied to them and their situation is unconstitutional.

Intermediate Scrutiny   Intermediate scrutiny applies in cases where the prohibited conduct was used to communicate a message or where government imposed a time, place, or manner regulation on expressive activities. Under intermediate scrutiny review, the burden is on the government to prove that the regulation does not restrict speech based on its viewpoint or the impact it is likely to have on the audience. A regulation is likely to be upheld under intermediate scrutiny if it is clearly content neutral and the restriction on the speech activity is negligible. With regard to time, place, and manner restrictions, the government must also show that ample alternative forums exist for communicating the message to its intended audience.

Judicial Review   The doctrine of judicial review gives judges the authority to strike down a law—to declare it null and void—if they determine the law is unconstitutional.

Judicial System   The judicial system or the judiciary refers to the organization, routines, and practices of US state and federal courts and the judges that sit on these courts. This system is responsible for interpreting and applying the law to case facts in order to resolve disputes.

Least Restrictive Alternative   Least restrictive alternative is a form of narrow tailoring that is applied in strict scrutiny review. It requires the court to examine whether a nonspeech alternative would work essentially as well as the speech restriction or whether a different option exists that would secure government's interest and burden less speech.

Marketplace of Ideas   The Marketplace of Ideas theory is the central organizing principle governing free speech law in the United States. The theory values an open marketplace where robust debate among ideas can freely occur and contends that public discussion, uninhibited by regulation, will lead to progressive results that are wiser, more useful, and more desirable than outcomes generated in speech-restrictive environments.

Narrow Tailoring   Narrow tailoring is a prong in both strict and intermediate scrutiny reviews. In the application of the narrowly tailored prong, courts examine how precisely the regulation has been crafted. A narrowly tailored regulation restricts no more speech than is necessary to advance the government's objective. Under strict scrutiny review, regulations will fail the narrowly tailored prong if they are over-inclusive, under-inclusive, or other options exist that limit less speech. Under intermediate scrutiny, regulations will fail the narrowly tailored prong if they are over-inclusive.

Nonpublic Forum   These forums are sometimes referred to as closed forums because they are not compatible with or intended for general access and unrestricted expressive activity. They are created to conduct the business of government or for some other non-expressive purpose. Because the primary function of nonpublic forums is administrative, government may impose reasonable restrictions on speech to preserve the forum for its intended use and purpose. Courtrooms, prisons, and military bases are examples of a nonpublic forum.

Opinion   A written document that details the decision and the reasoning for the decision. There are several types of opinions. With regard to the US Supreme Court, a majority opinion requires five or more justices to agree on the outcome of the case as well as the reasoning for that outcome. Justices who disagree may write a separate dissenting opinion explaining their decision and rationale for that decision.

Overbreadth   Under the overbreadth doctrine, the constitutionality of a regulation may be challenged on its face or as written. In overbreadth cases, a plaintiff will argue that some applications of the law are permissible under the First Amendment while others are impermissible. A statute will be struck down if it punishes a substantial amount of constitutionally protected speech along with the speech that government has a right to legitimately restrict.

Over-inclusiveness   A regulation will not pass strict or intermediate scrutiny review if it is over-inclusive. An over-inclusive regulation restricts substantially more speech than is necessary to advance government's stated objective.

Plaintiff   A plaintiff is the person or party that initiates the case by filing a complaint against the defendant. A plaintiff is sometimes referred to as the petitioner.

Precedent   The US legal system is built on the idea that alike cases must be treated alike. This requires courts to look to the past decisions of similar cases for guidance on how to decide the issue before it. The legal rules contained in those past cases are considered precedent and as such are applied to current cases with similar fact patterns. Under the idea of precedent, the rules handed down by the US Supreme Court must be followed by other courts. In this way, Supreme Court opinions become reliable guides upon which future cases are decided. Respect for precedent also fosters consistency in the legal system and becomes the mechanism through which the rules of law are established.

Prior Restraint   A prior restraint is a form of censorship that occurs when government reviews and suppresses speech before it is published or disseminated. A prior restraint may involve a court order—called an injunction—that prohibits speech under threat of criminal or civil liability. Permit or licensing schemes that require speakers to obtain permission to use a public forum are also a form of prior restraint. Because prior restraints prohibit ideas from ever entering the marketplace of ideas, they are regarded as a severe curtailment of free speech rights and presumed to be unconstitutional.

Public Forum   These forums are historically devoted to public assembly and debate or intentionally opened by government for unlimited public expression. In a public forum, content-based restrictions on speech, including regulations that exclude speakers based on their identity, are subjected to strict scrutiny review and content-neutral time, place, and manner regulations receive intermediate scrutiny review.

Rational Basis Review   A common form of judicial review that is applied in cases where fundamental rights or suspect classification are not at issue. Regulations reviewed under this standard are considered constitutional if they are rationally related to a legitimate government interest. Under rational basis review, the plaintiff has the burden of proving the regulation does not serve any conceivable government objective. Courts largely defer to government's judgment and do not seriously examine whether other ways of achieving the objective would be more effective.

Strict Scrutiny   Strict scrutiny is the most exacting form of review applied by courts. It is applied in cases where government restricted or compelled expression based on its content. Under strict scrutiny review, the burden is on the government to prove that the regulation is narrowly tailored to advance a compelling government interest. Regulations subjected to this heightened form of review are often declared unconstitutional.

Time, Place, and Manner Regulations   Government has the power to impose reasonable, content-neutral time, place, and manner regulations on where, when, or how speech activities may occur in a public forum. Time, place, and manner regulations are viewed as less restrictive of First Amendment rights because they are designed to reroute or readjust the speech within the marketplace rather than remove it. As a result, time, place, and manner regulations are adjudicated under intermediate scrutiny.

US Supreme Court   The US Supreme Court is the court of last appeal in the federal system. Nine justices—each with lifetime tenure—sit on the court. To become a Supreme Court justice, a person must be nominated by the president and confirmed by the Senate. If the Senate rejects the nomination, the person will not be able to sit on the court.

Under-inclusiveness   A regulation will not pass strict scrutiny review if it is under-inclusive. An under-inclusive regulation restricts substantially less speech than is necessary to advance government's stated objective.

Vagueness   Under the void for vagueness doctrine, the constitutionality of a regulation may be challenged on its face. In void for vagueness cases, a plaintiff will argue that the law is written so unclearly that people of common intelligence can only guess at what is prohibited. As a result, vague laws can punish people for speech they could not have known was illegal.

2

Commercial and Corporate Speech

In First Amendment law, speech receives its broad-base protection from government interference to advance public debate and achieve greater goals for a democratic society. However, not all classes of speech significantly further these core values. One such class of speech is commercial speech. The relationship between commercial speech and the First Amendment largely began in 1942 when the US Supreme Court held that pure commercial advertising was not deserving of free speech protection given that its primary purpose was to generate business profits.[1] This line of thought held until *New York Times v. Sullivan* was handed down in 1964.

At issue in *Sullivan* was a full-page advertisement that attempted to persuade the readers of the *New York Times* to financially support the Committee to Defend Dr. Martin Luther King Jr. and its mission. Although the advertisement was economically motivated, it also sought to educate the public on the civil rights movement. In the opinion, the *Sullivan* Court emphasized the content of the ad instead of its purpose and concluded that commercial speech can be used to further debate on public issues and when it does, it deserves robust First Amendment protection, including protection for false speech.[2] To view the facts otherwise, the court said, would cut off an important vehicle for the free flow of information.[3] The case also viewed the nonprofit fundraising organization that placed the ad[4] as an individual speaker whose participation in the marketplace was helping "to secure 'the widest possible dissemination of information from diverse and antagonistic sources.'"[5]

In *Sullivan*, the court shifted its legal analysis from the commercial purpose of the speaker to the marketplace value of the content. This created a split between purely commercial speech and public-issue speech of a commercial nature. "In the latter, the content is richer and more useful to the marketplace of ideas than purely commercial speech."[6] Once this split occurred, "it followed that the Court would find some value in purely commercial expression and, therefore, some First Amendment protection."[7]

RIGHT TO RECEIVE INFORMATION

By the mid-1970s, the court rejected the notion that pure commercial speech did not deserve First Amendment protection; it found that even speech that does no more than promote a commercial transaction provides useful information upon which intelligent decisions and opinions are based.[8] In carving out a place for pure commercial advertising within the free-speech clause, the court relied largely on the First Amendment right of the audience to receive information rather than an individual's right to speak. The **right to receive information** is considered a corollary right to the right to speak and publish information. Without recognition of the right to receive information, government could constitutionally restrict the free exchange of ideas by preventing the sharing of information it considers undesirable for public consumption. The power to withhold knowledge keeps people in the dark and works to manipulate behavior by suppressing valuable information. The best interests of the public, the court said, are achieved through open channels of communication that work to inform and educate all consumers and upon which sound economic decisions can be made.[9]

LESSER DEGREE OF FIRST AMENDMENT PROTECTION

While a purely economic intent by a commercial speaker no longer disqualifies speech from constitutional protection, the inherent profit motive in commercial information has prevented it from receiving the same degree of First Amendment protection afforded to noncommercial speech. Because commercial speakers have an economic incentive to provide consumers with false or misleading statements, the principle that false speech must be tolerated in the marketplace to ensure robust debate and public discussion does not apply to commercial speech. Instead, commercial speech is subjected to a standard of accuracy. The court based this standard on two characteristics of profit-driven speech.

1. Commercial speech can be easily verified by the speaker who has detailed, insider knowledge of the product or service.

2. Profit-driven speech is not as easily chilled as other classes of non-commercial speech. Because commercial speakers are economically motivated to engage in speech, they are viewed as more determined to overcome regulatory restrictions than other speakers. Consequently, it is unlikely that the threat of sanctions will deter them from participating in the ideas market. The same, however, cannot be said for political speakers who under the threat of punishment are quite likely to disengage entirely from the ideas market even though much of what they intended to say was not prohibited by any government regulation.

Based on these two distinctions, the court has concluded that the threat of sanctions for false or misleading statements would not chill commercial speech to the same degree it would political commentary or news reporting.[10] As a result, a two-tiered scrutiny standard, commonly referred to as the **Central Hudson standard**, was developed that denied constitutional protection to inaccurate commercial statements.

CENTRAL HUDSON STANDARD

The first tier of the Central Hudson standard seeks to sever false or misleading commercial speech from the constitutional protection the court affords inaccurate public-interest speech. In doing so, the standard asks whether the commercial speech in question concerns an unlawful activity or is false or misleading. Commercial speech that promotes an illegal activity or is false or misleading receives no First Amendment protection and may be regulated as government sees fit as long as the restriction is rationally related to a legitimate state objective.[11]

On the other hand, if the speech in question is truthful, nonmisleading commercial speech, it will fall within the protection of the First Amendment, and the government's attempt to regulate it will be scrutinized more intensely through an application of the second tier of the Central Hudson standard. The second tier consists of three prongs that require the government to show that the

1. Asserted governmental objective(s) is substantial.
2. Regulation directly advances the asserted objective.
3. Regulation is narrowly tailored to advance the asserted objective.[12]

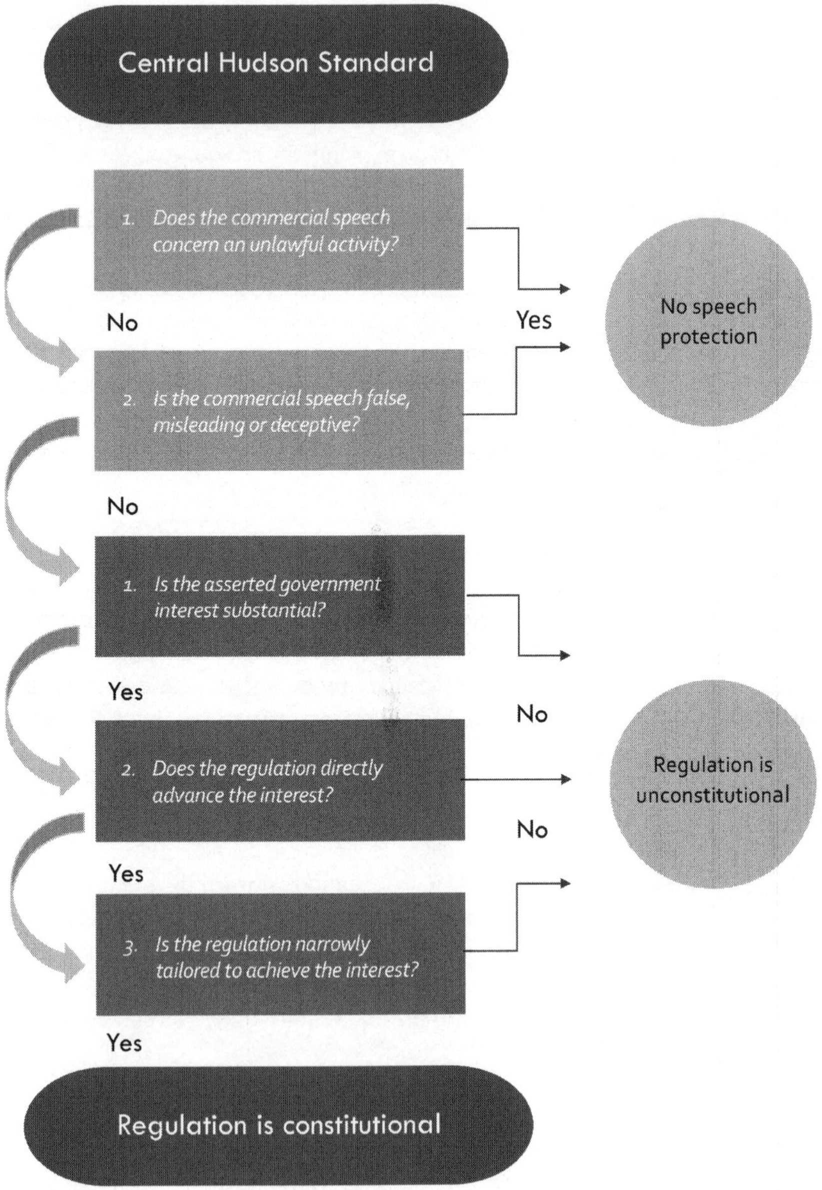

Central Hudson Standard

1. Does the commercial speech concern an unlawful activity?

No

2. Is the commercial speech false, misleading or deceptive?

Yes → No speech protection

No

1. Is the asserted government interest substantial?

Yes

2. Does the regulation directly advance the interest?

No

Yes

3. Is the regulation narrowly tailored to achieve the interest?

No → Regulation is unconstitutional

Yes

Regulation is constitutional

Figure 2.1.

Even though the Central Hudson standard is often referred to as a form of intermediate scrutiny, it differs from the intermediate scrutiny standard courts typically apply to noncommercial expressive conduct and time, place, and manner restrictions in one important aspect—the Central Hudson test does *not* contain a content-neutral requirement. This allows government to enact legislation that directly regulates the messages and information commercial speakers convey to the public.

The Central Hudson standard emerged from the court's opinion in ***Central Hudson Gas & Electric Corp. v. Public Service Commission***. At issue in the case was a New York state regulation that banned electric utilities from engaging in promotional advertising in order to curb energy consumption and encourage the conservation of energy resources. The Central Hudson Gas & Electric Corp. opposed the regulation, arguing that it violated the company's First Amendment commercial speech rights. The Supreme Court agreed with the utility.

To achieve this determination, the court reviewed the facts of the case in relation to the three prongs listed in tier two of the standard, and concluded that the state satisfied prongs one and two in that

1. The country is dependent on electricity, and given this dependency, energy conservation is an important objective for the government to advance.
2. An immediate connection exists between advertising and demand for a service, and thus a ban on utility advertising is directly linked to advancing energy conservation.[13]

In its application of the third prong, the court found that a complete ban on advertising was more extensive than necessary to advance the objective. Essentially, the ban was unconstitutionally over-inclusive. It reached all advertising, even that which "would cause no net increase in total energy use," such as advertising that promoted products and services that use energy efficiently.[14] Based on the state's failure to craft a restriction that was narrowly targeted to further energy conservation, the court struck down the commission's regulation on electric utility advertising.

Central Hudson is important not only for the standard that emerged but also for its words of warning on outright bans on truthful, nonmisleading commercial speech. Blanket bans on truthful information, the court said, need to be reviewed with special care.[15] Special consideration is necessary given the indispensable information commercial speech provides to consumers. **Blanket bans** cut off a source of information and manipulate product choice by keeping consumers ignorant of the very information and ideas a free market is intended to produce.

Vice Products

So-called **vice products**—for example, alcohol, tobacco, and gambling—are particularly vulnerable to blanket bans given the harmful effects associated with their overuse and abuse. To curb the usage of these lawful products, government typically levies taxes and enacts age restrictions. When these tactics do not provide enough of a deterrent, government has turned to directly restricting their promotion and advertisements.

A case in point—*Educational Media at Virginia Tech v. Insley*—involves a Virginia statute that prohibits college student newspapers from publishing advertisements for beer, wine, and mixed beverages unless the advertisement is promoting a dining establishment and does not reference particular brands of alcohol or the prices of such drinks. The statute was enacted to reduce underage drinking and over-consumption of alcohol products by college students.

The Educational Media Co., a nonprofit corporation that owns student newspapers at Virginia Tech and the University of Virginia, argued that the law as applied to the company's student newspapers could not satisfy the Central Hudson standard. The Fourth Circuit agreed and held that the statute as applied to Educational Media's college newspapers was unconstitutional. In its analysis, the Fourth Circuit found that the state's interest in reducing abusive underage alcohol consumption was a substantial interest that was directly advanced by the advertising ban. The court based its conclusion on the general correlation between product advertising and product demand. Given that advertising increases demand for a product, the court said that it is reasonable to conclude that a decrease in alcohol advertising would likely result in a decrease in alcohol consumption.[16] While the advertising/demand correlation is insufficient to justify advertising bans in every case, here, the court said, the association is particularly strong given the unique role student publications play on campus and the attraction they hold for alcohol advertisers.[17]

While the regulation cleared the first two prongs in tier two of the standard, the court found that it failed the last prong. Often referred to as the "narrowly tailored" prong, it requires the government to show that the challenged regulation is sufficiently limited in scope. Here, the court said that the regulation not only targeted readers who were under the legal drinking age, but it also prevented a large number of readers who are twenty-one years of age or older from "receiving truthful information about a product that they are legally allowed to consume."[18] In this case, some 60 percent of student newspaper readers were of legal age to consume alcohol,[19] and the statute violated their right to receive information as well as the newspapers' right to publish truthful, nonmisleading alcohol advertisements. In the end, the Virginia law failed Central Hudson review because it infringed the rights of a substantial number of people whose status and behavior were unrelated to the government's stated objectives.

Compelled Disclosure of Factual Information

Economic markets work best when consumers are equipped with perfect information about a product or service. Access to accurate and reliable commercial information allows the consumer to make a fully informed purchasing decision. Commercial interests, however, have an economic incentive to withhold unfavorable information about their product or service from the market. Nondisclosure often gives businesses a distinct advantage over consumers who do not possess the information or the time necessary to research commercial claims. As a result, consumers may be misled and eventually harmed by the economic choices they make.

Consumer protection is an important governmental interest and responsibility. To protect consumers and equip them with the knowledge they need to make informed choices, governments frequently require commercial speakers to disclose specific factual information about their products or services. Perhaps most notable is the warning statement on packs of cigarettes that was mandated by Congress in 1965 to inform the public of the severe health risks associated with tobacco use.

Compelled disclosure requirements, like blanket bans on commercial speech, allow the government to pick and choose what information it considers appropriate and inappropriate for individuals to consume. As such, both classes of regulation are subjected to First Amendment challenges and review. But, as the Supreme Court has noted, when it comes to First Amendment values, a material difference exists between regulations that prohibit truthful, nonmisleading commercial information from entering the market and disclosure requirements that compel the publication of such information.[20] Prohibitions directly assault First Amendment values by hindering the discovery of truth. However, compelled disclosure of purely factual and uncontroversial commercial speech promotes the free flow of accurate information to consumers. In short, disclosure requirements further the informational value upon which the First Amendment protection of commercial speech rests. As a result, disclosure regulations that are aimed at preventing consumer deception are generally subjected to a **rational basis review**, which is a more lenient review than the Central Hudson standard.[21]

Rational Basis Review

In rational basis review, courts do not seriously question or examine whether the government's objective is directly advanced by the requirement or whether the requirement is narrowly tailored to achieve the objective. Instead, a regulation will pass a rational basis review if it is reasonable to conclude that the regulation will further a legitimate government interest.[22] In *New York State Restaurant Association v. New York City Board of Health*, the Second Circuit upheld a New York City health code that required chain restaurants to post calorie information on their menus. The requirement was intended to reduce consumer confusion and deception and promote informed decision-making that would lead to reductions in obesity and the diseases associated with it. The court conducted a rational basis review and concluded that the city "plainly demonstrated a reasonable relationship" between the objectives it was attempting to achieve and the compelled disclosure of calorie information.[23]

A level of scrutiny akin to rational basis was first applied by the Supreme Court to a disclosure requirement in ***Zauderer v. Office of Disciplinary Counsel of the Supreme Court of Ohio***, a case that involved a state court rule requiring attorneys to fully disclose the total cost of contingency fee services in their advertisements. In the *Zauderer* opinion, the court noted that disclosure regulations that are "reasonably related" to preventing consumer deception are less violative of First Amendment values than "unjustified or unduly burdensome" requirements.[24] The court's distinction drew a line between mandated disclosures of factual, uncontroversial information as a means to prevent consumer deception and compelled speech restrictions that would force commercial speakers to express views and opinions with which they disagreed.

In *R.J. Reynolds v. FDA*, the DC Circuit Court found that the government crossed the line between mandating disclosure of factual information and ideological messages when it required cigarette manufacturers to display a new graphic warning label on the top 50 percent of the front and back panels of every cigarette package manufactured and distributed in the United States. The Department of Health and Human Services selected nine color images that included photos of horribly damaged teeth and lungs and a man exhaling smoke through a tracheotomy opening in his neck. Each image accompanied a larger text warning and the toll-free telephone number 1-800-QUIT-NOW. The graphic warning label was also required on all cigarette advertisements and would constitute 20 percent of the space in those advertisements.[25]

The *R.J. Reynolds* case tested the scope of the government's authority to force a cigarette manufacturer to carry a specific anti-smoking message.[26] In its analysis, the court found that the graphic warning labels were more problematic from a constitutional perspective than the disclosure requirements in *Zauderer* and *New York State Restaurant Association*. First, no findings demonstrated that the labels were necessary to address a problem with misleading cigarette packaging. And second, the "inflammatory images and provocatively-named hotline" could not reasonably be viewed as purely factual and noncontroversial information intended to prevent consumer deception. Instead, the court found that the warning labels were intended to "evoke emotion (and perhaps embarrassment) and browbeat" smokers into retaining the government's message. Given the unjustified and controversial nature of the warning, the regulation could not be subjected to a rational basis review.[27]

Figure 2.2.
FDA cigarette warning label via *FairWarning*

Courts have subjected disclosure requirements that fall outside Zauderer's lower level of scrutiny to strict scrutiny or the Central Hudson standard. The DC Circuit Court applied Central Hudson and determined that the government failed to show that the graphic warning labels would "discourage nonsmokers from initiating cigarette use and encourage current smokers to consider quitting." The court said that regulations that provide "only ineffective or remote support" for the government's objective would not satisfy prong two of the Central Hudson standard. Here, the FDA offered no evidence that the warning labels "*directly caused* a material decrease" in smoking rates in the countries that require them. Instead, survey data showed that such warnings merely caused a substantial number of respondents to "think—or think more—about quitting smoking."[28] Given that the First Amendment requires the government to show that the warning labels will reduce smoking rates, the disclosure requirement was **vacated**.[29]

More recently, the Supreme Court subjected a California disclosure requirement to intermediate scrutiny review. The statute at issue in *National Institute of Family & Life Advocates v. Becerra* required licensed crisis pregnancy clinics opposed to abortion to inform their clients that the state provides free or low-cost family planning services, including abortions. The government-mandated message also included contact information for obtaining such services. The court found that California's disclosure requirement was not limited to purely factual and uncontroversial information. The mandated message included controversial abortion-access information. As such the notification requirement fell outside Zauderer's lower-level scrutiny review.[30] Here, California enacted a content-based regulation that compelled crisis pregnancy clinics to deliver a message they sought not to convey. However, the court did not apply strict scrutiny review. Instead, it found that the regulation was not sufficiently crafted to satisfy even the less burdensome narrowly tailored prong of an intermediate scrutiny standard.

The court found that the regulation, which was intended to educate low-income women about state-sponsored services, was substantially under-inclusive in that it excluded, without explanation, most of the clinics and health centers that serve low-income women. Moreover, California could have conducted its own public information campaign, posting its notice on public property near crisis pregnancy centers, instead of forcing these centers to deliver a message that not only ran counter to their beliefs but also impeded the actual idea they were attempting to send.[31]

Defining Commercial Speech

Since **commercial speech** receives less protection than noncommercial speech, an important question in many disputes is whether the speech at issue actually constitutes commercial speech. While no definitive definition of commercial speech exists, the US Supreme Court in **Bolger v. Youngs Drug Products Corp.** looked to a combination of three elements—advertising format, reference to product, and economic motivation—as "strong support" for a determination of commercial expression, and noted that any one of the three would not by itself be sufficient to define speech as commercial.[32]

In **Kasky v. Nike**, the California Supreme Court relied on *Bolger* to craft a definition of commercial speech that examined whether the

1. Speaker was engaged in commerce or was acting on behalf of a person engaged in commerce.
2. Intended audience was actual or potential buyers or customers.
3. Content of the message involved representations of fact about the business operations, products, or services of the speaker, or the individual or company that the speaker represents.
4. Content was created for the purpose of promoting sales or other commercial transactions in the speaker's products or services.[33]

According to the *Kasky* court, these four elements are necessary to account for commercially motivated statements made in the context of a public relations campaign. Public relations campaigns, like the one at issue in *Kasky*, typically employ a variety of distinct communication tactics that are largely disconnected from a traditional advertising campaign but nonetheless are "intended to increase sales and profits by enhancing the image of a product or of its manufacturer or seller."[34] In *Kasky*, Nike distributed news releases and letters to athletic directors, university presidents, and newspaper editors to address adverse publicity concerning the company's labor policies and practices and the working conditions in the factories that produce Nike products. The tactics were also intended to maintain and increase sales and profits.[35]

Using the four elements, the California Supreme Court concluded that Nike was engaged in commercial speech, and thus precluded from making false or misleading statements in its response to public criticism. The court recognized that Nike's speech was intermingled with noncommercial speech, but stressed that references to public issues will not immunize false or misleading commercial speech from government regulation.[36] Here, the court noted, the alleged false and misleading statements involved commercial speech, namely wages, hours worked, employment conditions, and practices in factories that produce Nike's products, and that this information was readily verifiable and within the company's knowledge base.[37]

Kasky v. Nike raises the difficult question of when a business may be sued for making allegedly false or misleading statements. Nike argued that as a corporation it was engaged in public debate. In public debate, honest mistakes and misleading information are fully protected by the First Amendment. Here, the California Supreme Court decision gave Nike's noncommercial critics the upper hand in the offshore labor debate by forcing the corporation to defend its practices under the accuracy standard of the commercial speech doctrine. And while the US Supreme Court agreed to review the case, they eventually dismissed it on procedural grounds. This left the extent to which a corporation may constitutionally defend its practices against accusations of wrongdoing largely unanswered. The Public Relations Society of America was dismayed by the US Supreme Court's inaction, which allowed the state court's definition of commercial speech to stand. According to the organization, the California court's definition was so broad that it could be read to cover "any public statement made by a company about a topic related to what that company does."[38]

CORPORATE SPEECH

In *Kasky v. Nike*, the California Supreme Court recognized that Nike's speech on the public issue of overseas manufacturing of goods contained both commercial and noncommercial elements. The court concluded that while the allegedly false statements regarding working conditions in factories that produced Nike apparel constituted commercial speech, the company's wide-ranging discussion on corporate responsibility in foreign factories was noncommercial, fully protected speech.[39] The recognition that a business does not always speak with a commercial voice derives from a line of Supreme Court precedent that guarantees the rights of corporations as **legal persons** to participate in general public debate.

The court began fashioning a free speech right for corporations in 1978 in **First National Bank of Boston v. Bellotti**. At issue was a Massachusetts criminal statute that prohibited two banking associations and three corporations from spending money to publicize their views on a proposed ballot measure that, if passed, would have allowed the state to impose a graduated income tax on individuals.[40] The corporations believed that the adoption of the tax would materially affect their businesses by shrinking the disposable income of citizens and discouraging others from settling, working, and remaining in Massachusetts.[41] Consequently, they challenged the statute as a violation of the First Amendment rights of corporations.

In its analysis, the court focused on the inherent value of the information to the marketplace instead of the identity of the speaker. Here, the proposed expression sought to inform democratic decision-making. Given the importance of the expression to the marketplace, a prohibition targeting it would be unconstitutional if the restriction applied to an individual speaker. Using this line of thought, the court concluded that the same expression does not lose its value and thus its constitutional protection simply because the speaker is a corporation.[42]

In *Bellotti*, the court noted that in addition to fostering individual self-expression, the First Amendment secures "public access to discussion, debate and the dissemination of information and ideas."[43] **Corporate**

speech, irrespective of its political or commercial nature, enhances the First Amendment's role in advancing the free flow of information. While both types of corporate speech receive First Amendment protection, commercial speech receives a limited level of constitutional protection given its distinct characteristics and the government's substantial interest in consumer protection and a fully functioning economy. The same cannot be said when corporations speak as members of society. In their role as legal persons that engage in public discussion and debate, corporate speakers are accorded full First Amendment rights. As a result, content-based restrictions on corporate speech trigger strict scrutiny and require the government to demonstrate that the regulation advances a compelling state objective and that the means chosen to accomplish that objective are the least destructive of the corporation's free speech rights.

The statute at issue in *Bellotti* was enacted to prevent corruption of the electoral process and to protect the interests of shareholders from supporting views with which they disagreed. In applying strict scrutiny to the restriction, the court concluded that the state's objectives were neither implicated by the facts nor served by the prohibition. According to the court, the government failed to demonstrate that corporate participation in the discussion would exert undue influence on the referendum vote or threaten public confidence in the democratic process. With respect to shareholder interests, the court said the statute was both over-inclusive in that it prevented corporations from expressing the views of their shareholders on ballot measures and under-inclusive in that it prohibited expenditures with respect to a referendum but not with respect to proposed legislation.[44]

Corporate Funds and the Political Process

A corporation's economic power and the potential threat that power exerts on a freely functioning marketplace of ideas have been an ongoing concern ever since the Supreme Court handed down ***Buckley v. Valeo*** in 1976. In *Buckley*, the court ruled that spending money to influence an election is a form of speech,[45] and as such restrictions on those expenditures must undergo heightened constitutional review.[46] The court reasoned that laws that limit campaign spending harm the marketplace by reducing the number of issues discussed and the depth and breadth of that discussion.[47] Regulators and critics of *Buckley* have long countered that without spending limits, large corporations will use their aggregated wealth to distort and corrupt the political process for private gain. The conduct most feared is the use of vast amounts of corporate and personal wealth to unduly influence voters by skewing the perceived support for a candidate or political issue.

The Supreme Court took the issue of corporate speech in connection with political elections head-on in *Citizens United v. Federal Election Commission*. At issue in the case was the planned release of a ninety-minute documentary that was highly critical of Senator Hillary Rodham Clinton, a Democratic candidate in the 2008 presidential primary elections. Citizens United, a nonprofit organization that accepted corporate funding, wanted to make the film available free of charge to digital cable subscribers. The organization's plans, however, ran counter to the **Bipartisan Campaign Reform Act of 2002**, which prohibited corporations from using their **general treasury funds** on "electioneering communication." The act defined **electioneering communication** as "any broadcast, cable or satellite communication" that "refers to a clearly identified candidate for Federal office" and is made within thirty days of a primary or sixty days of a general election. In addition to BCRA, federal law also prohibited corporations from making **independent expenditures** advocating the election or defeat of a candidate.[48]

The federal government argued that the law was necessary to prevent corruption in the political process. The court rejected that objective, concluding that expenditures, including those made by corporations, that are carried out independent of a campaign, candidate, political party, and their agents "do not give rise to corruption or the appearance of corruption."[49] The court based its conclusion on *Buckley*, which ruled that the government interest in preventing *quid pro quo* **corruption** or the appearance of such corruption was inadequate to justify a ban on independent expenditures.[50] The *Buckley* court reasoned that unlike direct contributions to candidates, independent expenditures may not only provide little assistance to a campaign but may also prove to be counterproductive to the candidate.[51] As long as the expenditure was truly independent and made without any prearranged or coordinated efforts between the corporation and the candidate, no improper *quid pro quo* corruption transpired.

In addition to *quid pro quo* corruption, the government also feared that the large sums of money spent by the corporation would unfairly gain the company favoritism and influence from the public official. The court found that favoritism, influence, and increased access to elected officials are unavoidable in representative politics and did not constitute a legitimate justification for restricting corporate speech. Influence and favoritism are broad and largely limitless concepts that defy the precision needed to pass strict scrutiny review and the constitution's requirement that restrictions on speech must be narrowly tailored to achieve a compelling governmental objective.[52]

The ruling in *Citizens United* upended restrictions on political campaign spending by allowing all corporations (including nonprofit corporations and trade unions) to spend unlimited amounts of money to expressly advocate the election or defeat of a candidate for federal office. In doing so, the decision significantly altered the contours of debate within the marketplace by bringing the political voices of corporations within the framework of the First Amendment.

Compelled Disclosure and Corporate Speech

The Bipartisan Campaign Reform Act also required outside parties that placed televised election ads that referred to a candidate for federal office to clearly state and display the name and address or website of the person or group that funded the advertisement. In addition, any person who spent more than $10,000 on such electioneering communications is required to disclose their identity, the amount spent, the election targeted, and the names of certain contributors.

Citizens United, a nonprofit organization, challenged these requirements, but the court upheld the provisions based on a governmental interest in providing citizens with nonmisleading information about the sources of election-related spending. The requirements, the court said, help citizens make fully informed political decisions that give proper weight to the various speakers and messages they encounter as well as avoid confusion as to the involvement of a candidate or political party with the communication. Moreover, disclaimer and disclosure requirements are a less restrictive alternative to speech bans. Here, no one was prevented from speaking or even suggested that the regulation would chill future expression. And the requirements did not foreclose any lawsuits where compelled disclosure would subject contributors to threats, harassment, or reprisals from government or private entities.[53]

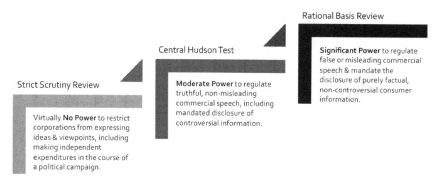

Figure 2.3. Government's sliding scale of constitutional power to regulate economically motivated speech.

CHAPTER SUMMARY

The court has struggled over the last half century to appropriately fit commercial and corporate expression into a body of free speech law built largely on an open and unregulated marketplace approach. In this effort, a mixed bag of constitutional review has emerged that embraces three levels of scrutiny and provides the government with a sliding scale of constitutional power to regulate economically motivated expression. On that scale, government's power is at its weakest point when it's used to restrict corporations from speaking out on matters of public concern and making independent expenditures in the course of a political campaign. It is at its strongest when it is preventing false or misleading commercial speech from entering the marketplace or requiring commercial speakers to disclose factual, noncontroversial information about their products and services to consumers.

At the intermediate level, the Central Hudson test was developed to review regulations and bans on truthful nonmisleading commercial information as well as mandated disclosures of controversial consumer information. The test, however, is not without its judicial critics, who say that stricter review standards should be applied when commercial speech bans are aimed at curbing the use of a legal product to manipulate consumer behavior. In the area of corporate speech, the court adopted a more speech-protective approach that allows corporations to fully engage in political debate. In doing so, it rejected the idea that corruption could include acts of favoritism and influence but upheld disclosure requirements intended to make citizens more fully informed and less susceptible to misinformation.

KEY TERMS

Bipartisan Campaign Reform Act of 2002 The Bipartisan Campaign Reform Act of 2002 expanded the scope of the campaign spending prohibitions on corporations. Under the act, corporations were prohibited from using general treasury funds on "electioneering communication,"—"any broadcast, cable, or satellite communication" that "refers to a clearly identified candidate for Federal office" and is made within sixty days before a general election or thirty days before a primary election. *Citizens United v. Federal Election Commission* overturned this part of the act but upheld the act's disclosure mandate that required outside parties engaged in electioneering communications to identify themselves as well as provide additional related information.

Blanket Bans on Commercial Speech   Regulations that prohibit the dissemination of truthful, nonmisleading commercial speech are referred to as blanket bans. These regulations aim to reduce the demand for a certain product by restricting its promotional advertisement. Because they seek to manipulate consumer choice by withholding truthful information from the ideas market, blanket bans need to be reviewed with special care.

Bolger v. Youngs Drug Products Corp.   A 1983 US Supreme Court decision that stopped short of providing a definitive definition of commercial speech. In *Bolger*, the court said that when speech is formatted as an advertisement, references a product, and is economically motivated, there is strong support that it is commercial speech.

Buckley v. Valeo   A 1976 US Supreme Court decision that established the idea that spending money to influence an election is a form of speech.

Central Hudson Gas & Electric Corp. v. Public Service Commission   A 1980 Supreme Court decision that fashioned the First Amendment review standard governing constitutional challenges to commercial speech regulations.

Central Hudson Standard   A two-tiered standard of review courts apply to constitutional challenges involving commercial speech restrictions. The first tier separates unprotected commercial speech from protected commercial speech. The second tier evaluates whether the restriction on truthful, nonmisleading commercial speech is constitutional. Here, the burden is on the government to show that the regulation is narrowly tailored to directly advance a substantial government objective.

Citizens United v. Federal Election Commission   A 2010 US Supreme Court decision that struck down federal restrictions on political campaign spending by corporations. In doing so, the court affirmed the First Amendment right of corporations to spend unlimited amounts of money to independently and expressly advocate the election or defeat of a candidate for federal office.

Commercial Speech

Accuracy Standard   Only truthful nonmisleading commercial information receives constitutional protection. The accuracy standard is not viewed as overly burdensome to commercial speakers because they can easily verify the truthfulness of their claims.

Chilling Effect   Commercial speakers are economically motivated to engage in speech and thus their speech is viewed as hardier and more able to overcome any chilling effect from regulatory restrictions.

Definition   No definitive definition of commercial speech exists. See *Bolger v. Youngs Drug Products Corp.* and *Kasky v. Nike.*

Compelled Disclosure Requirements   Factual, noncontroversial information that commercial speakers are required to disclose to protect consumers and equip them with the knowledge they need to make informed choices. An example would be health risk warnings on cigarette packages.

Corporate Speech   As legal persons, corporations have free speech rights that are comparable to the rights that individuals hold. Before *Citizens United* was handed down, corporations were restricted in their ability to advocate for or against a candidate for public office. That is no longer the case.

Electioneering Communication   Electioneering communication is defined as "any broadcast, cable, or satellite communication" that "refers to a clearly identified candidate for Federal office" and is made within sixty days before a general election or thirty days before a primary election.

First National Bank of Boston v. Bellotti   A 1978 corporate speech case that focused on the inherent worth of the speech to the marketplace rather than the economic strength of the speaker. Using this line of thought, the court recognized the First Amendment right of corporations to speak as members of society.

General Treasury Funds   These funds are amassed from the profits corporations earn. The *Citizens United* decision struck down restrictions on the use of these funds to influence the outcome of federal elections. Critics of the decision argue that access to such large amounts of money significantly advantages corporations and the political ideas they support.

Independent Expenditure   The money spent on political communications that expressly advocates the election or defeat of a clearly identified candidate. Independent expenditures differ from direct campaign contributions in that they are *not* made in coordination with any candidate or any committee, party, or agent authorized by the candidate.

Kasky v. Nike A 2002 California Supreme Court decision that provided a mechanism for defining commercial speech through an evaluation of four elements: the speaker, the intended audience, and the content and purpose of the message.

Legal Persons A nonhuman entity, such as a corporation, that has many of the same rights as natural persons and thus may sue for an alleged violation of those rights.

New York Times v. Sullivan A 1964 US Supreme Court opinion that recognized the public interest value in commercial speech. The case involved an advertisement that sought to educate the public on the civil rights movement as well as seek financial support for the Committee to Defend Dr. Martin Luther King Jr. At the time of the decision, commercial speech received no First Amendment protection. This decision knocked down that barrier and provided public-issue speech of a commercial nature with free speech protection.

Quid pro quo Corruption Quid pro quo is a Latin phrase meaning "a thing for a thing." In the political arena, quid pro quo corruption typically refers to the exchange of money or other things of value for an official act. The government's interest in guarding against this form of corruption has resulted in restrictions on direct contributions to candidates as well as independent expenditures advocating the election or defeat of a candidate. The *Citizens United* court, however, struck down regulations on independent expenditures, ruling that this form of campaign spending does not give rise to quid pro quo corruption or the appearance of such corruption.

Rational Basis Review A low level of scrutiny often applied to constitutional challenges of factual, noncontroversial disclosure requirements intended to protect consumers. Regulations reviewed under this standard are considered constitutional if they are rationally related to a legitimate government interest.

Right to Receive Information The right to receive information is a corollary right to the right to speak and publish information. This right prevents government from constitutionally restricting the sharing of information. The right of consumers to receive accurate commercial information underlies the First Amendment protection this form of speech receives.

Vacated To set aside or legally void a previous judgment.

Vice Products   Alcohol, tobacco, gambling, and products of this nature are vulnerable to blanket bans given the harmful effects associated with their use and abuse.

Zauderer v. Office of Disciplinary Counsel   A 1984 US Supreme Court decision that separated the mandated disclosure of factual, noncontroversial information to prevent consumer deception from compelled speech restrictions that force commercial speakers to express views and opinions with which they disagreed. The former, the court said, was less violative of First Amendment values than the latter.

3

Copyright

The evolutionary nature of a free and unfettered ideas market is a vital component in the advancement of science and expressive creativity. Throughout history, ideas from the past have been borrowed, reimagined, and reinvented into works of the present in an innovative process fueled by both freedom and restraint. The freedom to create and the right to restrain the use of that creation are inherent in the tension between the First Amendment's free speech guarantees and the restriction on expression that occurs with the ownership of a **copyright**. Copyrights—like free speech rights—aim to stimulate the production of creative works. They do so by granting an **intellectual property** right in products of the mind. This property right allows owners of creative works to realize the full economic benefits of their imagination and provides a means to punish others who illegally **appropriate** it.

The US Constitution gives Congress the power to promote the advancement of creative intellectual activity by giving to authors and inventors exclusive rights in their respective writings and discoveries for a limited time. Through the establishment of a marketable right in the creation of original expressive works, copyright law is viewed as an "engine of free expression"[1] intended to encourage and advance intellectual activity. Today, copyright law extends broad protection to authors of works that are

- Original: The work must be independently conceived and created by a human author. This allows two photographers, for example, to take a picture of the Grand Canyon from the same vantage point at approximately the same time on the same day, and each retain a copyright of the work produced. **Originality** also extends to a collection of unoriginal works if the choice or arrangement of those works by the compiling author is substantially original. While each work in the collection retains its own copyright protection, the compiling author may receive a copyright in the collection.

- Creative: The work must possess at least some minimal degree of **creativity**. According to the Supreme Court, even a slight amount of creativity is enough to clear this requirement. Works that closely resemble each other also maintain their originality as long as the similarities are inadvertent and not the result of copying.[2]
- Fixed in a Tangible Medium of Expression: The idea must be translated into a stable, sufficiently permanent copy that allows it to be perceived, reproduced, or communicated for more than a short period. Since the work stems from the author's creativity, the author is responsible for translating or directing the translation of the creative idea into a **fixed, tangible medium**.

Figure 3.1. This picture of a monkey is actually a selfie. That is, the monkey, a female Macaca, took the photo of herself after a photographer set up the camera. Because the photo is not original to the photographer and the U.S. Copyright Office does not register works created by animals, the picture is not eligible for copyright protection.

Photo via *Wikimedia Commons*.

EXCLUSIVE RIGHTS

A copyright exists in a creative work of original authorship once it is fixed in a tangible medium. The work may also be registered with the US Copyright Office. Registration is relatively easy and provides additional benefits, including a certificate of ownership. Once protected, the work becomes an intangible asset with an economic value that can be exploited through a set of **exclusive rights** granted only to holders of the copyright. Like other forms of property, these rights may be sold, assigned, and inherited. The copyright holder may subdivide them by transferring a portion or the entire set of rights to one or more entities through agreements that spell out the exact arrangement between the parties. In the end, these rights allow the copyright holder to control authorized and unauthorized uses of the work by permitting or preventing others from exercising the following rights:

Reproduction

The copyright holder maintains the exclusive right to reproduce the work and may prevent others from unauthorized copying of the entire work as well as limited or small portions of the work.

Creation of Derivative Works

A **derivative** is a new work of original authorship that is based on one or more preexisting copyrighted works. A derivative is created, for example, when a novel is turned into a motion picture. Because the intent of the motion picture is to make a film version of the novel, the film is considered a derivative of the book. Only copyright holders have the right to produce or authorize derivatives based on their original works.

Distribution

The right to distribute gives the copyright holder control over the sale, rental, lease, and lending of the work. However, this right is limited by the **first-sale doctrine** to the first sale or distribution of the work. Once a book is purchased, for example, the copyright holder is no longer able to control the book's distribution. The book could be rented, sold, or otherwise disposed of without permission of the copyright holder; however, it could not be reproduced, adapted, published, or performed without authorization. The first-sale doctrine applies to works lawfully made and sold under the US

Copyright Act. The rental of computer programs and sound recordings, and the destruction of certain types of artworks are exempted from the doctrine.

Public Performance

Copyrighted works that can be performed live or through analog or digital transmission by radio, television, and internet streaming are protected under the **public performance** right. This includes literary, musical, dramatic, choreographic, audiovisual, motion picture, and pantomime works. Under the public performance right, copyright holders can control when the work is performed publicly.

A performance is considered public when the work is performed in or transmitted to a "place open to the public or at a place where a substantial number of persons"[3] other than family or close friends are gathered. This includes everything from live concerts in venues that hold tens of thousands of fans to the recorded music played at small, private business or charitable functions.

Limited exceptions apply for certain religious and educational uses as well as smaller businesses that display audio-video performances from licensed radio, television, cable, and satellite services. The exceptions are very precise and take into consideration the size of the establishment, number of speakers, number and size of TV screens, whether an admission fee is charged, and whether the performance is retransmitted beyond the establishment.

The public performance right also covers the transmission or communication of a work to the public by "any device or process whereby images or sounds are received beyond the place from which they are sent."[4] According to the court, the purpose of this provision is to prohibit such activities as the unauthorized retransmission of a network broadcast to subscribers of cable service.[5]

Public Display

The public display right covers works that can be shown visually to others either directly, such as a painting on the wall, or indirectly by means of a film, slide, television image, or any other device or process. A **public display** right is similar to the public performance right in that the definition of "public" is the same for both. A display is also considered public when it is posted to the internet. That said, confusion between the two rights does occur with regard to audiovisual works. An audiovisual work is displayed rather than performed when its individual images are shown nonsequentially rather than in a sequence as in a performance.

COPYRIGHT AND FIRST AMENDMENT VALUES

The legal authority to prevent others from exercising these rights provides an economic incentive to create and produce original works of authorship. This incentive also links copyright protection to the First Amendment and its speech-oriented market values. As an engine of expression, copyright protects from further use of vast quantities of creative works of original authorship that exist in the marketplace. If taken to its extreme, copyright law, which seeks to stimulate creation, may in fact diminish the market by prohibiting the entry of new works based on the ideas of protected works. The court has acknowledged this concern and the fact that few, if any, creative works are entirely new and original throughout.[6] Instead, the creative process consistently builds and borrows from what is well known and used before.[7]

To secure a robust marketplace of intellectual and creative exchange, copyright law built in two First Amendment accommodations that limit the scope of the exclusive rights. The first distinguishes between ideas and expression and facts and expression. Referred to broadly as the **idea/expression dichotomy**, this accommodation confines copyright protection to those components and only those components of a work that are original to the author. Originality, the courts said, is the essential component of copyright.[8] This means that the underlying facts and ideas contained within the work are not copyrightable.[9] Only the original expression of those facts and ideas receives copyright protection. This limitation in copyright law stimulates the creation of original works in the first place while providing the breathing space necessary for the subsequent creations of original works built on the same or similar ideas and facts.

While the idea/expression dichotomy appears to be fairly straightforward, it is difficult to apply the doctrine to a particular situation because the Copyright Act does not define what constitutes a "fact," "idea," or "expression." The lack of a definitional boundary in the act hampers the ability of subsequent authors to precisely distinguish between a work's underlying ideas or facts and the expression of those ideas/facts. This uncertainty has the capacity to chill expression and encourage aggressive copyright claims that maintain that almost any borrowing from a protected work constitutes an actionable infringement.[10]

Facts, Ideas, and Expression

The court has explained that facts in and of themselves are discoverable and therefore do not owe their origin to an act of original authorship.[11] For example, the first person to find and record a fact did not create the fact—but merely uncovered the fact. This holds true regardless of how much time and money it took to unearth the fact. In copyright law, facts are special. They serve as the building blocks of new works and need to be freed from expression so that subsequent authors may restate, reshuffle, and reuse them. Moreover, the public needs access to facts. Given the public interest value in facts, facts lie outside the scope of copyright protection. Instead, it is the author's selection, arrangement, and compilation of facts that embody originality and subjectivity and thus receive copyright protection.

In compilations, authors need to choose the facts and determine their most effective placement and arrangement. These independent choices even in a factual work void of any written expression contain enough creativity and originality to warrant copyright protection in the components that are original to the author. The degree of protection in a fact-based compilation that contains no original expression is thin in that only the selection and arrangement of the facts are protected. In such works, subsequent authors are free to use the facts contained in another's publication even when preparing a competing work, but the written expression of those facts, that is, the exact words used to communicate them, may not be copied.

The Supreme Court tackled the interaction between uncopyrightable facts and protected compilations in *Feist Publications, Inc. v. Rural Telephone Service Co., Inc*. At issue in *Feist* were competing telephone directories. One listed the names, towns, and telephone numbers of a local telephone service area's subscribers and the other assembled the same information from eleven different service areas into a competing directory that covered a much wider geographic area. In its compilation, Feist Publications used most of the subscriber listings in the directory produced by Rural Telephone but modified some of the listings to include additional information, such as street addresses. Rural Telephone sued for copyright infringement.

The court held that as a purely factual compilation Rural's white page directory lacked originality and was not entitled to copyright protection.[12] The key consideration in determining whether an author of a compilation can claim originality is whether the selection, coordination, and arrangement of the facts are sufficiently subjective to merit protection.[13] Originality, the court explained, requires a subjective selection or arrangement of facts that exhibits some minimal level of creativity. The court acknowledged that the vast majority of compilations will pass this test, and only those works "in which the creative spark is utterly lacking or so trivial as to be virtually non-existent" will be denied copyright protection.[14] Rural's directory fell into that category. The court found nothing even remotely creative about arranging names alphabetically. Such an arrangement, the court said, is an "age-old practice, firmly rooted in tradition and so commonplace that it has come to be expected as a matter of course."[15]

The consideration of **fact v. expression** extends beyond the collation of basic information. In *Rentmeester v. Nike*, the Ninth Circuit regarded the individual elements that comprise a photograph as "unprotectable facts that anyone may use to create new works."[16] According to the *Rentmeester* court, photographs can be broken down into various creative choices related to subject matter, pose, lighting, camera angle, depth of field, and the like. These choices when viewed in isolation do not warrant copyright protection. The court explained that a *"photographer who produces a photo using a highly original lighting technique or a novel camera angle cannot prevent other photographers from using those same techniques to produce new images of their own."*[17] The same holds true with respect to the subject of the photograph. This means that the protection a photograph receives is limited to the particular selection and arrangement of the subject matter, pose, camera angle, and so forth.

Figure 3.2. When creative choices for product shots are quite limited, differences in camera angle, lighting, shadowing, etc., may be enough to protect a secondary work from an infringement claim.

Photos courtesy of Robert Whitmore and Brian Brosmer

That said, it is important to note that the extent of copyright protection can vary among photographs and other creative works. Works in which the range of creative choices available are quite limited are entitled to only **"thin" protection**. In *Ets-Hokin v. Skyy Spirits, Inc.*, the court determined that a series of product shots of a blue bottle of Skyy Vodka was entitled to thin protection given the limited number of ways one could photograph the item for a marketing campaign. As a practical matter, this meant that the original product shots were entitled to protection only against virtually identical copying.[18] In *Ets-Hokin*, the court found that while the photographs at issue shared the same concept, idea, and subject matter, they differed, within the constraints of the commercial product shot, in camera angle, lighting, shadowing, highlights, reflection, and background. These differences, the court ruled, were enough to protect the secondary work against an infringement claim.

Merger Doctrine and *Scènes à Faire*

Aspects of the photographs at issue in *Ets-Hokin* implicate the merger doctrine, a concept in copyright law that prevents the protection of a work if the underlying idea can be expressed only in one way. For instance, the symbol of a circle with a diagonal line crossed through it is one of only a few ways to visually express that an activity is not permitted. In this circumstance, the idea, which is to visually communicate that an activity is prohibited, is virtually indistinguishable and inseparable from the expression.

For that reason, the expression of the symbol lies outside copyright protection and may be legally used in a wide variety of contexts—for example, no swimming, no food or drink, no cell phone—by a wide range of creators.[19]

Figure 3.3. The idea that an activity is prohibited is inseparable from its expression. Because the two have merged, the symbol is not eligible for copyright protection.

To determine whether an idea and its expression have merged, courts begin by identifying the underlying concept of the work and considering the range of ways that the subject matter could be expressed.[20] When the entire range of conceivable artistic choices is severely limited, the variation of creative input by the author may be too trivial to meet the originality standard.[21] As a result, the expression of the idea receives no copyright protection. Courts have reasoned that granting copyright protection to a "merged" work would effectively allow the copyright holder to retain a monopoly on the idea underlying the work.

This line of reasoning also applies to the companion doctrine *scènes à faire*. Under *scènes à faire*, expressive elements that are "standard, stock or common to a particular subject matter or medium are not protectable under copyright."[22] This includes stock themes, scenes, character traits, and descriptions. For example, one would expect stories about college fraternities to contain parties, alcohol, coeds, and wild behavior.[23] As such, these elements of a story about a college fraternity may be freely used by all artists. Likewise, the doctrine covers commonly employed artistic elements and techniques that follow naturally from the idea.

An illustration of this point involves realistic depictions of animals in their natural surroundings. Such depictions will have commonly held expressive elements that no artist may copyright. For instance, an eagle with talons extended to snatch a mouse, a grizzly bear clutching a salmon between its teeth, and a brightly colored jellyfish swimming vertically through tropical waters are ideas first expressed by nature, and as such these ideas belong to the public.[24] This means that an artist who creates a glass-in-glass sculpture of a jellyfish may not prevent another artist from producing a glass-in-glass sculpture depicting a brightly colored jellyfish with a rounded head and tendril-like tentacles positioned vertically in the glass. Given that the second artist may use the natural expressive elements that follow the idea, the two works will have common unprotectable elements.

The glass-in-glass sculpture was at issue in *Satava v. Lowry*. In this case, the court noted that copyright protection may be extended to a combination of numerous unprotectable elements if their selection and arrangement are subjective enough to constitute a work of original authorship. When the court applied this holding to the plaintiff's glass-in-glass jellyfish sculpture, it concluded that the unprotected elements employed were too commonplace and typical to qualify for copyright protection. The court noted, however, that the artistic choices not governed by the natural physiology of the fish or the glass-in-glass medium, namely the distinctive curls of the particular tendrils, the arrangement of certain hues of color, and the unique shape of the jellyfish's head, were original elements that warranted copyright protection.

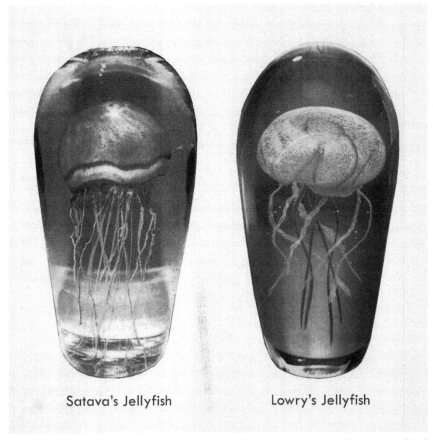

Satava's Jellyfish   Lowry's Jellyfish

Figure 3.4. The court found that the similarities between the two works were confined to a combination of the unprotectable lifelike elements of the jellyfish, i.e., tendril-like tentacles, rounded bells, bright colors and vertical swimming pattern. By contrast, the distinctive curls, unique shape of the bells and the hues of colors are original to the artists and protected by copyright.

Photo of Satava's Jellyfish courtesy of Richard Satava.
Photo of Lowry's Jellyfish courtesy of Christopher Lowry.

INFRINGEMENT

Dissecting a creative work into its protectable and unprotectable parts can be a difficult and complicated process. Courts engage in this process to determine whether any of the exclusive rights listed were infringed—that is, used without permission of the copyright holder. To prove **infringement**, a plaintiff bringing suit must show

1. Ownership of a valid copyright;
2. That the defendant copied from the plaintiff's work; and
3. That the defendant copied a substantial amount of protected expression from the plaintiff's work.

Copyright infringement is most easily established when an exact reproduction of the plaintiff's work has been created—for example, when a song is illegally downloaded, and the owner holds a valid copyright registration. Infringement becomes harder to determine when a defendant was inspired by an earlier work. In such cases, a plaintiff must establish that the defendant actually copied the plaintiff's work to create the allegedly infringing work. Proof of copying in stage one of the process ordinarily requires showing that the defendant had access to the plaintiff's work and that the two works resemble each other. Access can be established when the defendant had a reasonable opportunity to view or copy the plaintiff's work. This may be proven when the plaintiff's work has been widely distributed or a particular chain of events enabled the defendant to gain access to the work. In addition to access, the works must share certain similarities that prove or tend to prove copying.

In determining whether stage one copying occurred, courts may allow expert testimony and the dissection of works into their objective components.[25] For example, a book or screenplay could be separated into its plot; characters; themes; dialogue; setting, mood and place; and sequence of events. Such a dissection may not be necessary, however, if the similarities are so striking that they virtually preclude the possibility that the two works were created independently.[26] Evidence in this realm includes similarities that are "quirky or appear in unique or complex contexts, and common mistakes or idiosyncrasies that can only be explained by copying."[27] At this stage of review, both protected and unprotected elements of the plaintiff's work are considered. This first step is important given that an independent creation is a complete defense to copyright infringement.

Substantial Similarity

If stage one copying occurred, the court will then examine whether the defendant's actions went so far as to constitute unlawful copying from a protected work. This step of the process focuses on whether a **substantial similarity** exists between the protected elements of the copyrighted work and the defendant's work. In determining whether two creative works are substantially similar, the unprotectable elements of the plaintiff's work are filtered from the protected expression. This includes ideas and concepts; material no longer protected by copyright; and standard, stock, or commonly used

Substantial Similarity

Proof of Copying: Stage 1	Proof of Copying: Stage 2
• Need to show access to plaintiff's work & that the two works resemble each other.	• Need to establish that a substantial similarity exists between the protected elements of the two works.

Access:
- Plaintiff's work is widely distributed (or)
- Defendant gained access through a particular chain of events.

Resemblance:
- Both protected and unprotected elements of plaintiff's work are considered.
- Expert testimony & dissection of works into their objective components may be allowed.
- Dissection is not necessary if similarities are striking.
- Goal is to establish that defendant's work was not independently created.

Filter:
- The unprotected elements in the plaintiff's work are separated from the work's protected expression.

Compare Similarities:
- The protected elements from the plaintiff's work are compared to the corresponding elements of defendant's work.
- Courts look for quantitively and qualitatively meaningful similarities.

Figure 3.5.

expressive features. The protectable elements that remain form the basis of an infringement claim and are compared to the corresponding elements of the defendant's work to assess similarity and unlawful appropriation.

A case in point, *Rentmeester v. Nike*, involves Nike's iconic photo of Michael Jordan leaping toward a basketball hoop, left arm extended and hand clutching the ball in a slam dunk attempt. The origin of that image can be traced back to a photo conceived and produced by Jacobus Rentmeester. Rentmeester's initial image of Jordan appeared in an issue of *Life* magazine as part of a photo essay featuring US athletes who were set to compete in the 1984 Summer Olympic Games. Soon after its publication, Nike obtained a limited license for $150 from Rentmeester to use a color transparency of the photo in a slide presentation. A year later, Nike produced a similar photograph of Jordan and began using that photo as part of its marketing campaign for its new Air Jordan brand of shoes. In 2015, Rentmeester filed a copyright infringement claim against Nike, alleging that the Nike photo infringed his 1984 photo of Jordan. While it took a long time for the case to develop, it provides an illustrative backdrop to explore how courts determine copyright infringement.

In the case, the court found that Rentmeester's photograph was "highly original" given the unusual position Rentmeester instructed the basketball player to assume. The leap toward the basket mimicked a grand jeté ballet pose in which a "dancer leaps with legs extended, one foot forward and the other back."[28] Rentmeester coupled this unusual pose with a low camera angle that captured Jordan at the peak of the jump as a soaring figure silhouetted against a cloudless blue sky. Powerful strobe lights and a fast shutter speed allowed Rentmeester to capture a sharp image of Jordan contrasted against the sky and the glare of the sun "shining directly into the camera lens from the lower right-hand corner of the shot."[29]

In evaluating the facts of the case, the court concluded that the "Nike photo was the product of copying rather than independent creation" given the shoe company's access to Rentmeester's photo and the "obvious conceptual similarities between the two photos."[30] The remaining question of whether Nike copied enough of the original photo's protected expression to render the two works substantially similar would determine if the defendant crossed the line between lawful and unlawful copying. Determining how much copying is too much is a difficult question to answer. Congress, the Supreme Court, and the Copyright Act have not provided any real substantive guidance on this question.[31] Consequently, lower courts differ on how best to determine substantial similarity.

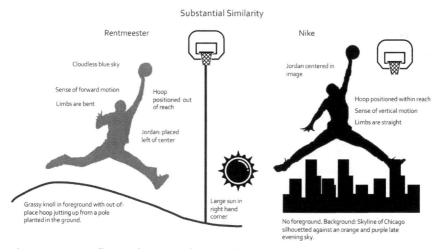

Figure 3.6. According to the court, the two photos share conceptual similarities, e.g., Jordan attempting to dunk a basketball, grand jeté-inspired pose, sparse outdoor setting, and lone basketball hoop. But the photos are not substantially similar given the distinct creative choices each photographer made in the selection & arrangement of these expressive elements.

Graphic includes Nike's Jumpman logo & silhouetted pose of Jordan as represented in Rentmeester's photograph.

The court reviewing *Rentmeester* focused on the similarities in the selection and arrangement of the photos' protected elements. While the two photos are similar in idea, concept, and subject matter, the court found that Nike's photographer made his own distinct creative choices concerning the highly original elements of Rentmeester's photo. Those elements included the details of the pose and the unusual outdoor setting Rentmeester chose. Both of these details were expressed differently in each photograph. For example, the court pointed out that the positioning of Jordan's limbs is different as well as the settings, the use of foreground, the height and positioning of the basketball hoops, and the arrangement of the elements within the frame of the photographs. These differences, the court said, affect the overall visual impact of the photos and preclude a finding of substantial similarity.[32]

"When works of art share an idea, they'll often be 'similar' in the layman's sense of the term. For example, two sets of stuffed, cuddly dinosaurs will be similar in that they are both stuffed, cuddly dinosaurs—but that's not the sort of similarity we look for in copyright law. 'Substantial similarity' for copyright infringement requires a similarity of expression, not ideas. The key question always is: Are the works substantially similar beyond the fact that they depict the same idea?"[33]

Ordinary Observer

In the end, the Ninth Circuit concluded that all Nike's photographer did was to build upon the ideas and information conveyed by Rentmeester's work. In coming to this conclusion, the court applied a type of **ordinary observer test** to determine whether the two photographs were substantially similar. This test assesses the ordinary observer's subjective reaction to the works and whether that reaction regards the aesthetic appeal[34] of the plaintiff's protected expression and the defendant's work as the same.[35] With this approach, the observer's reaction may not be aided by expert advice or an intent to detect the similarities or disparities in the two works. Instead, the test explores the question of whether the defendant took enough of the plaintiff's protected expression that a lay spectator or intended audience member[36] recognizes that the "defendant wrongfully appropriated something which belongs to the plaintiff."[37] In *Rentmeester*, the court found that Nike's photographer produced an image so unmistakably different in its choice of details that no ordinary observer could overlook the disparities between the two works.[38]

While the court ruled in Nike's favor, it acknowledged that no well-defined standard exists for assessing when **nonliteral similarities** become substantial.

Consequently, three discrete approaches to determine substantial similarity have been fashioned by the circuit courts. Often referred to as "tests," they are the ordinary observer, extrinsic/intrinsic, and abstraction-filtration comparison tests. In practice, each of the twelve circuits has used one or more of these tests with varying degrees of consistency and jurisdiction-specific modifications. As a result, multiple approaches framed in different language have developed.[39] These approaches, however, tend to follow a fairly common although not always recognizable path that involves the (1) identification of literal and nonliteral similarities; (2) separation of unprotected material from protected expression; and (3) comparison of protected elements for quantitatively and qualitatively meaningful similarities.[40]

The relative complexity of the aesthetic arts and the unique factual scenarios that develop make it nearly impossible to develop a hard and fast rule for determining substantial similarity. As a result, the American Bar Association advises copyright holders to use caution "when deciding whether to allege or defend infringement actions."[41] Before initiating a case, the ABA recommends that copyright holders examine how the chosen jurisdiction has applied and modified one or more of the above tests when assessing substantial similarity. In doing so, it is wise to review factually similar cases given that the application of these approaches can vary depending on the type of work at issue.[42]

In terms of photography, for example, Rentmeester illustrated this point in his petition requesting review of the Ninth Circuit's decision by the US Supreme Court. In the petition, he argued that the Ninth Circuit's approach, which limited copyright protection to the photographer's selection and arrangement of individual elements, deviated from the rulings of other circuit courts. In *Rogers v. Koons*, for instance, the Second Circuit noted that "[e]lements of originality in a photograph may include posing the subjects, lighting, angle, selection of film and camera, evoking the desired expression, and almost any other variate involved."[43] The Eleventh Circuit followed by concluding that "the selection of lighting, shading, timing, angle, and film" were all elements of a photograph that are protected by copyright law.[44]

Rentmeester argued that the most original elements of his photograph resulted from the artistic judgments he made concerning the positioning of Jordan, the selection and manipulation of lighting and landscape, and the employment of composition techniques involving the angle, lens, and depth of field.[45] These elements, the petition contended, were both meticulously created by Rentmeester and meticulously pirated by Nike.[46] Because the High Court declined to resolve the tension among the circuits, plaintiffs, like Rentmeester, are likely to fare better before courts that view copyright protection in a photograph as also extending to elements that express original, creative judgments by the photographer.

CONTOURS OF COPYRIGHT LAW

Copyright protection is extended to a wide array of original works of authorship that fall within the categories of copyright-eligible subject matter. Those categories can be broken into the following:[47]

- Literary: Works intended to be read through expression in words, numbers, or other verbal or numerical symbols or indicia. Includes books, articles, manuscripts, blogs, catalogs, advertising copy, directories, instructions, tests, and other such works.
- Visual Arts: A wide variety of two- and three-dimensional pictorial, graphic, sculptural, and architectural works. Includes paintings, illustrations and photographs; textile, fabric, flooring and jewelry designs; puppets, cartoon characters, toys, models and comic strips; prints, posters and reproductions; maps, charts, technical drawings and diagrams; product packaging, visual advertising, labels and logos; blueprints and buildings; and other such works.
- Performing Arts: Works intended to be performed either directly or by any device or process for an audience. A performance means to recite, render, dance, play, or act, and in the case of audiovisual works to show images in any sequence or to make the accompanying sounds audible. Includes music, lyrics, songs, music editing, musical arrangement, musicals (song/script), sound effects, beats, instrumentation, sound recordings, mixed tapes, sampling, karaoke, live concerts, vocal remixes and mashups; screenplays, scripts, stage plays, comedy routines, teleplays, dances, and choreography; podcasts, TV/radio broadcasts, and other such works.
- Audiovisual: Works that contain a series of related images and accompanying sound, if any, that are intended to be shown with a machine or device. Includes animations, documentaries, motion pictures, television shows, videos, multimedia works, commercials, banner advertisements, slide presentations (including PowerPoint), and other such audiovisual work.
- Other Digital Content: A wide variety of additional works that are used with computers, tablets, smartphones, videogame platforms, and other electronic devices. This category also includes works used or distributed on the internet. Includes websites and blogs; video games and virtual

reality environments; apps, computer programs, and screen displays; databases, spreadsheets, and other such works.

Works in these categories are eligible for copyright protection if they contain a minimum amount of creativity that is original to a human author and the expressive work is fixed in a tangible medium. To determine whether a work contains a sufficient degree of creative expression to satisfy the originality requirement, the US Copyright Office focuses on the actual appearance or sound of the work submitted for registration. In its evaluation, the office does not consider artistic choices and qualitative measures, such as the work's aesthetic appeal, value, or meaning; its look, feel, and material composition; the author's intent, design choices, skill, and experience; the time, effort or expense it took to create work; or the likelihood of commercial success. Works that do not fall within the permitted subject matter categories are not copyrightable.

As addressed earlier in this chapter, facts and ideas do not constitute copyrightable subject matter in that they are essentially the building blocks of original authorship. To prevent others from using the underlying facts and ideas in protected works would stifle creativity and inhibit free expression. Given the tension between protection and the production of new creative pieces, works that lack sufficient creativity or merely supply the raw materials on which copyrightable creations are built are also not eligible for copyright protection.

Processes, Procedures, Methods, or Systems

Any work or portion of a work that is an "idea, procedure, process, system, method of operation, concept principle, or discovery, regardless of the form in which it is described, explained, illustrated, or embodied" is not eligible for copyright protection.[48] This includes scientific and technological methods or discoveries; business operations; mathematical formulas, algorithms, or equations as well as the processes or procedures for making or building things and the concept for a creative work.[49] This exclusion does not include a written description or drawing of the idea or process. The expression of these concepts may be protected and that protection will prevent others from copying or distributing the work of authorship but not from using any procedures, processes, or methods described in the work.

Typeface, Fonts, and Lettering

For the most part, copyright law views typeface, fonts, and lettering as the building blocks of expression used to create works of authorship. In this regard, they generally exist outside the bounds of copyright protection no matter how novel and creative the shape and form of the typeface may be. This means that mere variations of typographical ornamentation or the simple arrangement of type on a page or screen cannot receive copyright protection. However, the creation of original pictorial or graphic elements that form, for example, the entire shape of a particular letter or number may fall outside this exclusion.[50]

Format and Layout Design[51]

The layout or format of a work is generally considered a template for expression and as such does not constitute original expression in and of itself. Copyright protection may be available for a sufficiently creative selection and/or arrangement of specific content, but it would not extend to the format and layout itself.

Uncopyrightable Elements

A large variety of elements commonly used in expressive works do not contain a sufficient amount of creativity. As a result, the Copyright Act does not protect common shapes, patterns, symbols, and designs as well as mere variations on color. Works comprised entirely of these materials will not receive copyright protection unless the selection, coordination, and/or arrangement of the elements constitutes an original work of authorship.

Names, Titles, Short Phrases

Names, titles, slogans, and other short catchwords, phrases, mottoes, and expressions do not contain a sufficient amount of creativity to qualify for copyright protection. This includes novel or distinctive words and phrases, such as a catchy ad slogan or product, stage, character, or domain name. However, words and phrases associated with a business may qualify for trademark protection.

Other Works That Lack Sufficient Creativity

Copyright protection is not available for

1. Works consisting entirely of information that is common property, such as standard calendars, schedules of sporting events, musical scales, and lists or tables taken from public documents.

2. Blank forms, such as time cards, graph paper, diaries, scorecards, address books, and order forms, that are designed for recording information.

3. The mere listing of ingredients or contents or a simple set of directions. This means that while a recipe consisting of nothing more than a set of ingredients and a process for preparing a dish is not copyrightable, the expressive material that accompanies the recipe, such as photographs, illustrations or a written description of the preparation process, is eligible for protection.[52]

4. A mere copy of another work of authorship without the addition of any original expression. This includes exact reproductions as well as photographs, photocopies, and scans of original works and also covers expressive works in the public domain.

5. US government works created by federal employees as part of their official duties.

Utility and Design

Visual art can be expressed in a fixed form in a multitude of ways. It can appear as free-standing artworks prominently displayed in homes and public places or as design elements on material objects, such as a chair or an article of clothing. The Copyright Act protects both types of pictorial, graphic, and sculptural works, with the latter receiving copyright protection if it was copyrightable before being applied to the useful article.[53] That said, industrial designs present somewhat of a conundrum for copyright law because the Copyright Act does not extend protection to the utilitarian aspects of a work. This means that the design work is eligible for copyright protection only if it can be separated from and has the capacity to exist independently of the useful purpose of the chair or article of clothing.[54]

In 2017, the Supreme Court weighed in to what the petitioners referred to as "the most vexing, unresolved question in copyright law: how to determine whether a feature of a useful article—such as a garment or piece of furniture—is conceptually separable from the article and thus protectable."[55] The question was especially vexing given that some ten different tests had been formulated and adopted by courts in a patchwork effort to determine separability.[56] The case before the court involved the two-dimensional designs appearing on the surface of cheerleading uniforms and other garments. The designs consisted of combinations and arrangements of chevrons, lines, curves, stripes, angles, diagonals, coloring, and shapes.

The court concluded that **separability** is met where (1) the design feature can be identified separately from the useful article and (2) the feature can

Figure 3.7. The design on this uniform qualified for copyright protection because it can exist separately as a two-dimensional work of art that is shaped like a uniform.
Design registration via court document.

Design 074

exist apart from the utilitarian aspect of the article.[57] Step one, the court said, is not onerous. In this case, a decision maker can identify the decorations on the uniforms as features having pictorial, graphic, or sculptural qualities. As for the second step, the court looked at whether those same designs could be separated from the uniform and applied to another medium, such as painter's canvas, and whether in this new medium they would qualify as a two-dimensional work of art without replicating the uniform itself.

Because the decorations are shaped to fit the uniform, Star Athletica argued they could not be fully separated from the article of clothing since the resulting artwork would be shaped in the outline of the cheerleading uniform. This fact, the court said, was not a barrier to copyright protection. A two-dimensional artwork does not lose its copyright protection "simply because it was designed to track the dimensions of the surface on which it was painted." In the end, the court ruled that the "two-dimensional work of art fixed in the tangible medium of the uniform fabric" is separable and eligible for copyright protection, but that the shape, cut, and dimensions of the cheerleading uniform itself are not protected, and as a result, anyone is free to reproduce the useful article itself.

Although art galleries throughout the United States showcase the work of fashion designers, fashion design is not a protectable category in copyright law. When it comes to copyright, the best the fashion industry can do is protect certain aspects of the design, such as a specific fabric pattern. This lack of full protection has spawned a copycat economy in which affordable and luxury brands knock-off trend-setting designs. During oral arguments, Justice Sotomayor observed that granting copyright protection to fashion designs would have the effect of killing off the knockoff industry.[58] To include fashion among the protected categories of copyright, an article of clothing would need to be considered original and expressive rather than simply a useful item meant to cover the body. Justice Breyer opened the door to that consideration when he commented that people wear clothes to make a statement about themselves. "They are saying who they are," he said. "The clothes on the hanger do nothing; the clothes on the woman do everything. And that is what I think fashion is about."[59]

Graphic and Literary Characters

As indicated, original literary and audiovisual works fall within the contours of copyright protection. In addition, courts have also extended copyright protection to sufficiently distinctive elements within these works, such as the characters in a comic book or television series.[60] As **characters** develop unique and recognizable attributes—for example, name, appearance, attitude, and personality traits—they become more delineated and move closer to receiving copyright protection that is independent from the work as a whole. Characters that contain unique elements of expression as displayed through consistent, widely identifiable traits and attributes are considered especially distinctive and copyrightable as a separately protected work.[61]

Popular graphic characters are especially suited for copyright protection given that their physical appearance and character traits are visually apparent.[62] In this way, they are differentiated from literary characters whose appearance and attributes largely develop in the reader's mind as the story unfolds. Since no two minds think alike, a fictional character may not be uniquely recognizable. Fictional characters that have gained copyright protection have developed unique attributes and personality traits over time. James Bond, for example, was first conceived as a literary character by Ian Fleming, a British journalist and novelist. Throughout the series of stories written by Fleming and the subsequent films that depicted him, Bond became known for his various character traits. These specific traits—cold-bloodedness, love of martinis, marksmanship, physical strength, and sophistication—remained constant despite the many actors who portrayed him. Bond's unique expressive attributes as delineated in a series of MGM films allowed the motion picture company to file suit against the Honda Motor Co. for an advertisement featuring a suave hero, attractive heroine, and menacing and grotesque villain in a fast-paced helicopter chase. [63]

Protected character status has also been extended to automobiles used in motion pictures. In 2008, the Ninth Circuit concluded that Eleanor, a car that appeared in the original and remake of *Gone in 60 Seconds*, possessed some key attributes of a copyrightable character.[64] Most recently, the same court ruled that the Batmobile as depicted in both the 1966 television series and the 1989 film is a protected character. The court applied a three-part test to determine whether a character in a comic book, television program, or motion picture is entitled to copyright protection. Protected characters, the court said (1) have physical as well as conceptual qualities; (2) are recognizable as the same character whenever they appear; and (3) are especially distinctive and contain some unique elements of expression.[65]

The court found that the Batmobile, which appeared first in comic books published by DC Comics and then as a three-dimensional car in a licensed television series and film, has physical and conceptual qualities. In addition, the car maintained a consistent, recognizable bat-like appearance that includes a bat-themed front end, batwing extensions, exaggerated fenders, curved windshield, and bat emblems along with its high-tech gadgets and weaponry. As a fierce crime-fighting machine, the Batmobile uses its twin flame-throwing jet engines and unique character traits to fly through the air, perform emergency reverse thrust rocket turns, fit through narrow openings, and tear up city streets like a cyclone. These identifiable attributes transform the car into a loyal sidekick that continually aids Batman in his quest to fight villains. According to the court, the Batmobile is not merely a stock character with indistinguishable and, therefore, unprotectable characteristics. Instead, the car is a copyrightable piece of expression that entitles DC Comics to prevent others from creating replicas of the 1966 and 1989 vehicles.

PUBLIC DOMAIN

He started out as a two-dimensional drawing and is now one of the world's most recognizable characters. At ninety-plus years of age, Mickey Mouse is an intellectual property powerhouse for the Disney Corporation and a driving force in copyright law. Copyright law is authorized by the US Constitution, which gives Congress the power to extend copyright protection to authors for a set duration of time. When that period ends, the work enters the public domain, and it can be copied and sold without authorization. For Disney, the expiration of Mickey's copyright would translate into a substantial loss in revenue. Thus far, however, Mickey has escaped this fate although at times it was a fairly close call.

Mickey first appeared on the scene in 1928 in the cartoon short Steamboat Willie. At the time, original works of authorship faced an initial term of twenty-eight years and a renewable term of twenty-eight years for a total of fifty-six years of copyright protection from the date of publication. This means Mickey would have entered the public domain in 1984. But luckily for Mickey Congress passed a new copyright act in 1976 that went into effect in 1978. The 1976 Copyright Act gave works an additional nineteen years to any work, like Mickey, that was created before 1978. Now Mickey could live until the ripe old age of seventy-five years as he was set to enter the public domain in 2003. As Mickey approached this fateful year, Congress acted once again, passing the **Copyright Term Extension Act** or what some referred to as the **Mickey Mouse Protection Act**. The CTEA extended Mickey's longevity another twenty years.

Under the current law, Steamboat Willie will lose its copyright protection in 2023. What this exactly means for Mickey whose character and stories have evolved over time is somewhat unclear. In a 2014 case involving the Sherlock Holmes series, the Seventh Circuit ruled that once a story falls into the public domain, its elements—including the characters covered by the expired copyright—become fair game for subsequent authors.[66] Arthur Conan Doyle wrote fifty-six short stories and four novels involving Sherlock Holmes. In 2014, only ten works remained under US copyright protection. The Conan Doyle Estate argued that Holmes was a multifaceted character whose full complexity was not developed and revealed until the final stories; thus the literary character should be protected until the last work expires in 2022. The court disagreed. Character alterations, the court said, "do not revive the expired copyrights on the original character."[67] Instead later works are considered derivatives of earlier works. As such, the copyright in the derivative covers the new material added and "has no effect one way or the other on the copyright or public domain status of the preexisting material."[68]

In relation to the Holmes character as created by Arthur Conan Doyle, what remains protected in the works still under US copyright protection are the additional character features and story elements that are original to those works. This means that storylines, dialogue, characters, and character traits newly introduced in a later work that is under copyright protection, such as Sherlock Holmes's retirement from his detective agency, which was first described in the 1926 short story "The Lion's Mane," may not be used without permission until that particular work enters the public domain.[69] This remains true for other derivatives of Holmes as well, such as the film renditions of the story and its characters.

Because Mickey's catalog of protected works is vast, including animated works, comic strips, and computer games as well as the three-dimensional character in Disney theme parks and touring productions, the copyright power of the mouse extends far beyond Steamboat Willie. If Steamboat Willie is allowed to fall into the public domain, the story elements and character features in the cartoon short would lose their copyright protection. But while Steamboat Willie would enter the public domain, later versions and adaptations of Mickey would not. That said, graphic characters that serve as an identifier of their creator are eligible for trademark protection. Because Mickey is synonymous with Disney, he is also protected by multiple trademarks. In the end, it is hard to identify a single work of art that has had a greater impact on copyright law than Mickey. The extensions in term limits that he helped usher in has provided ninety-five years of protection for the multitude of characters that were created and published in his lifetime.

Duration of Copyright

Works created on or after January 1, 1978:

- Single author: Life of author plus seventy years.
- Two or more authors: Seventy years after death of longest-living author.
- Works made for hire[70] or anonymous and pseudonymous works: Ninety-five years from first publication or 120 years from date of creation, whichever is shorter.

Works created before January 1, 1978:
Published between 1924 and 1963 with notice:

- Twenty-eight years with renewal for an additional sixty-seven years for a total of ninety-five years.
- Works copyrighted in 1924 will enter public domain on January 1, 2020.
- Works published without notice or expired works are in the public domain.

Published between 1964 and 1977 with notice:

- Ninety-five years; renewal extension of sixty-seven years is automatic.
- Works published without notice are in the public domain.

Created before 1978 but not published or registered:

- Protected as of 1978.
- Life of author plus seventy years or until end of 2002, whichever is longer.
- Otherwise, duration is calculated as works created on or after January 1, 1978.

Created before 1978 and not registered but published between 1978 and 2002:

- Protected as of 1978.
- Life of author plus seventy years or until end of 2047, whichever is longer.

CHAPTER SUMMARY

Copyright law is intended to encourage creative activity. It does so in several ways. First, it gives authors of original, expressive works the exclusive right to prohibit unauthorized uses of their creative expression. Second, it realizes that the creative process builds and borrows from earlier works. To incentivize the creation of new works, the law allows authors to use the underlying facts and ideas contained within a protected work. This means that just the original expression of those facts and ideas is protected and thus unlawful copying can only be found if a substantial similarity exists between the protected elements of a copyrighted work and the defendant's work. In addition, the law does not prohibit the use of creative elements that are standard, stock, or common to a particular subject matter or medium or where the idea and its expression have merged. Works that lack sufficient creativity or have fallen into the public domain also receive no copyright protection.

KEY TERMS

Appropriate   To take or use a protected creative work without permission or authorization.

Characters   Graphic or fictional characters may receive copyright protection if they (1) have physical and conceptual qualities; (2) are recognizable when they appear; and (3) are distinctive and exhibit some unique elements of expression.

Copyright   A property right granting broad protection and exclusive rights to authors of original, creative works. Copyright protection is available to a wide array of original works of authorship, including literary, musical, dramatic, choreographic, pictorial, graphic, sculptural, and architectural works; motion pictures and other audiovisual works; sound recordings; and other digital content that is expressed in a fixed, tangible medium.

Copyright Term Extension Act of 1998   This act extended the term of copyright protection in the United States. Works created today receive the life of the author plus seventy years or ninety-five years from date of first publication or 120 years from date of creation, whichever is shorter.

Creativity   To receive copyright protection, a work must possess at least some minimal degree of creativity.

Derivative work   A new work of original authorship that is based on one or more preexisting copyrighted works.

Exclusive Rights   The owner of a valid copyright has the exclusive right to control the reproduction, distribution, and adaptation of the work, and if applicable, the right to publicly perform and display the work. These exclusive rights are the mechanism by which creative works are turned into intangible assets with an economic value that can be exploited by the copyright holder. Like other assets, these rights may be sold, inherited, reapportioned, and subdivided through agreements that spell out the exact terms and conditions of the reassigned use.

Fact v. Expression   Facts in and of themselves are discoverable and therefore do not owe their origin to an act of original authorship. This means that the underlying facts in a work will not receive copyright protection. Only the original expression of those facts is eligible for copyright protection.

First-Sale Doctrine   Under the first-sale doctrine, the exclusive right of distribution is limited to the first sale or distribution of the protected work. This means that the purchaser of the book may lend, rent, or sell the book to someone else without infringing the rights of the copyright holder.

Fixed, Tangible Medium   To receive copyright protection, the work must be translated into a fixed, tangible medium. This means that the author is responsible for converting the expressive work into a stable, sufficiently permanent copy that allows it to be perceived, reproduced, or communicated for more than a short period of time.

Idea v. Expression   To foster the creation of intellectual and expressive works, copyright protection is limited to the original expression of an idea rather than the idea itself. This means that others are free to use the underlying idea contained with a copyrighted work, but not the original expression of that idea.

Infringement   An unauthorized use of a work's protected elements that violates a copyright holder's exclusive rights constitutes infringement. When such an act has likely occurred, copyright holders may sue for copyright infringement.

Intellectual property   Products of the mind are referred to as intellectual property. Intellectual property includes works that receive copyright protection as well as designs and creations covered by trademark and patent law.

Merger Doctrine   A concept in copyright law that prevents the protection of a work if the underlying idea can be expressed in only one way. The symbol of a circle with a diagonal line crossed through it is an example of an idea that is virtually indistinguishable and inseparable from its expression.

Mickey Mouse Protection Act   Some refer to the Copyright Term Extension Act of 1998 as the Mickey Mouse Protection Act because the CTEA extended the term of Mickey's copyright protection in the United States an additional twenty years.

Nonliteral Similarities   Nonliteral similarities arise when the new work is inspired by the protected work. To determine whether an infringement has occurred, courts need to determine whether the nonliteral similarities are substantial.

Ordinary Observer Test   No well-defined standard exists for assessing when nonliteral similarities become substantial. Ordinary observer test is one of three approaches courts use to determine substantial similarity. All three approaches, however, tend to (1) identify the literal and nonliteral similarities; (2) separate the unprotected material from protected expression; and (3) compare the protected elements for meaningful similarities.

Originality   Originality is the essential component of copyright. This means that the underlying facts and ideas contained within the work are not copyrightable. Only the original expression of those facts and ideas receives copyright protection. To be original, a work must be independently conceived and created by a human author.

Public Performance or Display   A work is performed or displayed publicly when it is transmitted to or visually shown in a "place open to the public or at a place where a substantial number of persons" other than family or close friends are gathered. An audiovisual work is displayed rather than performed when its individual images are shown nonsequentially rather than in a sequence as in a performance.

Scènes à Faire   This concept in copyright law prevents the protection of expressive elements that are "standard, stock or common to a particular subject matter." Realistic depictions of animals in the natural surroundings are examples of the *scènes à faire* concept.

Separability   Because copyright protection does not extend to the usefulness of such articles as chairs and clothing, industrial designs are eligible for copyright protection only if (1) the design feature can be identified separately from the useful article and (2) the feature can exist apart from the utilitarian aspect of the article.

Substantial Similarity   Unlawful copying from a protected work occurs when there is a substantial similarity between the protected elements of the copyrighted work and the defendant's work. To determine whether two creative works are substantially similar, the unprotectable elements of the plaintiff's work are filtered from the protected expression. The protectable elements that remain form the basis of an infringement claim and are compared to the corresponding elements of the defendant's work to assess similarity and unlawful appropriation.

Thin Protection   "Thin" copyright protection is given to works in which the range of creative expressive choices are quite limited. Examples include product shots of a bottle of vodka or fact-based work that contains no original expression and where only the selection and arrangement of the facts are protected. As a practical matter, these works are protected only against virtually identical copies.

4

Fair Use and Transformative Works

Judicial thought dating back to the mid-1800s recognized that few things in literature, science, and art are strictly new and original throughout. Accordingly, courts have acknowledged the central role **appropriation** plays in the creation of new works. "Every book in literature, science and art borrows," the court noted, "and must necessarily borrow, and use much which was well known and used before."[1] While the right to quote, as Judge Pierre N. Leval asserted, "is essential to the progress of knowledge,"[2] copying more than the ideas or facts contained in a protected work establishes an infringement claim that by its very nature stifles the creativity the law was designed to foster. To ease the tension between ownership rights and the chill on expression that occurs with every grant of a copyright, the law provides for a **fair use** defense that allows subsequent authors to borrow from protected works.

Fair use is an **affirmative defense** that formally comes into play after an infringement complaint is filed. In such cases, the complaint establishes that unauthorized copying occurred by the defendant. The defendant is then left to prove that the use of the work was fair. If the defendant is successful, the court will rule that no infringement took place. Because fair use is an affirmative defense, it requires a case-by-case analysis. At a minimum, that analysis must consider four factors identified in the Copyright Act as being especially relevant in determining fair use. Those four factors are

1. Purpose and character of the secondary use, including whether the use is of a commercial nature or is for nonprofit education purposes.
2. Nature of the copyrighted work.
3. Amount and substantiality of the portion used in relation to the copyrighted work as a whole.

4. Effect of the use upon the potential market for or value of the copyrighted work.

PURPOSE OF COPYRIGHT LAW

The degree of significance each of these factors has received has varied over time, making it difficult to predict whether an appropriation constitutes actionable infringement or a new creation in its own right. The Copyright Act, in turn, does not provide any actual direction on the application of the factors, but notes that the use of a protected work for purposes such as criticism, comment, news reporting, teaching, scholarship, and research *may* qualify as a fair use.[3] As a result, determinations often appear inconsistent and subjective. In 1990, Judge Pierre N. Leval drew attention to this problem in an influential law review article that exposed the lack of consensus among judges concerning what fair use actually means. The Copyright Act and the fair use factors, he maintained, provided little guidance for distinguishing between acceptable and excessive levels of copying. Consequently, court decisions were not constrained by governing principles. This left judges free to rely on instinctive reactions to individual fact patterns. The resulting outcomes were often more responsive to private property concerns than the foundational purpose of copyright law.[4]

Leval's observations reflected a trend that had developed from 1960 to 1990, in which courts largely viewed fair use as an exception for secondary uses that do not harm the potential market for the original. This view fit well with the understanding of copyrights as intangible assets that have actual economic value an individual or company can use to generate revenue. When considered in this light, factor four, which examines the impact of the taking on the market value of the original, became the single most important factor of fair use analysis. Courts using this approach emphasized the economic value of the copyright owner's work rather than the informational and cultural contributions of the **secondary work**.

Judge Leval's article challenged the state of fair use law and provided a way forward that was grounded in the foundational principles of copyright. He asserted that copyright law and the exclusive rights it grants to authors acknowledge the vital connection between creative intellectual activity and the well-being of society.[5] This acknowledgment, he explained, is furthered by the fair use defense, which "is a necessary part of the overall design"[6] of copyright and its ability to "stimulate creativity for public illumination."[7] Under Judge Leval's approach, a finding of fair use "turns primarily on whether, and to what extent, the challenged use is transformative."[8]

Transformative works are works that use protected material in a different manner or for a different purpose. According to Leval, quoted matter that is used as raw material and transformed into a creative work consisting of "new information, new aesthetics and new insights and understanding . . . is the very type of activity that the fair use doctrine intends to protect for the enrichment of society."[9]

Leval's emphasis on the transformative nature of the secondary work shifted the analysis from the economic effects of an unconsented use to the purpose and character of that use. In *Campbell v. Acuff-Rose*, the Supreme Court embraced the transformation standard and rejected the notion that the commercial nature of the secondary use is the determining factor. The court's decision gradually ushered in a new understanding of fair use centered on the concept of **transformation** and the role fair use plays in protecting freedom of expression and securing the breathing space necessary for art and culture to develop.

Campbell v. Acuff-Rose

Campbell is, conceivably, the most influential and widely cited case in the reformulation of the fair use defense. The case centered on a song written by the rap group 2 Live Crew. The song, "Pretty Woman," was a commercial **parody** of Roy Orbison's hit "Oh, Pretty Woman." In the parody, the rap group copied the opening bass riff and a line of lyrics from the original.[10] While 2 Live Crew offered to pay Acuff-Rose for the right to do so, the music publisher refused, and the group released "Pretty Woman" without authorization. Acuff-Rose filed suit nearly a year later.

The case called on the court to determine whether "Pretty Woman" was a fair use of Orbison's song. The District Court ruled that it was, reasoning that "Pretty Woman" was a parody of "Oh, Pretty Woman." The trial court noted that the group substituted predictable lyrics with shocking ones by using a play on words that commented on the blandness and banality of the Orbison song.[11] The Court of Appeals, on the other hand, returned to the pre-Leval interpretation of fair use and reversed by weighing the rap song's "blatantly commercial purpose" and thus its potential for economic harm as the most important factor.[12] Dismissing the appeals court's analysis, the Supreme Court ruled that the four factors are not to be isolated from one another. All the factors, the court said, "are to be explored and the results weighed together in light of the purposes of copyright."[13] Accordingly, the court criticized the Sixth Circuit for confining its review and the resolution of 2 Live Crew's fair use claim to essentially "one relevant fact, the commercial nature of the use."[14]

Factor One

In its opinion, the court crafted a well-defined defense standard that aligned strongly with Judge Leval's approach. The court began its explanation of why an overtly commercial work like "Pretty Woman" could be considered fair by investigating factor one and the significance of the concept of transformation. Factor one, the court said, requires a determination of whether the new work merely replaces the original or instead transforms it into a new expression with a different character and purpose.[15] Transformative works used for purposes such as criticism, comment, news reporting, teaching, scholarship, or research expand the information, insights and/or artistic expression in the marketplace.

In *Campbell*, the court categorized parody as a form of comment or criticism that requires some of its victim's imagination to make a point. New works where the **parodic character** is reasonably perceived are more likely to be considered transformative[16] regardless if the work is or is not labeled as a parody.[17] As for "Pretty Woman," the court found that the critical intent in the song was to "ridicule the white-bread original,"[18] but refused to assess the quality of the work. Whether the parody is of good or bad taste, the court said, "does not and should not matter to fair use."[19]

When determining the purpose and character of the secondary work, the Copyright Act explicitly references commercial versus nonprofit educational as an element of a factor one examination. As a part of its first factor inquiry, the court extinguished the view that commercial uses are categorically unfair. Congress, the court said, resisted attempts to create presumptive categories of fair use. Instead, each particular use, regardless of its category or type, is subjected to an independent examination of the four factors that concentrates on the relevant evidence and context of the taking. This means that the commercial or nonprofit educational character of a work is not conclusive but rather is an element to be considered and weighed along with other facts in a fair use decision. To that point, the court succinctly addressed this common misconception of fair use when it wrote that "the mere fact that a use is educational and not for profit does not insulate it from a finding of infringement, any more than the commercial characters of a use bar a finding of fairness."[20]

Factor Two

The finding of "Pretty Woman" as a transformative parody helped the song work its way through factors two, three, and four. Factor two assesses the nature of the original work in relation to the expressive creativity copyright law is intended to spur. This element takes into consideration that some works are closer to the core of intended copyright protection than others. This factor often weighs against a finding of fair use when the original work is "crea-tive, imaginative and original," and represents a "substantial investment of time and labor that was made in anticipation of financial return."[21] Given the creative and artistic nature of "Oh, Pretty Woman," the court recognized that factor two favored *Acuff-Rose*. Nonetheless, the court cautioned that this fact was not much help to the music publisher because parodies invariably copy widely distributed expressive works.[22]

Factor Three

The purpose and character of the secondary use is also a consideration in factor three. Some secondary works, such as a parody, require a more robust taking than other creative endeavors in order to achieve their intended pur-pose. In factor three, courts determine whether the amount and creativity taken is appropriate and proportional in relation to the nature and character of the new use. A secondary work composed primarily of material taken from the original work, much of it verbatim with little to no original additions or changes, is more likely to replace the original rather than transform it into a new expression with a different meaning and message. In such a case, there is a greater likelihood of market harm and a finding of infringement. Applying this understanding to parody is difficult. According to the court, parody's humor or biting comment springs from the tension between a known orig-inal and its distorted imitation. To successfully implement this technique, the **parodist** must take enough of the original's most distinctive and memorable features to make its targeted victim recognizable to an audience. Once iden-tification has been assured, how much more is reasonable will depend on the extent to which the secondary work's aim is to comment on the original or supplant it in the marketplace.[23] Works in which the parodic element is great and copying is small are more likely to constitute a fair use than works where the taking is extensive and the parodic element is small.

In *Campbell*, 2 Live Crew took the opening riff and the first line of the lyrics to "Oh, Pretty Woman." It may be argued that these distinctive and memorable artistic elements constitute the heart of the original work. The court explained that merely copying the heart of an original for a parodic purpose does not render the taking excessive. According to the court, if the group had copied lesser-known elements, it would be unlikely that the parodic character would have come through. However, the court warned that a self-described parodist cannot simply "skim the cream and get off scot free."[24] Context is every-thing in these cases as courts will examine the extent to which the parodist contributed original elements to the secondary work. The court noted that 2 Live Crew departed markedly from the Orbison lyrics and, while the group repeated the opening bass riff from the original, they also added distinctive sounds that included "interposing 'scraper' noise, overlaying the music with solos in different keys, and altering the drum beat."[25] This is not a case, the court concluded, where a substantial portion of the parody is comprised of verbatim copying or where the parodic element is so insubstantial in comparison to the taking that the third factor must be resolved against the parodists.[26]

Factor Four

With factors one and three weighing in favor of fair use and factor two indecisive, the court turned to the remaining factor—the extent of market harm not only to the original but also to its market for **derivative works**. While the Court of Appeals presumed market harm given the commercial nature of "Pretty Woman," the Supreme Court held that such a presumption does not apply in cases where the new work extends beyond a mere duplication of the original. When the secondary use is transformative, market substitution is less certain and market harm may not be inferred. This is especially the case in terms of a parody. A true parody is not a substitute for the protected work it targets. Therefore, it resides in a different market than the original. Even when a highly critical parody severely reduces the demand for the original, it does not cause the type of market harm that copyright law protects. This means that copyright law does not protect original works from criticism and does not recognize parodies or other similar works as infringing on the derivative markets for originals. Instead, the market for derivative uses of a protected work extends only to those uses that the copyright holder would in general develop or license others to develop.[27]

TRANSFORMATIVE WORKS

Satire versus Parody

Not all works that label themselves a parody are transformative. Courts are much more suspect of works that have "no critical bearing on the substance or style" of the protected work but nevertheless claim a right to borrow extensively in order to comment on the original.[28] A case in point involved the children's book *The Cat in the Hat* by Dr. Seuss and a secondary work that extensively used Seuss's distinct rhyming scheme and whimsical illustrative style to satirize a murder trial involving ex–NFL football star O. J. Simpson. The authors of the secondary work, *The Cat NOT in the Hat! A Parody by Dr. Juice*, claimed the taking was a fair use. The Court of Appeals disagreed, holding that *The Cat NOT in the Hat!* was not a parody. The Ninth Circuit explained that a parody needs to mimic the protected work it is targeting in order to make its point.[29] This allows the parodist to claim fair use when the parodic character of the new work is reasonably recognizable. A **satire** that uses a copyrighted work to poke fun at a different target must justify its borrowing because it has no need to conjure up the protected material. This means that a defendant has a stronger claim to fair use when the copyrighted work is the principal or at least partial target of the secondary work.

Figure 4.1. The Cat NOT in the Hat! used Dr. Suess' rhyming scheme and illustrative style to ridicule the O.J. Simpson double murder trial. Because the critical bearing of the book focused primarily on Simpson rather than Seuss, the court found that the defendants were not justified in their extensive use of Dr. Seuss's expressive style.

Image via court document.

The Cat NOT in the Hat! mimicked the distinctive style of at least three books created by Theodor S. Geisel, the author and illustrator known as Dr. Seuss. Both the trial court and appellate court noted numerous similarities in text and illustrations between Geisel's work and the defendants' work. For example, Geisel's famed "one fish / two fish / red fish / blue fish" became "one knife? / two knives? / red knife / dead wife" in the secondary work. The cover art of *The Cat NOT in the Hat!* contained a whimsical illustration of O. J. Simpson that imitated an illustration of Geisel's Cat in terms of positioning, facial features, unnaturally long and flat feet, and the Cat's signature

red and white stove-pipe hat.[30] In all, Simpson was depicted thirteen times
in the Cat's distinctively scrunched and somewhat shabby hat and yet the
substance and content of *The Cat in the Hat* was not evoked by the secondary work's focus on the double murder trial.[31] Instead, the authors of *The
Cat NOT in the Hat!* relied on Geisel's creative artistry in their retelling of
the controversial murder trial. In *Campbell*, the court warned against such
techniques. A fair use defense, the court said, diminishes and may vanish
altogether for defendants who borrow from protected works to simply "get
attention" or "avoid the drudgery in working up something fresh."[32]

Advancing a Broader Artistic Purpose

Courts are more likely to find fair use when the author of the secondary work
has a "genuine creative rationale for borrowing" the protected material.[33]
A case in point involves Jeff Koons, a visual artist who uses appropriated
images found in popular media in his finished artwork, and Andrea Blanch,
a professional fashion and portrait photographer. In 2000, Deutsche Bank in
collaboration with Guggenheim commissioned Koons to create a series of
seven paintings titled *Easyfun-Ethereal*. To create the paintings in this series,
Koons scanned into a computer photographs he took as well as images he
found in advertisements and fashion magazines. The scanned images were
then digitally combined and layered over pastoral landscapes and used as
templates to create the large-scale oil paintings.[34] One such painting, titled
Niagara, became the subject of a copyright infringement suit.

 Niagara depicts the dangling feet and lower legs of four women. The
legs are placed side by side over an image of a large brownie topped with
ice cream. Niagara Falls and a grassy field appear behind the brownie and
two other plates of sweets. The painting triggered a lawsuit because the pair
of legs positioned second from the left originated from a photograph composed, staged, and shot by Blanch. In the photograph, titled *Silk Sandals by
Gucci*, the image of a woman's lower legs and feet is positioned upward at a
forty-five-degree angle across the frame. The woman's feet are adorned with
bronzed nail polish and glittery sandals that hang detached from the heels.
Her ankles are crossed and relaxed as they rest on a man's lap. Koons adapted
this image for *Niagara* by stripping out the background and altering the ori-
entation of the legs so that they dangle vertically downward on the canvas.

 At issue in this case was whether Koons's appropriation of the image was
fair use. In applying the first factor of the defense, the court noted that a secondary work is considered transformative when it uses the protected work
as raw material to further distinct creative or message-based objectives.[35]
Secondary works are not transformative when their purpose is to repackage

the original. Examples include a secondary work that turned a television series into a set of trivia questions and a television episode that used a poster as part of a set decoration. Neither the trivia book nor the set decoration transformed the protected materials used. The trivia book merely repackaged the television series to entertain the show's fans,[36] and the television episode used the poster for its intended purpose as a wall decoration.[37]

In *Blanch v. Koons*, Koons did not argue that his work was transformative solely because it is a painting and Blanch's work is a photograph or because his work is displayed in museums and her photo was published in a fashion magazine. According to the court, such an argument would have been ill-advised.[38] Instead Koons argued that the juxtaposition of the food, landscape, and legs serves as a comment on the appetites and indulgences of society that are encouraged by promotional images of food, entertainment, fashion, and beauty.[39] Koons said that he wants viewers of the painting to think about their personal experiences with these products and to gain some new insight into how these objects affect their lives.[40] The court found that Koons had a "sharply different" objective in using the photograph than Blanch had in creating it. Blanch wanted to interject an erotic sense into the photo, which, as part of a six-page feature on metallic cosmetics, was composed to call attention to the bronzed nail polish on the model's toes.[41] Given these two different objectives, the court concluded that Koons used Blanch's image as raw material for his commentary on the consequences of mass media and that the use was transformative.

The court also addressed the fact that Koons's message targets the genre of fashion images instead of the photo itself. This means that the painting's purpose is satire (not parody) and that Koons needed to justify why he took the image rather than create one of his own.[42] Koons explained that the photograph was necessary because it represents a ubiquitous style of images that can be found in almost any glossy magazine and other media. To Koons, the legs are a fact in the world that everyone experiences constantly and not anyone's legs in particular. By using the existing image, Koons contended that he is able to not only comment "upon the culture and attitudes promoted and embodied in *Allure Magazine*" but also to ensure that his commentary is authentic and understood.[43] "[I]t is the difference between quoting and paraphrasing," he said.[44] In the end, the court accepted Koons's explanation, writing that there was no reason to question his justification that the use of Blanch's photograph advanced his artistic purposes.[45] With a ruling of fair use, *Blanch v. Koons* illustrates the importance of a perceptible transformative purpose.

In an earlier case, however, Koons was not so convincing. This case involved a sculpture that mimicked a black-and-white photograph of a couple holding eight German Shepherd puppies. Koons ran across the photograph in a card shop and purchased a set of notecards on which the photo, titled "Puppies," appeared. He then gave one of the notecards to a group of artisans who were instructed by Koons to turn the two-dimensional image into a three-dimensional polychromed wood sculpture.[46] In guiding the creation of the sculpture, Koons provided the woodcarvers with written instructions, in which he repeatedly stressed that the finished work must faithfully replicate the features and details of the photograph. In his production notes, he told artisans that the "work must be just like photo."[47] Throughout the process, his reviews of the work underscored the need to copy the details of the photo. He wrote that the "puppies needed detail in fur . . . [j]ust like Photo!" and that the "girl's nose was too small," telling the artists to "[p]lease make [it] larger as per photo."[48]

Art Rogers, the photographer who created "Puppies," learned about the sculpture, *String of Puppies*, after it appeared in the Sunday edition of the *Los Angeles Times*. A lawsuit ensued in which Koons claimed that the sculpture was a satire or parody of society at large. Koons said he belonged to a school of artists that incorporate mass-produced images into works of art to comment critically on the social system that created them.

In the case, the court expanded on the use of a protected image as a means to make a statement on some larger aspect of society. Secondary works that use original material for a broader artistic purpose must, at least in part, comment upon the protected work, the court said. Otherwise, there is no need for the secondary work to copy the original work. By requiring that the copied work is in some way targeted by the secondary work, the audience is aware that an original and separate expression, attributable to a different artist, underlies the new work. "This awareness," the court said, "may come from the fact that the copied work is publicly known or because its existence is in some manner acknowledged" by the secondary work.[49] Without such an awareness, the court asserted that no real boundary to fair use can be established. In the end, the court noted that the problem with *Rogers v. Koons* is that even though *String of Puppies* may be perceived as a satirical critique of a materialistic society, it is difficult to discern how it comments on the photograph itself. Without such a connection between the two works, it is more likely that the copying was done in bad faith for profit-making objectives.[50]

A New Purpose

Courts often afford fair use protection to biographical, historical, and other such works that contain original source material to advance the treatment and understanding of their subjects. Again, the key consideration in the analysis is whether the incorporation of such source material is transformative. A case in point involves the reproduction of seven thumbnail images of Grateful Dead concert posters. The images are accompanied by descriptions of the concerts they depict and appear in chronological order in *The Grateful Dead: The Illustrated Trip*, a 480-page biography of the musical group. Bill Graham Archives owns the images and argued that simply placing the images along a timeline without comment or criticism related to the artistic nature of the image was not a transformative use.

The appellate court disagreed. The court compared the original creative purpose of the posters with their new usage. When the posters were originally created, each image fulfilled the dual purpose of artistic expression and promotion. The posters were created to increase public awareness of the band as well as to provide information about concert dates and times. These purposes, however, contrast with their use in *The Illustrated Trip*. In the book, the images are used as "historical artifacts to document and represent the actual occurrence" of the live events highlighted on the timeline.[51] In this form, the images enhance the reader's understanding of the text or serve as historical artifacts that graphically represent the importance of the concert to the timeline.[52] Both types of uses are separate and distinct from the original creative purposes.

The court found that the purposes between the original and secondary works were further distinguished by the manner in which the images were displayed in the book. In the book, the publisher significantly reduced the size and expressive value of the images by displaying them as thumbnails that are positioned at angles and blended into a prominent timeline containing textual material and original illustrative work.[53] The court pointed out that the treatment of the posters is similar to transformative uses of television clips that play for only a few seconds to reference the material a narrator or interviewee is describing.[54]

This type of usage stands in contrast to nontransformative treatments that play clips of artists without much interruption or reference. In nontransformative uses, the purposes of the original and secondary works are essentially the same. This means that a biography of Michael Jackson, for example, would not be able to use clips of his concerts merely as means to entertain the audience. A biographer that did so would simply be recreating the protected expression for its original purpose. The transformative treatment of the posters also prompted the court to conclude that the amount and artistic significance of the taking was sufficiently limited.[55] In this regard, the court additionally referenced the fact that the seven images constituted only a trivial portion of the 480-page book. Coupled together, these creative decisions meant that the third factor, which evaluates the quantity and quality of the appropriation in relation to the work as a whole, did not weigh against a finding of fair use.

Despite these findings, Bill Graham Archives argued that the taking harmed the established licensing market for the images. As a result, the company said it suffered direct revenue and opportunity losses from the secondary use. Here, the court found that Bill Graham Archives was entitled to potential licensing revenues from traditional markets, as opposed to transformative markets. In traditional markets, the appropriated use serves as a substitute or replaces the original. By serving as a replacement for the original, the secondary use directly impairs the copyright holder's right to develop a licensing market. In such cases, factor four will weigh heavily against a finding of fair use. This is not the case, however, with transformative uses. Transformative uses exist in a fair use market, and copyright holders cannot prevent others from entering a fair use market. This means that the copyright holder is not entitled to potential licensing revenue from transformative uses of its own creative work. In these cases, courts conclude that copyright holders, like Bill Graham Archives, have not suffered market harm due to the loss of licensing fees.[56]

An Entirely Different Aesthetic

While fair use is most often extended to works that comment on, critically reference, or historically relate to the original works, the law does not require that a work do so to be considered transformative.[57] In *Cariou v. Prince*, the Second Circuit determined that a series of secondary works that express an entirely different aesthetic than the original was transformative. At issue in the case were thirty pieces of art in a series titled *Canal Zone*. The series was created by Richard Prince, who incorporated partial or whole images from a book of black-and-white portraits and landscape photography titled *Yes Rasta*. The photographs were taken by Patrick Cariou during the six years he spent living among the Rastafarians in Jamaica. Prince, a widely known **appropriation artist**, pieced together large reproductions of Cariou's images into the paintings in the *Canal Zone* series. Some of the paintings consisted almost entirely of the photograph while others used torn photos along with other images to create oversized collages. Additionally, the images used were often altered with stark circles and other forms of over-painting that obscured and distorted the facial features of the individuals depicted in the photo. Colored tints and random elements were also added to some photographs.

Figure 4.2. The court contrasted the serenity and natural beauty depicted in Patrick Cariou's photographs with the crude, jarring, and distorted human features in Richard Prince's work. The court said that the different character of Prince's artwork gives the original photographs a new expression and constitutes a transformative use.
Images via court document.

In all, the court concluded that twenty-five of the artworks involved an "entirely different aesthetic from Cariou's photographs." Where Cariou deliberately composed the portraits to depict the natural, serene beauty of the Rastafarians and their surrounding environment, the court found that Prince used the photographs to create "crude and jarring works" that come across as "hectic and provocative." Moreover, the court remarked on the differences in composition, presentation, scale, color palette, and media. One particular factor the court observed was the comparative size of Prince's artwork, which measured between ten and nearly one hundred times larger than the 9.5-by-12-inch *Yes Rasta* book.[58] The court also noted that the *Canal Zone* series was produced on canvas using inkjet printing, acrylic paint, and paste-on elements. Inkjet printing is typically used to transfer images onto a canvas where they can then be customized with paint and other artistic treatments. In the customization process, Prince chose to incorporate color and distort the features, forms, and settings the images depicted. Cariou, by contrast, made creative choices involving equipment, staging, composition, and developing techniques and processes.

In the end, the court found that the distinct character of the artworks gave
the photographs a new expression. This finding ran counter to Prince's own
admission that he was not trying to create works with a new meaning or,
for that matter, with any message at all. Nevertheless, the court concluded
that the critical component is how the work may reasonably be perceived
by the observer and "not simply what an artist might say about a particular
piece or body of work."[59] Here, the court examined the works side by side
and concluded that twenty-five of the pieces employed new aesthetics that
transformed them into their own distinct creations but that five contained
minimal alterations and needed to be reevaluated by the lower court to appropriately determine whether they constituted a new expression. Because the
court's ruling expanded the scope of fair use, it also warned that the decision
did not mean that any cosmetic change or modification to an original work
would be considered transformative.[60]

Armed with the finding that most of the artworks constituted a transformative use, the court followed a typical path of analysis with regard to factors
two, three, and four. In considering factor two, which assesses the nature of
the original works, the court recognized that the photographs were both creative and published and, thus, fell well within the core of protection provided
by copyright law. While this finding weighed against fair use, the court concluded that the factor is of limited usefulness where the secondary work is
transformative.[61]

Transformativeness also shaped the court's analysis of the final two
factors. In determining whether the quantity and quality of the taking was
excessive, the court acknowledged that certain pieces in the series contained
key portions of the photographs, but that fair use does not require an artist
to take "no more than is necessary." Instead, the amount taken as well as its
quality and importance to the original work will vary with the purpose and
character of the secondary use.[62] Here, twenty-five of the pieces transformed
the photographs into something new and different and thus factor three
weighed heavily in their favor.

Last, with regard to factor four, which examines the potential impact
of the artworks on the market for the photographs, the court stressed that
infringements occur where the target audience and the nature of the new work
are the same as the original. In this case, the court found that Prince's artwork "appeals to an entirely different sort of collector than Cariou's."[63] Given
that certain pieces of the *Canal Zone* series sell for more than one million
dollars, Prince's works are marketed to wealthy individuals. The court noted
that the invitation list for a dinner associated with the opening of *Canal Zone*
included famous musicians, athletes, and actors, such as Beyonce Knowles,
Tom Brady, and Brad Pitt, among others. Cariou's photographs, on the other

hand, had not been actively marketed or sold for significant sums of money. Moreover, the court found nothing in the record to suggest that Prince's artwork ever impacted a market for the photographs or that anyone would forgo purchasing Cariou's work or nontransformative derivatives of his works as a result of the market for Prince's work. And, finally, because Prince did not intend to capture significant revenues as a direct result of the unauthorized use of the photographs, the commercial nature of his artworks did not weigh against a finding of fair use.[64]

TAKEDOWN NOTICES AND FAIR USE

Digital technology presents special challenges for copyright law given the ease of which it allows protected materials to be reproduced, manipulated, and distributed online. The technological ease coupled with the sheer volume of internet activity creates an outsized liability risk for websites, like YouTube and Instagram, that host user-generated material. If left unchecked, the costs associated with infringement claims would cripple online companies and the growth of the internet. In 1998, Congress attempted to address this problem by enacting the **Digital Millennium Copyright Act** (DMCA). The DMCA was intended, in part, to shield internet companies from massive liability claims resulting from infringing activity that occurs on their sites.

Known as the **Safe Harbor provision**, section 512 of the DMCA protects **internet service providers** (ISP) from liability for storing the content of its users. To receive this protection, ISPs must expeditiously comply with the notice and takedown procedure set forth in the act. The procedure requires the ISP to remove or disable access to the material upon notification from the copyright holder and to take reasonable steps to notify the user that the material has been removed or disabled. The user may then file a **counter notice** if it is believed that the removal was a mistake or the material was misidentified. Upon receipt of this notice, the ISP is required to inform the copyright holder that the alleged infringing material will be replaced in ten to fourteen business days unless a lawsuit is filed. Copyright holders who abuse the system by knowingly misrepresent the material in the takedown notification are liable for damages.[65]

The staggering amount of online infringement and the speed at which it reappears after removal places a heavy burden on copyright owners.[66] As a result, companies often turn to automatic search devices to scan for and identify infringing activity. While these artificial intelligence programs enhance the efficiency of the identification process, they also increase the probability that inaccurate **takedown notices** will be filed.[67] Such notices may target work that constitutes fair use or does not otherwise infringe copyright. If litigation ensues, both parties are facing a long and costly process. It took some ten years to resolve a lawsuit filed by Stephanie Lenz against Universal Music Group. In this suit, Lenz argued that a twenty-nine-second home video of her then thirteen-month-old son dancing to the song "Let's Go Crazy" by Prince was a fair use. Lenz's claim called into question whether the DMCA requires rights holders to undertake a fair use analysis of the material before filing a takedown notice.[68] The Ninth Circuit held that it did and that failure to do so will result in damages.[69] The case was appealed to the US Supreme Court, but the High Court declined to review it. This leaves the Ninth Circuit as the only federal circuit to require rights holders to engage in a fair use analysis before issuing a takedown notice.[70]

Because the DMCA Safe Harbor provision was designed to protect the companies that host content, it has been criticized for the burdens it places on rights holders. The process is cumbersome in comparison to the volume and speed at which infringement occurs and can be especially problematic for independent artists and creators who don't have the resources to find the infringing uses of their work in the first place. Once an infringing work is found, a takedown notice should be sent to the website that is hosting the use. While most major online host companies have specific pages devoted to helping rights holders file notices, finding links and contact information for smaller host sites can be difficult. Organizations like the *Art Law Journal* offer step-by-step instructions and are a good starting point in the process.[71]

DE MINIMIS EXCEPTION

The ***de minimis*** concept is derived from the legal maxim *de minimis non curat lex* (the law does not concern itself with trifles). In the copyright context, *de minimis* most often means that the copying is so insignificant that it is not recognized as an actionable infringement.[72] To be an actionable infringement, the secondary use must be substantially similar to the original work. This means that the use must be qualitatively and quantitatively sufficient enough to prove that substantial similarity exists between the works. In cases involving the *de minimis* exception, defendants are essentially arguing that the quantity or amount of copying is so slight that the allegedly infringing use is not substantially similar to the original.[73] This argument is different from the fair use defense, which is employed after an actionable infringement has been established. The *de minimis* exception is especially relevant in cases involving exact copying[74] given that unlawful infringement does not occur when copying is *de minimis*.

While the *de minimis* exception has been applied to a variety of creative fields, it can be especially useful in audio-video productions where set designs, background scenery, and the use of short clips of video and other copyright-protected materials can prompt lawsuits. In such cases, the quantitative component of substantial similarity is concerned not only with the amount of copying but also with the observability of the copied work. In determining observability, courts consider the length of time the protected material is visible as well as creative decisions impacting clarity of the use, such as focus, lighting, camera angles, and prominence. Two recent cases illustrate this point.

The first case involves CBS and Steven Hirsch, a photojournalist who actively licenses his photographs to media outlets for a fee. Back in 2010, Hirsch took a photograph of Justin Massler outside a courthouse in Manhattan. At the time, Massler had been accused of stalking Ivanka Trump, and this notoriety prompted the *New York Post* to license the photograph from Hirsch and use it in an online article titled "Ivanka's Stalker Ordeal Featured Crazed Talk, Threats and Blood pix."[75] Seven years later, CBS aired and made available online an episode of *48 Hours* devoted to the "horrors of stalking."[76] One segment from the episode focused on Massler and included an unauthorized screenshot of Hirsch's photo and the *New York Post* headline. The screenshot appeared slightly skewed to the left, rotated clockwise slowly for two seconds, and ended slightly skewed to right.

During the time it appeared on screen, roughly only the top half of the photo was exposed. As a result of the cropping, Hirsch's photo credit did not appear in the segment.[77] Hirsch sued for copyright infringement, and CBS argued that its use of the photo was *de minimis*. Even though the photo was observable for approximately two seconds, the court disagreed and invalidated the notion that a short, quick clip is nonactionable.[78] The court explained that the idea that a brief use in and of itself will be regarded as *de minimis* is not supported in law.[79] Instead, the court found the following facts decisive: (1) a substantial proportion of the photo was visible; (2) the portion shown was in clear focus; and (3) the photo occupied most of the screen.[80] Based on these findings, the court concluded that a reasonable jury could find that CBS's use of the photo was quantitatively substantial and, therefore, not covered by the *de minimis* exception.[81]

HBO addressed a similar claim before the same court less than a year later. This lawsuit involved a two- to three-second depiction of graffiti in a background scene from an episode of the series *Vinyl*. In the scene, the graffiti is never pictured by itself or up close. Instead, the camera focuses on a well-lit actress who is pictured in the foreground in an "eye-catching bright red dress."[82] By contrast, the graffiti is depicted at an angle in low, uneven light;

is never fully visible, legible, or noticeable; and plays absolutely no role in the plot. The court found that the graffiti was "next to impossible to notice when viewing the episode in real time" and hard to notice even when the video is paused. In the end, the court concluded that given the manner in which the graffiti was filmed, no plausible claim for copyright infringement existed.[83]

When evaluating creative decisions that determine how much of the protected work to show, consider how noticeable and identifiable the work is to the reasonable viewer. According to attorneys Lee S. Brenner and Allison S. Roher, case law indicates that a number of factors shape the outcomes of infringement claims.[84] The factors listed next incorporate their research with additional findings from case law.

Length of Time:
   The exact number of seconds/minutes image appears in total and each time it appears.
   The amount of time the image appears in comparison to the length of the defendant's work.
Visibility:
   Placement: background, foreground, full screen, close-up, partially obscured, etc.
   Focus: blurred, distorted, sharp, etc., in real time and freeze-frame
   Camera angle and its effect on visibility
   Lighting: degree to which image is well-lit and noticeable or dimly lit and shadowy
   Description of visibility: unidentifiable, barely noticeable, clearly observable, legible, etc.
Portion used:
   Fragment, partial, majority, entire, etc.
   Degree to which use represents a substantial portion of the plaintiff's work
   Degree to which use represents a substantial portion of the defendant's work
Prominence:
   Degree of importance to defendant's work
   Role plaintiff's work plays in defendant's work: e.g., incidental, significant to plot, etc.
Intent and Injury:
   Degree to which use is a means to profit from the plaintiff's materials or ensure the success of the defendant's work
   Extent to which royalties would be required under regulations of the Librarian of Congress

CHAPTER SUMMARY

The use of copyrighted material in the creation of new works with a new purpose, meaning, and expression advances the principles upon which copyright law was built. Through a fair use analysis that rests largely on whether a secondary work is transformative, copyright law has provided a mechanism to protect and encourage free expression by creating a breathing space for culture to develop. In doing so, it has recognized that a protected work can have more than one meaning, one aesthetic, and one understanding. Because the law provides a fair use defense, it is important for artists to comprehend the purpose and character of their work and how the elements they use comment on and transform the protected work. Today works that bring about new information, aesthetics, and insights are largely protected against a copyright infringement claim. In this way, the fair use defense works together with the protection provided by copyright law to stimulate creativity for the enrichment of society.

KEY TERMS

Affirmative Defense A set of facts presented by the defendant that if true would defeat the plaintiff's claim. In copyright law, the fair use defense is considered an affirmative defense.

Appropriation The act of taking or using a protected creative work without permission or authorization.

Appropriation Artist An appropriation artist uses recognizable objects or images with little to no transformation in the creation of new works of art. Appropriation artists commonly use mass-produced objects or images that an audience could easily identify. Often, the artist's goal is to comment upon some aspect of consumer culture.

Counter Notice A signed document that disputes the takedown of creative material from the internet. This document asserts that the material does not infringe the rights of a copyright holder and was removed by mistake or through misidentification. Upon receipt of a counter notice, the ISP must inform the copyright holder that the alleged infringing material will be replaced in ten to fourteen business days unless a lawsuit is filed.

Derivative Work   A new work of original authorship that is based on one or more preexisting copyrighted works.

De Minimis   Derived from the legal maxim *de minimis non curat lex* (the law does not concern itself with trifles), in a copyright context, it means that the copying of a protected work is so insignificant that it is not recognized as an actionable infringement.

Digital Millennium Copyright Act   A law passed by Congress in 1998 that is intended, in part, to shield internet companies from massive liability claims resulting from infringing activity that occurs on their websites. The DMCA contains a safe harbor provision that insulates ISPs from copyright claims based on material posted to their sites.

Fair Use Defense   An affirmative defense used to defeat a finding of copyright infringement. The defense asserts that the use of the plaintiff's work was fair in that its use was transformative and thus served to create an original expressive work with new insight and meaning.

Internet Service Provider   Any company or organization that provides users with internet access or other internet-related services that allow them to participate in online activities.

Parodic Character   The critical intent of a parody. To claim a fair use defense, the critical intent of the parody should be directed at the protected material the defendant used rather than at an unrelated target.

Parodist   A creator of parodies.

Parody   A parody pokes fun at, comments on, or criticizes a copyright-protected work. In this way, a parody needs to borrow in order to conjure up the protected material and comment on it. This means that a defendant has a stronger claim to fair use when the copyrighted work is the principal or at least partial target of the secondary work.

Safe Harbor Provision   Section 512 of the Digital Millennium Copyright Act is known as the safe harbor provision. Section 512 protects ISPs from copyright liability for storing the content of its users. To receive this protection, ISPs must expeditiously comply with the notice and takedown procedure set forth in the act. This procedure calls on the ISP to remove or disable access to material upon notification from the copyright holder and to take reasonable steps to notify the user that the material has been removed.

Satire   Satire uses a copyrighted work to poke fun at or ridicule a different target. In this way, a satiric work must justify its borrowing because it has no need to conjure up the protected material.

Secondary work   A secondary work refers to a new work that has been created through the use of original copyright-protected material.

Takedown Notice   A notice informing ISPs that infringing material is hosted on their platform. Once the notice is received, the ISP is required to remove or disable access to the material and take reasonable steps to notify the user of this action.

Transformation   The concept of transformation is a central component of the fair use defense. It rests on the idea that copyright law's intended purpose is to stimulate creative intellectual activity. To fulfill this purpose, a fair use analysis needs to be focused on the transformative nature of the new work rather than its economic effect on the market for the plaintiff's work.

Transformative Works   Transformative works use copyrighted material as a component or building block in the creation of a new work. A transformative work provides new information, aesthetics, insights, and understanding and differs in its purpose from the protected work.

5

Right of Publicity

Right of publicity can be traced back to the emotional and physical distress a young woman suffered when she was informed that her likeness was used without her consent on some twenty-five thousand lithographic advertisements for Franklin Mills Flour. Abigail Roberson found herself confined to bed in humiliation from the "jeers and scoffs" she experienced from people who recognized her face on advertisements prominently posted in stores, warehouses, saloons, and other public places throughout the country. Given her physical and emotional suffering, Roberson brought suit in 1900 seeking damages of $15,000 and a court order prohibiting the defendants from "using in any manner whatsoever" her likeness. At issue in the suit was whether the flour company had the right to print and circulate Roberson's lithographic image for commercial gain without her consent. Franklin Mills argued that Roberson was powerless to prevent them from using her likeness to sell flour. No law, they said, existed that could protect her[1] and in 1902 New York's highest court agreed.[2]

In her lawsuit, Roberson was arguing for a **right of privacy**—a new legal principle predicated on a right to be let alone. Although a closely divided New York Court of Appeals rejected her claim, criticism and outrage over the decision prompted the adoption of the right by other courts and the enactment of state statutes prohibiting the unauthorized use of an individual's name or likeness for commercial purposes.[3] By the 1950s, the right of privacy was increasingly accepted throughout the country and could be asserted to not only stop the **misappropriation** of one's name or likeness but also to recover reputational, emotional, and economic damages.[4] In the decades that followed, as the country's celebrity culture developed and more public figures sought to commercialize their image, a separate **right of publicity** that addressed

Figure 5.1. Abigail Roberson was completely humiliated when she discovered her photo printed on this poster-sized advertisement for flour. At the time, no law prevented the company from misappropriating her image. Her lawsuit would usher in a right of privacy.

the type of harm public figures experienced began to take shape. Lawsuits and court decisions reasoned that public figures, who actively promote their images and seek publicity, suffer more economic than emotional damage from the misappropriation of their identity. As it emerged, the right of publicity increasingly focused on public figures and their ability to protect the commercialization and economic value of their likeness. Today, the right is largely viewed as **intellectual property** in which one's **persona** is distinct from the right of privacy and its emphasis on dignitary and emotional stress injuries.

RIGHT OF PUBLICITY LAW

The right of publicity is generally viewed as a right to prohibit unauthorized commercial uses of one's identity. The right allows individuals to safeguard the commercial value of their fame and prevent the unjust enrichment of others who seek to profit from it. Bringing suit for an unauthorized use, however, can be confusing given there is no federal right of publicity law. Instead, the right to control unauthorized uses of one's identity exists through a patchwork of various state **statutes** and **common law**. This means that laws vary widely across jurisdictions. In some states, the only **cause of action** open to **litigants** is privacy-based common law.[5] In other jurisdictions, well-defined right of publicity statutes form the basis of a legal action. States that recognize statutory and/or common law right of publicity as well as common law right to privacy provide litigants with the opportunity to bring multiple causes of action.[6] While a majority of states provide at least some protection for the misappropriation of one's likeness, a few states have rarely considered such claims and have not explicitly recognized either a right of publicity or a right to privacy.[7] As expected, inconsistencies in state law have created much uncertainty as to which state's law applies, what that law explicitly prohibits, and whether the use at issue actually violates the law.[8] Given this confusion, creative decisions are often based on the most expansive, speech-restrictive publicity laws.[9] In this vein, right of publicity statutes in Indiana, California, and Tennessee are notable. The dimensions contained in those laws are discussed next and form the primary basis of this chapter.

Establishing Identity

In general, right of publicity laws recognize the property interest in a person's **identity**. To establish a claim for right of publicity, plaintiffs need to prove their identity was taken and used without their consent. How broadly state law defines "identity" is a source of some controversy. Commonly, privacy-based misappropriation laws confine identity to a person's name or likeness, such as a portrait, photograph, or drawing. A number of states have expanded that list to include voice and signature.[10] In addition, personality,[11] distinctive appearance,[12] gestures,[13] and mannerisms[14] are considered as well in a few states. Moreover, the scope of what actually constitutes identity has been further enhanced by the courts. In their application of state law, courts have concluded that identity is established by look-alike and sound-alike characterizations and uses that simply evoke the person's image in the public's mind.[15] Altogether, these wide-ranging definitions of identity have effectively prohibited a variety of uses that go well beyond a person's name and image. These uses include a host of indicators uniquely associated with an individual. Courts have concluded that the unauthorized use of such items enables others to reap the commercial value of the person's identity. Unauthorized uses that have established identity and triggered valid publicity rights claims include

- An advertisement for Ford Lincoln Mercury in which the song "Do You Want to Dance?" was sung in a manner that imitated Bette Midler's voice.[16] The sound-alike recording allowed Midler to establish identity.

- A stock color photograph depicting several racing cars on a racetrack. A racecar driver established identity because his car appeared in the foreground, and although his facial features were not visible, a court found that his image was evoked from the appearance of his car.[17]
- A couple of three-dimensional animatronic figures placed in airport bars. The bars were modeled on the television set from the show *Cheers*. The figures evoked the images of Norm and Cliff, two characters in the show. The actors brought suit, establishing identity in their likeness from the figures used to represent the characters they played on the show.[18]
- A robot dressed in a wig, gown, and jewelry posed next to a recognizable game board from the TV show *Wheel of Fortune*. The court concluded that the robot evoked the image of game show host Vanna White, who stood in a similar position while turning block letters on the board.[19]
- The phrase "Here's Johnny," which was used on a late-night talk show to introduce Johnny Carson, the show's host. The court held that use of the phrase by Here's Johnny Portable Toilet company appropriated Carson's identity.[20]
- Several humorous references to musician Don Henley in two different print ads for henley shirts. In one ad, the copy used Henley's last name to describe the shirt and first name to identify the model in the advertisement. The copy read, "This is Don's Henley. Sometimes Don tucks it in; other times he wears it loose—it looks great either way. Don loves his henley; you will too."[21] The court concluded that the play on words was intended to appropriate Henley's identity.[22] In another shirt advertisement, the copy urged customers to "DON A HENLEY and Take it easy."[23] Henley settled this suit with retailer Duluth Trading Company for using both his name and the title of a signature song performed by the band the *Eagles*, of which Henley was a founding member.
- The use of a deceased comedian's last name on a line of bicycles with oversized tires. A lawsuit settled by Chris Farley's family and Trek Bicycle Corporation accused Trek of misappropriating Farley's fat guy image and style of comedy by naming its fat-tire bikes "Farley."[24]

The Value of One's Identity

Generally speaking, right of publicity claims are concerned largely with the commercial value of one's identity, whereas right to privacy misappropriation claims tend to deal with the personal harm suffered by the plaintiff.[25] The connection to commerce and the monetary value in one's identity raises questions with regard to an individual's celebrity status and whether noncelebrity plaintiffs can assert a right of publicity claim. In a handful of states, right of publicity suits are largely limited to individuals with commercially significant identities.[26] However, a host of other states allow individuals who do not have an independent monetary value in their identity to file suit.[27] In *Fraley v. Facebook*, the Ninth Circuit allowed a group of Facebook users to proceed with their right of publicity suit against the social media company. The plaintiffs asserted that Facebook violated their statutory right of publicity when the company created endorsement advertisements that used their names and profile pictures and the fact that they clicked "like" in relation to a specific product or brand. Once created, these commercial endorsements appeared on the news feed of the plaintiffs' friends in an attempt to prompt those friends to purchase the product.[28]

Based on the uncompensated use of their identities in these ads, plaintiffs filed a right of publicity claim for economic injury under California's right of publicity law. At issue in the case was whether the Facebook members could bring suit without demonstrating some preexisting commercial value in their name or likeness. The court concluded that California's right of publicity statute applies to both celebrities and noncelebrities and that even obscure individuals can have a commercial value in their likeness. Here, the court found that the identities of the plaintiffs were commercially valuable to their friends and that, like celebrities, Facebook users have a right to control the exploitation of their identities. In the past, the court noted, a noncelebrity's endorsement carried little weight with advertisers. But today, targeted marketing techniques have made friend endorsements a valuable advertising tool that when exploited allowed this group of plaintiffs to bring suit for economic damages under California's right of publicity statute.[29]

Proving Economic Injury

While the plaintiffs in *Fraley* were successful in showing that their identities had value in the context of the endorsement ads, they also needed to establish actual economic injury to receive compensation for the unauthorized use.[30] In right of publicity suits, damages are usually limited to the resulting harm the publicity inflicted on the commercial value of plaintiff's identity. Harm can be measured by the fair market value of the use, the loss to future earnings or publicity opportunities, or the profits made by the defendant from the appropriation.[31] While it is generally perceived that the "greater the fame or notoriety of the identity appropriated, the greater will be the extent of economic injury suffered," the *Fraley* court also noted that appropriating the identity of a relatively unknown individual may also result in economic injury or create economic value in an identity that was previously valueless.[32]

Elements of a right of publicity claim

1. Defendant used plaintiff's "identity"—for example, name, picture, voice, likeness, mannerisms.
2. Without plaintiff's consent.
3. Use of plaintiff's identity "advantaged" defendant. Examples include uses of identity
    - On or in connection with goods, services, or commercial activities.
    - For advertising or soliciting purchases of goods or services, or for promoting commercial activities.
    - For the purpose of fundraising.
4. Use resulted in economic injury that may be measured by
    - Fair market value of use.
    - Loss to future earnings or publicity opportunities.
    - Profits made by the defendant from appropriation.

Postmortem Rights and Transferability

When Elvis Presley died in August 1977, his death set off a series of lawsuits regarding whether the rights to his name and likeness survived the rock 'n' roll icon's death. During the nearly ten years following Presley's death, a legal battle ensued that was fueled in part by a Supreme Court decision handed down only a few months prior.[33] In *Zacchini v. Scripps-Howard*, the High Court aligned the right of publicity with the goals of intellectual property. This alignment was based on the rationale that the right of publicity is primarily intended to protect the economic benefits of one's endeavors rather than their personal feelings or reputation.[34] The court's rationale effectively separated publicity rights from the right to privacy and formed the justification for treating publicity rights in a person's name and likeness similar to copyright and other forms of intellectual property that could survive death and be passed on to one's heirs.

While the *Zacchini* decision provided the justification for a **descendible** right of publicity, it was up to Presley's home state of Tennessee to adopt the reasoning. In 1984, the state enacted a statutory law that created an assignable, licensable, and descendible right of publicity. Three years later, a state appeals court recognized a descendible right of publicity under Tennessee common law. In doing so, the appeals court embraced the idea that the right of publicity is an intangible piece of property that can be possessed, used, assigned, subjected to contract, and inherited at death.[35] The court's decision meant that Presley's estate could stop the sale of unauthorized in-memoriam merchandise and secure for his heirs the hundreds of millions (and possibly billions) of dollars this and other such merchandise earns through direct sales and **licensing agreements**.[36]

Today, approximately twenty-five states have laws protecting a person's right of publicity after death.[37] The remaining states have either not considered the question or limited claims to living individuals.[38] Of the states that do provide a **postmortem right**, most reserve that right for legal residents of the state. A few states, however, have an "all comers" policy that recognizes the postmortem rights of nonresidents as well. This means that entities could be sued for unauthorized uses of a deceased individual's likeness in states like Indiana, Washington, and Hawaii that have adopted broad-based postmortem rights that cover residents and nonresidents alike. In addition to residency, the length of time the postmortem right survives an individual's death differs among the states. In some states, the duration is relatively long. Indiana, for example, recognizes the right for one hundred years after death. California and Hawaii provide seventy years of protection, and Tennessee law potentially extends the right as long as the identity is being commercially exploited.[39]

Because the right of publicity emerged in a piecemeal fashion across the various **jurisdictions**, its underlying purpose had not been universally set. This and other inconsistencies among the states have prompted calls for a federal right of publicity statute.[40] Until such a law materializes, the question of exactly why a right to publicity exists has been left up to the states and the judiciary. In *Zacchini*, the US Supreme Court had the opportunity to determine Ohio's interest in permitting a publicity right. At issue in the case was a broadcast of Hugo Zacchini's human cannonball act at a county fair. A broadcasting company aired the act on a local television's news program, and Zacchini sued for damages.[41]

The court reasoned that under Ohio law the right of publicity was intended to provide an economic incentive for entertainers, such as Zacchini, to "make the investment required to produce a performance of interest to the public."[42] The same consideration, the court said, underlies copyright law. By providing just compensation for the time and effort Zacchini invested in his act, others are encouraged to follow suit and thereby enrich the public welfare through their talents. In addition to the incentive to invest in one's persona, the court noted that publicity rights allow entertainers and other individuals to reap the rewards of their hard work and prevent others from free-riding or unjustly enriching themselves by appropriating the commercial value of another's fame. Here, the news media broadcast Zacchini's entire act without his consent and, therefore, hampered his ability to collect admission fees.[43] The court's emphasis on commercial gain in its reasoning further prompted states and the judiciary to consider the right as a fully assignable property right rather than a nontransferable privacy right.

INFRINGING USES AND EXCEPTIONS

Given the connection of right of publicity to the commercial exploitation of one's identity, state statutes typically limit infringing actions to those involving some form of commerce or exchange. Depending on the state, infringing actions may consist of unauthorized uses for commercial, trade, advertising, promotional, fundraising, solicitation, and/or endorsement purposes. A host of states also include as actionable uses on products, merchandise, services, or goods.[44] While the commercial nature of a use is viewed as a limiting factor, the true scope of a statute's breadth lies in how broadly courts interpret terms like "trade" or "commercial." Some courts have defined these terms narrowly to cover only those cases in which a person's identity is employed to directly promote a product or service.[45] Because commercial speech receives a lower level of constitutional protection, an unauthorized use of a person's identity to sell an unrelated product often violates right of publicity laws.[46] The more difficult cases, however, involve nonadvertising uses that merit stronger First Amendment protection. In this regard, a court's definition of terms like "trade" and "commercial" can be a decisive factor in cases involving expressive works. Under Florida law, for example, courts have ruled that the use of a person's name or identity in expressive works, such as publications, song lyrics, and motion pictures, does not constitute a commercial, trade, or advertising purpose simply because these items are sold for a profit.[47] This means that such uses of a person's identity are **nonactionable** in that they lie outside the boundaries of the state's right of publicity law.

In California, on the other hand, the law is written more broadly. In addition to advertising or selling purposes, the statute covers unauthorized uses "on or in products, merchandise, goods or services,"[48] and the state's common law right of publicity recognizes all uses that advantage the defendant commercially or otherwise.[49] Under California law, expressive works used in or on products and merchandise are considered actionable. As a result, courts have found that unauthorized uses of a celebrity's likeness on t-shirts, lithographs, and greeting cards, and in video games established viable claims under California's right of publicity laws.[50] The same court system, however, has not clearly concluded whether the unconsented use of a person's identity in a motion picture would violate either the state's statutory or common law.[51] In *De Havilland v. FX Networks*, as an example, the court asked but did not answer the question of whether books, films, and television shows are merchandise or products.[52]

Broad-based applications of the right of publicity are worrisome to free speech advocates, artists, media organizations, and the like. The more the law is considered to be an absolute right to prevent uses that in some way advantage the defendant, the more speech these laws prohibit or sanction. To help curb the expansive nature of right of publicity, many state statutes contain exceptions that address First Amendment concerns. These exceptions commonly exempt newsworthy, public affairs, and political works. Depending on the state, exemptions may also include musical, artistic, audiovisual, and historical works as well as works of fiction or nonfiction and works connected to the broadcasting of sporting events.[53] Along with the exemptions, defendants often invoke the First Amendment as a defense against broad applications of right of publicity law. In doing so, they also bear the burden of establishing that their use of a person's identity was protected by the First Amendment or a stated exemption.

First Amendment Defenses

Because right of publicity lawsuits are routinely brought against expressive works, such as books, films, songs, paintings, and prints,[54] courts have recognized the need to limit the right in order to accommodate First Amendment concerns and preserve a robust marketplace of ideas.[55] While courts acknowledge that some sort of balance needs to be struck between free speech rights and the right of publicity, what that balance exactly looks like has vexed courts and legal scholars alike. As a result, no clear **precedent** has emerged that establishes how much the First Amendment limits the right or what test should be applied when resolving a particular publicity dispute.[56] Instead, at least five different First Amendment approaches have been developed by federal and state courts. Not surprisingly, an assortment of results has materialized from the inconsistent application of these standards across jurisdictions. This inconsistency has left creators and publishers uncertain about what they may say and how they may use an individual's identity as an expressive component in a larger work.[57] Even First Amendment legal scholars are perplexed by the outcomes of free speech challenges to right of publicity claims. They point out that the decisions in such cases are often unsupportable under free speech principles that largely favor the speaker and the speaker's choice of what to say and how to say it.[58]

While the right of publicity is largely viewed as an intellectual property right like copyright, it lacks an overarching directional purpose that shapes the boundary between a fair use and an infringing use of a person's identity. In copyright law, that boundary is largely defined by the law's underlying purpose, which is to stimulate creative activity for public enrichment. With this rationale as a guidepost, courts consider whether the law's purpose would be better served by allowing the secondary work or prohibiting it. In this way, copyright law encourages transformative creative expression that builds on protected works without inhibiting the economic incentive the law gives to the creators of those protected works. The state-structured right of publicity has not been successful at creating a comparable fair use defense. This has prompted courts to balance publicity and speech interests through judicial intuition and a variety of "tests" that differ across the jurisdictions. This practice often leads to outcomes that favor traditional forms of expression, such as news reports, direct criticisms, historical or biographical works, and the like, and disadvantages works that judges view as an unfair exploitative use of a celebrity's fame.[59]

Transformative Use Test

In *Comedy III Productions v. Gary Saderup*, the California Supreme Court squarely addressed the constitutional clash between artistic expression regarding celebrities and laws that prohibit the unauthorized use of their identity. The case involved a charcoal drawing by artist Gary Saderup of the deceased comedy group, the Three Stooges. Saderup used the drawing to produce and sell high-quality, beautifully detailed lithographic prints as well as silkscreened t-shirts bearing the likeness of Moe, Curly, and Larry. Comedy III, owners of the rights to the Three Stooges, sued, claiming the use was a violation of California's statutory right of publicity law. Saderup responded that a judgment against him would violate his right of free speech. In the case, the court acknowledged that Saderup's artistic expression and the reproduction of that expression received a high degree of First Amendment protection and that Comedy III had a legitimate economic interest in the commercial value of the group's identity.[60] To reconcile these two interests, the court formulated a balancing test derived from the **transformative use** analysis of the fair use defense in copyright law. The court reasoned that because the First Amendment and copyright law have a common goal of encouraging free expression and creativity, an artist facing a right of publicity challenge may also raise an **affirmative defense** that the work in question contains significant transformative elements or that its value is not derived primarily from the celebrity's fame.[61] An inquiry into whether a work is transformative is appropriate, the court said, given that "when a work contains significant transformative elements, it is not only especially worthy of First Amendment protection, but it is also less likely to interfere with the economic interest protected by right of publicity."[62]

Figure 5.2. The artistic merit of Gary Saderup's portrayal of the Stooges did not help the drawing fend off a right of publicity challenge. Instead, the court signaled that realistic depictions of celebrities are generally nontransformative, whereas works that use distortion, subtle social criticism and careful manipulation of context are more likely to receive First Amendment protection against a publicity claim.
Photo courtesy of Gary Saderup.

Using a framework drawn from the transformative use element in the fair use defense, the *Comedy III* court indicated that the following factors need to be evaluated when determining whether a work is transformative. According to the court, a work in question will most likely be considered sufficiently transformative if

1. The celebrity's likeness is one of the raw materials used to create the new work.
2. The new work is primarily the defendant's own expression rather than the celebrity's likeness. The *Comedy III* court stressed that the defendant's expression needs to be "something other than likeness of celebrity." In a later case, the Ninth Circuit said that this factor may require an examination of the purchaser's motivation and whether that

motivation is driven by the celebrity's image or the expressive work of the artist.[63]

3. The defendant's creative elements dominate the work. The *Comedy III* court clarified that a literal or imitative representation of a celebrity, "even if accomplished with great skill," may infringe a celebrity's publicity right, especially if that depiction is the very sum and substance of the work in question.

4. The marketability and economic value of the new work are not primarily derived from the fame of the celebrity depicted.[64] Here again, the Ninth Circuit weighed in, adding that it is irrelevant that the producer of the new work seeks to profit from it. The only question is whether the new work is transformative, not how it is marketed.[65]

In their analysis, the *Comedy III* court refused to take into account the artistic merit of Saderup's drawing or the work's subtle expressive qualities. Instead, courts should not consider the quality of the artist's work, the *Comedy III* court wrote, stressing that "vulgar forms of expression fully qualify for First Amendment protection."[66] The *Comedy III* court also noted that a work is not transformative if the artist's skill and talent are used to create a "conventional portrait of a celebrity so as to commercially exploit his or her fame,"[67] but clarified that celebrity portraits by artists like Andy Warhol are an exception. Warhol, the court explained, "convey[ed] a message that went beyond the commercial exploitation" of the celebrity's image. Through distortion and careful manipulation of context, Warhol was able to transform the image into a "form of ironic social comment on the dehumanization of the celebrity itself."[68]

Turning to Saderup's work, the court discounted the artistic merit exhibited in the drawing and focused instead on how the Three Stooges were depicted in the work. Here, the court concluded that because the drawing consisted of a conventional portrayal of the Three Stooges, Saderup's intent was to exploit the comedy group's fame.[69] Moreover, the court pointed out that the economic value of the t-shirts and lithographs is derived primarily from the fame of celebrities depicted. "While this fact alone does not necessarily mean the work receives no First Amendment protection, we can perceive no transformative elements in Saderup's works that would require such protection," the court wrote.[70] To hold otherwise, the court concluded, would strip the right of publicity of its ability to protect the economic interests of celebrities in most all cases except those involving falsified celebrity endorsements.[71]

The *Comedy III* court's transformative use standard has been applied by the Third and Ninth Circuits to a series of cases involving the use of a celebrity's likeness in a video game. Like the *Comedy III* court, the Circuits concluded that the First Amendment protects uses that sufficiently transform a person's identity and that works consisting of a mere copy or imitation of the celebrity's identity are vulnerable to a right of publicity challenge.[72] They applied this line of thinking to three cases involving video-game manufacturers that created virtual football games with digital avatars that realistically portrayed former players.

In *Hart v. Electronic Arts*, for example, the Third Circuit noted that the avatar matched football star Ryan Hart in terms of hair color, hairstyle, skin tone, and the accessories he wore when he was a football player at Rutgers University. Moreover, the court pointed out that "[d]igital Ryan Hart does what the actual Ryan Hart did while at Rutgers: he plays college football" in recreated stadiums that are filled with all the trappings of a college football game.[73] While video games are expressive works protected by the First Amendment, the Third Circuit held that the *NCAA Football* game is not transformative in that it does not alter or transform Hart's identity in a significant way. Instead it allows Electronic Arts to benefit from the respective fan bases for the various teams and players depicted in the games and their rivals who have the ability to change the outcome of bitter defeat.[74] The Ninth Circuit followed this line of reasoning in cases involving the *NCAA Football* and *Madden NFL* series of video games, and a California Appeals Court used it to strike down a game maker's transformative use defense in a video game that contained literal recreations of members of the rock band *No Doubt* doing "the same activity by which the band achieved and maintains its fame."[75]

While the economic value of the video games was drawn primarily from the fame of the celebrities depicted, this factor was not implicated in a case involving a comic book company and its five-volume comic miniseries featuring the fictional anti-hero Jonah Hex. The case centered on the creation of Johnny and Edgar Autumn, two characters that appeared in volumes four and five of the miniseries. Johnny and Edgar Winter, two well-known musicians, sued, claiming that the names and the depictions of the Autumn brothers violated their right of publicity under California law. In the miniseries, the Autumn brothers were drawn with pale skin and long white hair to evoke the albino features of the Winter brothers. In addition, the character Johnny Autumn wore a tall black top hat that resembled the black hats often worn by Johnny Winter. The court contrasted these "less than subtle" similarities with the significant expressive content of the miniseries. The court wrote, "The Autumn brothers are but cartoon characters—half-human and half-worm—in a larger story, which is itself quite expressive."[76] The court concluded that the miniseries' portrayal of the Winter brothers did not greatly threaten their publicity rights given that Winter brothers' fans would not find the Autumn brothers a satisfactory substitute for a conventional depiction of the musicians.[77]

While the *Comedy III* and *Winter* decisions represent bookend examples of the transformative use test, a painting commemorating Tiger Woods's dramatic victory at the Masters Tournament in Augusta, Georgia, in 1997 falls somewhere in the middle. The painting, titled *The Masters of Augusta*, consists of three dominant images of Tiger Woods playing golf. The center image shows Woods as he completes a golf swing. On each side of this image, Woods is seen crouching as if he is lining up a putt. Next to the crouching images on both the far right and far left sides of the painting, a partially visible caddy stands. Behind these foreground figures, the Augusta National Clubhouse sits against a blue sky filled with subtle images of famous golfers and the Masters leader board. The artist, Rick Rush, published and marketed 250 serigraphs and 5,000 lithographs of this painting. Woods challenged the work as a violation of his right of publicity under Ohio law.

Figure 5.3. The court found that Rick Rush transformed three images of Tiger Woods into a story that described the significance of the young golfer's 1997 Masters Tournament win. Rush accomplished this by showing Woods in action along with his caddy and his partner's caddy as he works toward a record-setting 12-stroke victory. The Augusta National Clubhouse, a collage of golfing greats, and the Masters leader board appear in the background. The court said that the depiction and placement of these elements celebrate an historical event without capitalizing on Woods or his fame.
Photo courtesy of Rick Rush.

The Sixth Circuit applied the transformative use test and noted that Rush's work contained significant transformative elements that made it especially worthy of First Amendment protection. First, Rush did not capitalize solely on a literal depiction of Woods. Instead, the artist added a collage of images to illustrate that Woods, as the youngest golfer to win the Masters, achieved a historic victory. In a more intuitive balancing approach, the court also noted how celebrities involved in these events symbolize certain ideas and values in our society that make them an important vehicle for cultural expression. Balancing societal interests against a celebrity's publicity rights, the court reasoned that like most celebrities, Woods generates substantial amounts of income from activities, such as authorized appearances and endorsements, that are unrelated to his right of publicity. And while he has the right to enjoy the fruits of his labors, in this case it is not clear that Rush's artwork will reduce the commercial value of Woods's likeness. However, it is quite clear, according to the court, that if Woods's publicity right is allowed to trump Rush's freedom of expression, the artist's ability to profit from his creative talents would be extinguished. In this vein, the court concluded that the informational and creative elements of Rush's work outweighed any adverse effect on Woods's right of publicity and the market that comes from his fame.[78]

Rush's transformation of Woods from a present-day celebrity athlete into a historic figure in the saga of the Masters tournament can be contrasted with a Hallmark card that depicted Paris Hilton as a cartoon waitress serving a plate of food to a customer. On the cover of the birthday card, Hilton says, "Don't touch that, it's hot," and the patron asks, "What's hot?" Hilton replies with her signature phrase, "That's hot." The image of Hilton as a waitress is a play on an episode of the reality television show *The Simple Life*. On the show, Hilton is placed in situations that she would most likely not find herself given her privileged background. In one episode, Hilton is working as a car hop at a fast-food restaurant, serving orders on roller skates and occasionally remarking that a person or something is "hot." Hallmark contended that the cartoon based on this episode was transformative, but the Ninth Circuit disagreed. The court noted that the restaurant style, food served, caricature drawing of Hilton's body, and the meaning of her catchphrase differed from the episode, but countered that the basic setting was the same in that "we see Paris Hilton, born to privilege, working as a waitress."[79] The court explained that defendants are only entitled to a transformative defense if no trier of fact could reasonably conclude that the use in question was *not* transformative. The court then compared the Hallmark card to *Winter*, where a comic book company transformed a celebrity's likeness into a fanciful creature, and found that the cartoon did not rise to this level and could not be deemed transformative.[80]

The Relatedness Test

The **relatedness test** is particularly applicable in situations where the name or other identifying characteristics of a celebrity is used in the title of an expressive work. The test, also known as the artistic relevance or *Rogers* test, was developed by the Second Circuit in a case involving a claim filed by dancer and actress Ginger Rogers against the Italian filmmaker Federico Fellini for a film he released titled *Ginger and Fred.* Rogers objected to the use of her name in the title, arguing that it violated her publicity right. In *Rogers*, the court ruled that the right of publicity does not prevent an artist from using the name of a celebrity in a movie title unless the title and the underlying work is (1) "wholly unrelated" to the celebrity or (2) a "disguised advertisement" used to market or get attention for the commercial project.[81] The film in question in the case centered on two retired cabaret performers named Pippo and Amelia, who in their younger years imitated Rogers and her longtime dance partner Fred Astaire. The fictional dance couple's imitation of Rogers and Astaire earned them the nicknames "Ginger and Fred" by their fans. Fellini contended that the film was a bittersweet story of a televised reunion of Pippo and Amelia many years after their retirement as well as a satire of contemporary television variety shows.[82] In its decision, the court found that the title was an entirely truthful representation of the film's fictional protagonists, who were known as Ginger and Fred to their Italian audience. Moreover, the film contrasts and satirizes the elegance and class of American cinema in the 1930s and 1940s with the gaudiness and banality of contemporary television. In this way, Fellini's movie was clearly related to Rogers and not a disguised advertisement. The use of Rogers's name in the title was, therefore, protected by the First Amendment and not a violation of her publicity right.[83]

Since *Rogers*, the relatedness test has also been adopted by the Fifth and Sixth Circuits. In *Parks v. LaFace Records*, the Sixth Circuit addressed the question of how closely related a celebrity's name needed to be to the underlying work to pass the relatedness test. The case emerged from the song *Rosa Parks* by the rap group OutKast. Rosa Parks, the civil rights icon who refused to give up her seat on a segregated bus to a white passenger, sued the group for violating her publicity right. In determining whether the title was protected by the First Amendment, the court evaluated the degree to which Parks's name was artistically related to the lyrics of the song. The group claimed that Parks's name was used as a symbol for the lyrics, which included the repeated phrase "move to the back of the bus." The court found, however, that in the context of the lyrics, the phrase had "absolutely nothing to do with Rosa Parks" and that the lack of relevancy of the phrase to Parks would not change no matter how many times "move to the back of the bus" was repeated in the lyrics.[84] This finding was reinforced by a group member who admitted that the phrase was not about Parks but was directed at the rap group's competitors. In the end, the court concluded that "crying 'artist' does not confer carte blanche authority to appropriate a celebrity's name" and that crying "symbol" does not change this.[85]

The Predominant Purpose Test

To better address right of publicity cases where the speech at issue is both expressive and commercial, the Supreme Court of Missouri developed the **predominant purpose test**. In *Doe v. TCI*, the state court noted that the threshold legal question in most right of publicity cases is whether the unauthorized use is "expressive" and fully protected by the First Amendment, or "commercial" and generally unprotected. To answer this question using the predominant purpose test, a court would need to assess whether the expressive products in question predominantly exploit the commercial value of a celebrity's identity or whether they mostly make a comment on or about that individual. If a court concludes that the former is correct, the unauthorized use would be a violation of the right of publicity, and if the latter is established, the use would weigh more in favor of a First Amendment defense.[86]

Armed with this legal framework, the court analyzed Anthony "Tony" Twist's right of publicity claim against Todd McFarlane Productions. Twist, a preeminent hockey player who earned the reputation as tough-guy enforcer, brought the claim in 1997 after he learned that a villainous character in the comic book *Spawn* was named "Anthony 'Tony Twist' Twistelli." Todd McFarlane, an avowed hockey fan, created *Spawn* in 1992. A year later, he added Twistelli to the storyline. In the comic book, Twistelli is a Mafia don who has committed multiple murders, abducted children, and frequented prostitutes. Although Twistelli bears no physical resemblance to Twist aside from their shared nickname, the fictional character, like Twist, has a similar tough-guy reputation. At trial, McFarlane denied that the fictional character was based on Twist even though evidence emerged that McFarlane marketed *Spawn* to hockey fans by "producing and licensing Spawn logo hockey pucks, hockey jerseys and toy Zambonis."[87] On one occasion, McFarlane appeared at a sponsored "Spawn Night" at a minor league hockey game and distributed products, including those that contained the Twistelli character.[88] In applying the predominant purpose test to the facts, the court found that the reference to Twist had "very little literary value compared to its commercial value" and that the use of the hockey enforcer's name was "predominantly a ploy to sell comic books and related products rather than an artistic or literary expression."[89] Under these circumstances, the court ruled that McFarlane's free speech defense must give way to Twist's right of publicity interest.

The Third Circuit was asked to apply the predominant use test in *Hart v. Electronic Arts*, and declined to do so, explaining that the test is at best "subjective" and at worst "arbitrary." In either case, the court said the test "calls upon judges to act as both impartial jurists and discerning art critics," and that "[t]hese two roles cannot coexist."[90] In *Hart*, the plaintiff argued that the *NCAA Football* game fails the predominant purpose test because, like the addition of the Twistelli character in *Spawn*, the inclusion of the Ryan Hart avatar does not enhance the artistic expressiveness in the video game. In fact, the game has the same level of expressiveness with or without Hart's likeness, and, therefore, the use of Hart's avatar is not shielded by the First Amendment from a right of publicity challenge. The Third Circuit rejected this argument, explaining that it is improper for a court to selectively analyze elements of a work "to determine how much they contribute to the entire work's expressiveness."[91]

Ad Hoc Balancing Test

Several circuits, including the Eighth, Tenth, and Eleventh, have engaged in a fact-based **ad hoc balancing** approach when evaluating First Amendment challenges to right of publicity claims. In one such case, the Eighth Circuit ruled for an online fantasy baseball game company that used players' names, biographical data, and statistics. The company, CBC Distribution and Marketing, had been licensing the information through the Major League Baseball Players Association but lost the contract after it expired. CBC brought suit arguing that it had a First Amendment right to use the information without a license. The court agreed, reasoning that the information used was readily available in the public domain. "It would be strange," the court wrote, "that a person would not have a First Amendment right to use information that is available to everyone" regardless of whether the information is for entertainment or newsworthy purposes.[92] The Players Association countered that an unlicensed use would violate the players' publicity rights under Missouri law.

In its balancing treatment, the court examined the economic harm the unlicensed use would inflict upon the players and determined that even in the absence of licensing fees for fantasy baseball games, major league players are handsomely rewarded for their participation in games and can, in addition, earn large sums of money from endorsements and sponsorship arrangements.[93] In the end the court held that the CBC's First Amendment rights in offering its fantasy baseball products trumped the players' right of publicity. Although CBC won its First Amendment claim, scholars have contended that if the Eighth Circuit would have applied Missouri's predominant purpose test, the case would have likely led to the opposite given that the identities were used for commercial gain.[94]

Public Interest Defense

Several states recognize a **public interest exception** for uses of a person's identity that are linked to the publication of newsworthy matters. This exception is used primarily in cases involving newspapers and other media outlets that publish or report information. For example, it has been used to uphold the right of a newspaper to turn the pages of its Super Bowl special edition into posters for sale to the public despite a right of publicity claim by the winning team's star quarterback. The court reached its decision because the quarterback's name and image "appeared in the posters for precisely the same reason" that they appeared in the newspaper—that is, he was a major player in a newsworthy sports event.[95] While the use of a person's identity in valid news coverage lies at the heart of this defense, it is not always a successful strategy even for defendants whose work can be deemed a public interest. A case in point is Hallmark's dispute with Paris Hilton. Under California law, Hallmark was effective at showing that the birthday card it created concerned a matter of public interest given that it focused on a person in the public eye (Hilton) and a topic of widespread public interest (Hilton's public persona and trademarked catchphrase). [96] However, the Ninth Circuit noted that the defense itself was not helpful because it is reserved for the "publication of matters in the public interest," and because the birthday card does not publish or report information, the public interest defense did not apply to Hallmark.[97]

The public interest defense was also problematic for Senator John McCain, the Republican National Committee (RNC), and the Ohio Republican Party (ORP) in a suit brought by singer and songwriter Jackson Browne. Browne, a public supporter of the Democratic Party and President Barack Obama, sued for the unauthorized use of his song, *Running on Empty*, in a web video paid for by the ORP that criticized Democratic presidential candidate Obama and his energy policy. Browne was successful in proving that he had a legitimate right of publicity claim under California common law. While the use at issue was a political and not a commercial advertisement, Browne only needed to establish that the appropriation "advantaged" the defendant "commercially or otherwise." Browne presented evidence that McCain may have received increased media attention for his presidential candidacy from the commercial that appropriated his song. The RNC claimed the use was exempted under the public interest defense but failed to show how its use of the composition was a matter of public interest. Because the commercial did not comment on or target the composition or Browne, a federal district court in California found that the exception did not apply.[98]

In a somewhat similar claim under Colorado law, a same-sex couple lost their challenge involving the unauthorized use of their engagement photo in political advertisements. The photo showed the couple holding hands and kissing each other on the lips and was used in a mailer that attacked state politicians who supported same-sex unions. Public Advocate of the United States, the sender of the advertisements, opposed same-sex marriage. The court found that the use of the photograph was primarily noncommercial and that the mailers were reasonably related to a matter of legitimate public concern given that they centered on the issue of same-sex marriage.[99] As such, the court said the public interest exception barred the couple's misappropriation claim.

CHAPTER SUMMARY

A common criticism of right of publicity is its lack of a unifying ratio-nale that places meaningful limits on the right. In *Zacchini,* the High Court tied the rationale to preventing the unjust enrichment that occurs when a defendant takes some marketable aspect of the plaintiff without paying for it.[100] This rationale has allowed plaintiffs to successfully establish a claim without showing that the unauthorized use caused them any reputational or personal harm. Consequently, celebrities are left to presume that they are "entitled to every cent of commercial value" that emanates from the use of their identities regardless of the broader public benefits that flow from the defendant's work.[101] With no clear fair use mechanism, courts turn to the First Amendment and a host of legal standards to resolve disputes involving expressive uses of a celebrity's identity. This approach has provided seem-ingly inconsistent outcomes involving similar types of expressive works that send a mixed signal to speakers and artists.

While no one First Amendment test is dispositive in right of publicity law, the most well-developed are the transformative use test and the relatedness test. Both require a clear connection between the artistic purpose and the use of the identity that is not primarily tied to the fame of a celebrity or a ploy to get attention. Courts have also cautioned against literal or imitative representations of an individual, especially those that place a celebrity in a familiar setting or capitalize off the person's fanbase. Right of publicity is an unwieldy area of law and its reach, while widely contested by media organizations, artists, legal scholars, and the like, presents considerable risk to individuals thinking about creating and selling an expressive product that evokes a celebrity's identity.[102]

KEY TERMS

Ad Hoc Balancing   Ad hoc balancing is an approach judges use to evaluate a First Amendment challenge to a right of publicity claim. With ad hoc balancing, a judge examines the interests of both parties and weighs those interests against each other to determine which interest is more important to society to protect. With this approach, free speech interests carry considerable weight.

Affirmative Defense   A set of facts presented by the defendant that if true would defeat the plaintiff's claim. An example of an affirmative defense is the fair use defense in copyright law.

Cause of Action   The basis on which a lawsuit is filed. The cause of action gives the plaintiff a right to sue the defendant. The cause of action may be based on a statute, common law, constitutional law, or other sources of law.

Common Law   Common law is derived from case law. Case law is created when a judge renders a decision, writes an opinion detailing the reason for the decision, and publishes the opinion. Because common law stems from case law, it is referred to as judge-made law and contrasts with statutory law, which is enacted by a lawmaking body, and constitutional law, which develops from federal and state constitutions.

Descendible   Descendible property can be inherited upon the death of the original property owner. Right of publicity is viewed as a property right in one's identity. Thus, in some states, the right may be inherited upon death.

Identity   Right of publicity recognizes the property interest in one's identity. State law can define "identity" broadly to encompass much more than one's name or picture. Voice, signature, mannerisms, gesture, distinctive appearance, and personality are descriptions of "identity" contained in state law.

Intellectual property   Products of the mind are referred to as intellectual property. Intellectual property includes works that receive copyright protection as well as designs and creations covered by trademark and patent law.

Jurisdiction   Jurisdiction is the power a court possesses to hear and rule on a specific legal matter. In a legal dispute, one of the first questions to resolve is which court has jurisdiction over the legal matter. Jurisdiction is often limited by the geographical area of a court's legal authority. For example, state courts in Montana do not have jurisdictional power over legal matters that occur in Nebraska. Jurisdiction may be limited by the parties involved. This is called personal jurisdiction.

Licensing Agreement   A licensing agreement is a contract between two parties that spells out the terms under which one party may use the property of another party. Licensing agreements are commonly used with intellectual property, including publicity rights. These agreements detail the exact parameters of the permitted use, including where, when, and how the intellectual property may be used by the licensee.

Litigant   A litigant is a person who is engaged in a lawsuit.

Misappropriation   The unauthorized use of another person's name, picture, or likeness in a manner that advantages the defendant and harms the plaintiff. Commonly, the unauthorized use is for commercial or promotional purposes.

Nonactionable   Nonactionable refers to uses of one's identity that are not prohibited by state law.

Persona   Persona refers broadly to the recognized features or indicators of one's character.

Postmortem Right   A postmortem right extends the ability to control unauthorized uses of one's identity after death. Postmortem rights are an important part of the right of publicity given the capacity of celebrities to generate revenue long after they have died. As a result, it is common for right of publicity laws to recognize a postmortem right.

Precedent   A past decision or a series of decided cases that serve as the basis for resolving a current dispute with a similar fact pattern or issue.

Predominant Purpose Test   This test is applied to works that use a celebrity's identity and are both expressive and commercial. Here, the court asks whether the work in question predominantly exploits the commercial value of the celebrity's identity or whether it predominantly makes a comment on or about the celebrity. If the former is established, the unauthorized use would violate the celebrity's publicity right. If the latter was confirmed, the use would be protected by the First Amendment.

Public Interest Exception   Under this exception, uses of a person's identity linked to the publication of valid news coverage are exempt from liability for misappropriation. Several states recognize this defense.

Relatedness Test   The relatedness test is another means by which courts weigh free expression interests against publicity rights. This test is primarily used in cases where the name of a celebrity is used in the title of an expressive work. Here, the title will most likely be protected expression unless the underlying work is entirely unrelated to the celebrity or a mere promotional tool for a commercial endeavor.

Right of Privacy   Right of privacy is based on a right to be let alone. It grew out of a 1902 case involving the use of a young woman's picture on an advertisement for flour. Since that time, right of privacy has developed as a state-based right that allows individuals to bring suit for unauthorized commercial uses of one's identity. In the broad sense, right of privacy laws differ from right of publicity laws in that they aim to protect the integrity of one's identity rather than its monetary value. As a result, privacy laws are designed to compensate the individual for personal suffering rather than economic damages. Because not all states recognize a right of publicity, litigants also sue for misappropriation of their identity under right of privacy laws.

Right of Publicity   Right of publicity is a state-based right that varies from state to state. Right of publicity laws allow a person to bring suit for unauthorized commercial uses of one's identity. In this way, right of publicity laws protect the monetary value of a person's identity. Damages are most often determined based on the value of the unauthorized use.

Statutes   Laws enacted by legislatures or other lawmaking bodies.

Transformative Use   In right of publicity, some courts have embraced the idea that transformative works are not only worthy of First Amendment protection but are also less likely to interfere with the economic interests protected by publicity rights. Building on this idea, courts have developed a four-part test to determine when a secondary work involving the identity of a celebrity is transformative and thus protected expression. A transformative use is likely to be found where the (1) celebrity's likeness is used as a raw material in the creation of a new work; (2) new work is primarily the defendant's own expression; (3) defendant's creative elements dominate the work, and (4) economic value of the new work is derived from the defendant's creativity rather than the celebrity's fame.

6

Trademarks

Trademarks are an integral part of a well-functioning economic market-place in that they enable consumers to quickly identify the source and quality of familiar products and services. This key purpose of trademarks reduces the time and cost it takes to search for the right product or service. For example, a consumer who has enjoyed a cup of Starbucks coffee in the past and wants to replicate that experience only needs to look for a green, twin-tailed mermaid positioned in the center of the cup. This mythical siren provides a reservoir of information to consumers acquainted with the types, flavors, and quality of Starbucks coffee. In this way, she helps to prevent market confusion and protect consumers from purchasing the wrong product. The Starbucks mermaid and other such logos also symbolize the character, cultural image, and market strength of their associated brand. Today, brands, especially famous ones, embody the goodwill of a company and are viewed as an important asset with their own substantial market worth. The Starbucks brand, for example, was valued by Interbrand in 2020 at more than $11.2 billion.[1] No other coffee company comes close. In this way, the seafaring siren also signals the market dominance of the company.

Trademark law recognizes that a company's brand is a complex entity that goes beyond a graphic element or logo and that organizations invest considerable amounts of resources in developing and maintaining their image. Consequently, trademark law has been designed and expanded to protect much more than the source-identifying marks associated with products and services. This expanded protection helps ensure that producers like Starbucks (and not some counterfeit enterprise) reap the financial and reputational rewards associated with their products.[2] In this role, the law aims to combat deceptive, imitation practices that capitalize on the desirability of well-known brands. This protection, in turn, is thought to incentivize the production of quality products and foster fair competition.[3]

FEDERAL TRADEMARK LAW

Since its inception in 1946, the scope of the federal trademark statute, known as the **Lanham Act**, has grown substantially based largely on the consumer protection goals of preventing misinformation and market confusion. Although the Lanham Act exists alongside state statutes and common law unfair competition, it has become the primary and most extensive source of trademark protection in the United States. This chapter focuses on federal trademark law, specifically trademark and trade dress infringement and false association. Other areas of law designated by the Lanham Act will be discussed in chapters 7 and 8.

Distinctiveness

At the heart of traditional trademark law is the concept of **distinctiveness**. Distinctiveness indicates the degree to which a designator—that is, letters, words, logos, images, slogans—invokes the source of the product or service in the mind of the consumer. In trademark law, distinctiveness is determined by the uniqueness of the text, visuals, and other symbols that are used to identify the origin of a good or service. This means that terms like "pain killer" or "lite beer" that indicate the basic nature of a product are useless. Because trademark protection effectively prohibits others from using certain words, no producer is allowed to trademark words commonly used within a specific industry. Even slang words are covered by this rule as Harley-Davidson found out when they tried to trademark the word "hog," which the dictionary defines as a large motorcycle. Allowing Harley-Davidson to trademark this word would have prevented the Hog Farm, a motorcycle parts and accessories shop, and other such businesses from using the term to identify their businesses. Courts consider how the term is used by competitors and the news media to determine its relevant public understanding. This means that misspelled words—for example, "Kleener" for a cleaning product—will also be deemed generic.

To receive federal trademark protection, a mark must be distinctive. Thus, all federally registered marks have been declared distinctive by an examining attorney working for the **United States Patent and Trademark Office** (USPTO). However, not all marks are equally distinctive. USPTO attorneys and courts group marks into one of the following five categories depending on the relationship between the underlying product or service and the mark.

Generic Marks

As discussed, **generic marks** basically denote the product itself and are considered extremely weak source identifiers. As a result, generic marks will not receive trademark protection. Registered marks may also become **genericized** over time. This occurs when the mark is so ingrained in the language that it now signifies the product itself and not the source of the product. Examples of once registered trademarks include "elevator," "aspirin," "thermos," and "teleprompter."

Today companies fear losing their legal protection and brand value to trademark erosion. Even powerhouse Google was forced to defend its trademarked name against a challenge from two individuals who argued that the word "Google" had become a generic term and that the company's trademark registration should be canceled. The court found that the word "Google" had four distinct meanings: (1) Trademarked name; (2) Verb that described the act of searching using the Google search engine; (3) Verb that described the act of searching using any search engine; and (4) Common descriptive term for search engines in general. Google showed that more than 90 percent of consumers understood definition one. The court concluded that the term Google was not generic because it still functions as a source designator.[4]

To combat **trademark erosion**, the mark should be used as an adjective rather than a noun or verb.[5] Avoid uses such as "Please hand me a Wet One" or "Just Google it." Some companies have added the word "brand" after the trademarked name—for example, Lysol brand. Others have paired the trademark with a descriptive term or phrase, such as "Kleenex brand tissues" or "Play-Doh—modeling compound." Extending the product line associated with the trademark, so the mark appears on more than one product, also helps.[6]

Descriptive Marks

Trademark terms in this category immediately convey some aspect of the underlying good. Courts have defined this category as marks that describe a "function, use characteristic, size or intended purpose of the product."[7] While a descriptive mark does not completely depict the good, it will feature at least one major characteristic of the product that is likely to influence a consumer's purchasing decision.[8] Marks are more likely to be categorized as descriptive when

1. The dictionary definition of the word corresponds with the mark's meaning and context;
2. No imagination, thought, or perception is required to understand the nature of the goods;
3. Competitors need to use the same terms in describing their products; or
4. Others have used the same term in marketing a similar service or product.[9]

Familiar marks held to be descriptive include "Holiday Inn," "All Bran," and "American Girl."[10]

Descriptive marks do a poor job of distinguishing one source from another and cannot be registered at inception. Instead, they must acquire a **secondary meaning** to become distinctive enough to warrant full trademark protection.[11] A secondary meaning is established when the consuming public mentally associates the descriptive mark with the source of the product. Take Kentucky Fried Chicken and American Airlines, for example. The words "Kentucky" and "American" are geographically descriptive terms that indicate the place of the product. To achieve trademark protection, these companies need to show that consumers largely recognize these terms as **source identifiers** for a specific brand of fried chicken and a particular airline rather than the places of Kentucky and America.[12] Once a descriptive mark is shown to be a source identifier, it has acquired a secondary meaning and is considered distinctive enough to be registered. Courts determine whether a mark has acquired a secondary meaning by examining a host of factors, including consumer testimonies and surveys; sales and advertising efforts; length of time mark has been in use; exclusivity of that use; volume of sales and the number of customers; use of mark in trade journals; size of the company; presence of the mark in the market; and proof of actual confusion.[13] This can be a lengthy and expensive process for any company trying to establish secondary meaning or defend a descriptive mark in a trademark suit.[14]

Personal Names

Many people like using their last name to identify their business. Because multiple people share the same last name, the party requesting exclusive rights to the **surname** needs to demonstrate that the name actually functions as a trademark. This means that step one of the process concentrates on how the public would likely recognize the surname. Surnames that the public regards as someone's family name cannot be registered without an acquired secondary meaning, whereas surnames that the public perceives as a trademark are eligible for registration upon application. In determining which surnames can be registered upon application, the following five factors are typically examined:

1. Is the name rare? A rare surname weighs in favor of registration.
2. Is the name connected to the applicant? Last names that are not associated with the applicant are less likely to be considered primarily a surname.
3. Does the name have other recognized meanings? A surname like Washington, which has historical and geographical significance, is less likely to be perceived as merely a surname. Conversely, names that have no meaning are more likely to be considered primarily a surname.
4. Does the structure and pronunciation of the mark look like a surname? Marks that look like a person's last name are more likely to be considered primarily a surname.
5. Does the stylization and design of the mark signal that it is a trademark and not primarily a surname? An elaborate design can disguise the fact that the mark is a surname.

The combination of surnames, for example, Abercrombie & Fitch, and the use of personal names—that is, first names and first names used with last names—are generally not considered as surnames for federal registration. The addition of initials to the surname also may convey to the public that the mark is a personal name rather than a surname.[15] But because trademarks function as source indicators, actual names and pseudonyms must identify and distinguish a specific set of goods or services in the minds of the consumers.[16] The extent to which a personal name functions as a mark, the more likely it will receive trademark protection. This means that individuals cannot trademark their name in isolation of any business activity.

The same holds true for celebrities, who need to show that the consuming public associates the personal name (1) with the celebrity and not just any person with that name and (2) with a specific set of goods or services. While fame helps to establish number one, a celebrity still needs to show that the public connects the name to a specific set of goods or services to register it as a trademark. This is easier when the products or services are in some way associated with the person's fame.[17] Think Michael Jordan and Air Jordan athletic shoes. But regardless of whether a trademark is a surname, first name, or full name, names are generally regarded by courts as descriptive terms that require proof of secondary meaning in trademark disputes.[18]

Suggestive Marks

Suggestive marks, like descriptive marks, use words associated with the product's characteristics or intended use. These two categories, however, part company when it comes to the mental leap consumers need to make to understand the relationship between the mark and the product or service it represents. While no imagination, thought, or perception is required to tie a descriptive mark to its product, the same cannot be said about a suggestive mark. Courts have explained that suggestive marks allude to or evoke (rather than describe) some quality, ingredient, or characteristic of the product and thus require the consumer to exercise imagination and perception to actually determine the nature of the good. Marks considered to be suggestive include Coppertone (sunscreen); Orange Crush (orange-flavored soft drink); L'eggs (pantyhose);[19] Extend Your Beauty (eyelash extensions);[20] and Microsoft (software for microcomputers).

Suggestive trademarks are popular with marketing professionals because they bring to mind the nature and attributes of the product. The seed these marks plant in a consumer's mind also reduces the time and resources needed to build brand awareness. But because this connection is shadowy, suggestive marks are considered inherently distinctive and may be registered at inception. While suggestive marks seem like a good option for marketing professionals, the problem lies in the blurry distinction between descriptive and suggestive marks and the stakes at issue in that distinction. Given that descriptive marks are unprotected at inception, a great deal of litigation revolves around this categorical question. Moreover, the outcomes often seem inconsistent. Take the mark "Work-n-Play" for a van that converts from a mobile office into a camper. The Seventh Circuit categorized the mark as descriptive because it describes the product category—that is, vans used for both work and play.[21] On the other hand, the Second Circuit found that "Wet Ones" was suggestive even though the defendant argued that the mark described the product category of wipes that are wet and dispensed one by one.[22] These two cases illustrate the risk companies take when creating suggestive marks. What a marketing team thinks is suggestive, a court or the USPTO may deem descriptive.

Arbitrary Marks

Arbitrary marks use common words in an imaginative way. Take the word "apple," for example. Its everyday meaning conjures up images of a round, red, crispy fruit that's good for you. Steve Jobs, the co-founder of Apple computers, apparently came up with this name for the company after returning from an apple orchard, thinking it sounded "fun, spirited and not intimidating."[23] Today, it is one of the most recognizable arbitrary trademarks

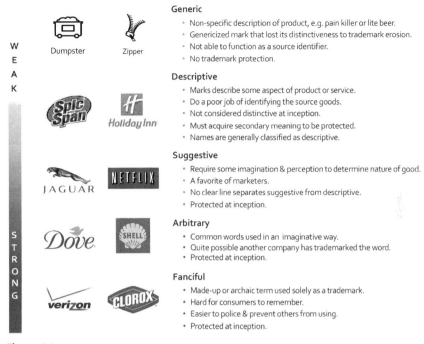

Generic
- Non-specific description of product, e.g. pain killer or lite beer.
- Genericized mark that lost its distinctiveness to trademark erosion.
- Not able to function as a source identifier.
- No trademark protection.

Descriptive
- Marks describe some aspect of product or service.
- Do a poor job of identifying the source goods.
- Not considered distinctive at inception.
- Must acquire secondary meaning to be protected.
- Names are generally classified as descriptive.

Suggestive
- Require some imagination & perception to determine nature of good.
- A favorite of marketers.
- No clear line separates suggestive from descriptive.
- Protected at inception.

Arbitrary
- Common words used in an imaginative way.
- Quite possible another company has trademarked the word.
- Protected at inception.

Fanciful
- Made-up or archaic term used solely as a trademark.
- Hard for consumers to remember.
- Easier to police & prevent others from using.
- Protected at inception.

Figure 6.1.

in the world. Because arbitrary trademarks rely on words with everyday meanings entirely unconnected to the products or services they identify, these marks are quite strong, inherently distinctive, and registered at inception. The one downside to using a common word like apple is it's quite possible that another company has already adopted it. This rang true for Jobs, who found himself in a nearly thirty-year, on-off trademark dispute with Apple Corps, a multimedia corporation that owned Apple Records.

Fanciful Marks

Considered the most distinctive category of marks, **fanciful trademarks** are made-up or archaic terms used solely for the purpose of identifying a particular product or source. Because they have no meaning other than as a trademark, they are the strongest category of marks. This makes it easier to police the mark and prevent competitors from exploiting it.[24] But because the word is invented and doesn't mean anything to consumers, it's harder to remember, making marketing efforts more of a challenge. Fanciful marks are also subject to trademark erosion. Think aspirin, escalator, and perhaps even one day Google. Famous fanciful marks include Pepsi, Exxon, and Clorox.

Registration

A mark does not need to be registered to receive protection. Trademark rights begin the instant a mark is first used in commerce. That said, federal registration is highly advised for the advantages it bestows on a trademark holder. For example, only federally registered marks have the right to use the registered symbol ®. This indicates that the holder has the exclusive nationwide right to use the mark in commerce and that the use of substantially similar marks is prohibited by the USPTO. Moreover, after five years of continuous use from the date of registration, the mark becomes incontestable. Registration also allows the holder to bring suit in federal court and to overcome claims by subsequent users of the mark.

Registered marks are protected as long as they remain distinctive, are used in **commerce**, and registration is renewed periodically. For marks that have been created but are not in use, an intent-to-use application can be filed. Under this application, the USPTO grants temporary rights to the mark for six months. These rights may be extended for a total of thirty-six months. But while the rights provided by registration can last indefinitely, they can also be lost. Most commonly, this occurs through **abandonment**. A mark is abandoned when the trademark holder stops using it and has no intent to resume its use. Three years of nonuse is clear evidence of abandonment. The cancellation of an abandoned trademark is necessary to prevent parties from warehousing marks that others could use.

Marks also lose their protection when they fall into the public domain as generic terms. A word mark becomes generic when a substantial majority of the public thinks of it in broad general terms—for example, as a type of product (aspirin) and not a specific brand (Bayer). Courts often take into account the dictionary's definition of the term and its use in the media when determining whether the word mark has attained generic status. Courts may also consider whether the rights holder attempted to police the mark against misuse. Because marks can erode over time, trademark owners have an obligation to police their mark to ensure that it remains a source identifier and thus helps to protect consumers from confusion.

Symbols: What to use?

Trademarks identify and distinguish goods while service marks identify and distinguish services. When identifying marks that are not federally registered, use the ™ symbol for trademarks and ˢᴹ symbol for service marks. These symbols alert others that the mark is your intellectual property. The ® is not permitted until the USPTO has issued a Certificate of Registration for the mark. Once this certificate has been granted, replace the ™ or ˢᴹ symbol with ®.

Trade Name v. Trademark or Service Mark

A trade name is basically the company's name. Trade names are not protected under trademark law. However, they may function as a trademark or service mark if they also serve as a source identifier.

BIG MAC®—Trademark—Source identifier for a product (hamburger)
MCDONALD'S ®—Service mark—Source identifier for a restaurant chain that serves food.
GOLDEN ARCHES LOGO—Trademark—Source identifier for the products provided under this particular logo.
MCDONALD'S—Trade name of a publicly traded corporation headquartered in Chicago, Illinois.

Disparaging and Immoral Marks

While a wide variety of words, designs, sounds, and even smells can receive trademark protection, federal registration is not extended to marks that would be perceived by the public as the US flag, the insignia of the United States, or flags and insignias of any state, municipality, or foreign nation. This does not include marks that are merely suggestive of these symbols.[25] Until recently, registration has been withheld from immoral, scandalous, deceptive, or disparaging names. A mark is deemed disparaging if the meaning of the word refers to identifiable people, institutions, beliefs, or national symbols and is disparaging to a substantial component of the group referenced.[26] The **disparagement clause** is intended to prevent underrepresented groups from being "bombarded with demeaning messages in commercial advertising."[27] Consequently, two groups of Native Americans petitioned the USPTO to cancel the registered mark "Redskins." The mark, which was first registered in 1967 as the name for the pro football team in Washington, DC,[28] prompted a twenty-five-year legal tussle with the owner of the Washington Redskins, who promised that he would never change the NFL team's registered mark.[29] In 2015, a federal district court judge found the mark to be disparaging to Native Americans and ordered its cancellation. Two years later, the case was put to rest when the US Supreme Court declared that the disparagement clause was unconstitutional.

In *Matal v. Tam*, a plurality of justices found that the main thrust of the government's argument for maintaining the disparagement clause was to prevent speech that offends.[30] Denying registration to marks that offend members of a certain group, the plurality said, discriminates based on viewpoint. "Giving offense is a viewpoint," they explained, and the First Amendment does not permit the suppression of ideas "simply because society finds the idea itself offensive and disagreeable."[31] After *Tam,* the USPTO clarified that trademark applications would no longer be subjected to a disparagement examination and that past applicants denied under the clause could reapply.[32]

In July 2020, Washington retired its controversial trademarked name and logo after major sponsors threatened to pull their support unless the name was changed and large retailers began dropping team merchandise from their stores and websites amid a wave of national antiracist protests.[33] The team did not adopt a new nickname but opened the 2020 season as the Washington Football Team with a new logo featuring a stylized letter W.

With the bar against disparaging trademarks removed, the court turned its focus on a case that challenged the "immoral" or "scandalous" provision. The case, *Iancu v. Brunetti*, developed after an attempt to register the trademark "FUCT" for use on clothing was rejected. Brunetti, who developed the edgy streetwear brand, argued that the acronym also means Friends U Can't Trust. However, the trademark office found that the brand name would be perceived as the phonetic equivalent of the F-word, especially given that Brunetti's products contained sexual imagery, misogyny, and violence.[34] Under the **immoral or scandalous clause**, the USPTO rejects marks that the public would view as "shocking to the sense of truth, decency, or propriety"; "calling out for condemnation"; "offensive"; or "disreputable."[35] With regard to FUCT, the **Trademark Trial and Appeal Board** (TTAB) found the mark to be "highly offensive" and "vulgar" given its "decidedly negative sexual connotations."[36] The court, however, held that the clause itself was viewpoint based in that it "distinguishes between two opposed sets of ideas: those aligned with conventional moral standards and those hostile to them."[37]

In the end, *Brunetti* reaffirmed *Tam* and the principle that the "government may not discriminate against speech based on the ideas or opinions it conveys"[38] even when it comes to trademark registration. Whether the court would accept a more limited statute that restricts certain highly vulgar modes of expression remains to be seen. For now, it appears that federal trademark protection can no longer be denied on the basis of whether an examining attorney finds the mark immoral or scandalous. As Justice Sotomayor wrote in her dissent in *Brunetti*, the government has "no choice but to begin registering marks containing the most vulgar, profane, or obscene words and images imaginable."[39] This means that it is up to consumers to decide whether to purchase the goods or services associated with such marks.

Appealing USPTO Denials

The four most common reasons marks are refused registration are

1. The mark deceptively misdescribes the good or service.
2. It is merely descriptive.
3. It is primarily a surname.
4. The mark creates a likelihood of confusion with an existing registered trademark.[40]

To deny an application for a mark, the examining attorney must present clear evidence that may include internet discussions, articles, and dictionary definitions. Moreover, the refusal to grant an application may be appealed to the USPTO's Trademark Trial and Appeal Board. Applicants who are not happy with the TTAB order may bring a lawsuit in a US District Court, where the court can consider any new evidence either party presents. A direct appeal to the **US Court of Appeals for the Federal Circuit** is also an option. The Federal Circuit reviews the case as it was presented to the TTAB. No additional evidence is presented in this appeal.

Trade Dress

The Lanham Act describes a trademark in the broadest of terms as "any word, name, symbol, or device, or any combination thereof" used to identify and distinguish goods or services from those produced or sold by others.[41] Since almost any symbol or device is capable of carrying meaning, trademark protection has been extended to the product's total image or overall appearance. This includes shapes, sizes, colors, or color combinations that make up a product's packaging; the designs and placements of words, graphics, and decorations on a product or its packaging; and even the décor, environment, or façade of the building in which a service is provided. Basically, anything that makes the presentation of a product or service distinctive may be protected as long as the elements were designed specifically to identify the product and are "**nonfunctional**."

Trade dress claims can be broken into three categories: product packaging, product configuration or design, and color. The three differ with regard to distinctiveness. Like word marks, trade dress must be distinctive to receive trademark protection, but only product packaging can be inherently distinctive upon inception. Product design and color, like descriptive marks, must acquire a secondary meaning to become distinctive enough to warrant trademark protection. Courts have reasoned that the very purpose of packaging is to identify the source, and because the choices for encasing a product are almost unlimited, inherently distinctive packaging is feasible. The same, however, cannot be said about product design and color, which are almost always intended to make the product more useful or appealing.

Product Packaging

Let's start with product packaging. Because only nonfunctional elements can receive trade dress protection, the first thing to note is that a lot of product packaging is purely functional in that it is essential to dispensing the product. Think of the commonly used plastic bottles for soda and the shape and design of packaging that dispenses disinfectant wipes. Or the shape of containers of sunscreen and other lotions. All of these packages are commonly used throughout the industry because they allow the product to be consumed. This means that they are essential to the use or purpose of the product. And if these packages were protected—and other companies in the industry could not use them—those companies would be at a serious disadvantage. So, these styles of packaging will not qualify for trade dress protection.

We also know that only distinctive elements can receive trade dress protection. This means that commonly used lettering, styles, geometric shapes, colors, and descriptive elements will not be eligible for trade dress protection. Here, think of the commonly used green plastic bottle for lime-flavored soda. The color green is descriptive of the flavor of the soda and thus nondistinctive. The color yellow on lemon-scented disinfectant wipes and on a bottle of sunscreen is also viewed as descriptive and nondistinctive. Likewise, an illustration of the sun on a bottle of sunscreen will most likely be seen as descriptive and nondistinctive because it describes the product.

Let's contrast the common packaging styles with one of the most recognizable product packages in the world. The now iconic contoured Coca-Cola bottle was developed as a way to create a "bottle so distinct that you would recognize it by feel in the dark or lying broken on the ground."[42] Back in 1915, the Coca-Cola company needed a distinctive bottle to prevent consumer confusion from competitors who were attempting to pass off their products as Coca-Cola. The contoured bottle that we know today was originally designed by the Root Glass Company of Terre Haute, Indiana. Over the years it has become the "perfect liquid wrapper"[43] because it serves two functions. It is both functional and nonfunctional.

On the one hand, it is an effective container and dispenser for the product. It allows a consumer to hold the product and either drink it out of the bottle or pour it into a glass. But its unique shape and ribbing are nonfunctional in that these features are not necessary for the bottle to perform its functions. No other glass container is shaped and ribbed like the Coca-Cola bottle. It is inherently distinctive and nonfunctional and, thus, protected by trade dress law.

The same can be said for Maker's Mark Bourbon which, like Coca-Cola, is distinguished in the marketplace by its unique product packaging. Since 1958, Maker's Mark has covered its bottle caps with red, wax-like coating that trickles down the neck of the bottle in a freeform irregular pattern. The bourbon distiller registered this dripping-wax-seal element and brought suit against Jose Cuervo for imitating it. Cuervo argued that preventing the tequila maker from using a similar technique put it at a significant nonreputation-related disadvantage. Here, the court disagreed, saying that there is more than one way to seal a bottle and make it look appealing and that it should not be difficult or costly for Cuervo to find alternative ways to seal its tequila bottles.[44]

Product Design or Configuration

A product's design or configuration and its color are almost always intended to make the product more useful or appealing. Take the M&M candy product, for example. Its product design is both useful and appealing. As we know, the color-coated candy allows the milk chocolate to melt in your mouth and not in your hand. The bright colors, which can coordinate with different holidays, certainly make the candy more appealing. Because the round, hard shell design is functional, other brands of candy are similarly designed. The same, however, cannot be said about the Hersey's Kisses.

Two good examples of products that receive trade dress protection are the Hershey's Kisses and Pepperidge Farm Goldfish cracker. Pieces of chocolate and crackers can be sold in a variety of shapes, and most are produced in simple geometric rectangles, squares, or circles. As we know, shapes that are common to a class of goods do not qualify for trade dress protection because they are not distinctive and will never function as a source identifier. The same cannot be said about the Hersey's Kisses and the Goldfish cracker.

These companies deliberately gave their products a unique design intended to identify and distinguish them at first glance. As a result, these product configurations are examples of distinctive, nonfunctional product designs and as such they are protected by trade dress. Other examples of protected product design include Vans checkerboard shoe, Converse high-top shoes, the Burberry check pattern, and the Birkin bag.

Non-Protected Trade Dress
Functional & Non-Distinctive

- Makes product more useful or appealing
- Not intended as source identifier
- Commonly used packaging, shapes, styles, colors, etc.
- Mere refinement of such designs

Protected Trade Dress
Non-Functional & Distinctive

Product Packaging Inherently Distinctive or Secondary Meaning	**Product Design** Secondary Meaning	**Color** Secondary Meaning
• Coca-Cola bottle	• Gold Fish cracker	• Louboutin – red
• Voss water bottle	• Vans checkerboard	• Tiffany & Co. – blue
• Maker's Mark red wax	• Converse high tops	• T-Mobile – magenta

Figure 6.2.

Color

Like product packaging and design, a particular color may also serve as a source identifier. In fact, even a single color placed just right on an item can be a powerful source indicator. Today, simply the flash of a red lacquered sole on a pair of high heels signifies designer Christian Louboutin. The idea for a glossy red sole came to light when Louboutin saw one of his assistants painting her nails red. Thereafter, the color and its placement on the outer sole of a pair of stilettos became internationally recognized as the Louboutin brand of luxury footwear. But whether the color is merely a way to make the shoe more visually appealing or whether it is truly a distinctive color mark came to a head when Yves Saint Laurent prepared to market a line of mono-chromatic shoes that included a red shoe with a red outer sole.

In the case, the court concluded that the red sole had achieved a secondary meaning as an identifying mark "firmly associated" with the Louboutin brand, but that the distinctiveness of the trade dress did not extend to shoes with red uppers. The court reasoned that it was the contrast between red outsole and the upper leather that caused the color to pop and distinguish its creator.[45]

However, the court noted that the protection of ornamental features (including color) can significantly hinder competition by limiting the range of alternative design choices for other players in the industry. In such cases, the court said, ornamental features are considered functional and barred from trademark protection.[46] Here, the red sole mark would significantly hinder design choices if it prevented competitors from using a red outsole in *all* situations.[47] This meant that Louboutin could not prevent Yves Saint Laurent from marketing a monochromic red shoe, but that the company could prevent competitors from using a red lacquered outsole that is paired with an upper of a different color.

In general terms, trade dress is functional and cannot serve as a trademark if it

1. Is essential to the use or purpose of the product;
2. Affects the product's cost or quality; or
3. Would put competitors at a significant nonreputation-related disadvantage.[48]

Without the nonfunctional requirement, trademark law could be used to inhibit legitimate competition by giving one producer monopoly control over a useful, functional product feature.[49] This would be especially problematic given that trademark protection has the potential to last in perpetuity and, thus, could effectively upend one's right to compete through imitation.[50]

Like Christian Louboutin, a variety of brands have been successful at using color as a source identifier. Think UPS and brown, Tiffany & Co. and robin egg blue, and Home Depot and orange. That said, not every color that consumers associate with a particular product will receive trade dress protection. General Mills discovered this when they tried to register the precise shade of yellow the cereal company uses on boxes of regular Cheerios. While the company's efforts to create an association between the color yellow and its doughnut-shaped, oat-based cereal were substantial and well documented, they were outweighed by the fact that twenty-three cereal products—some of which were ring-shaped and oat-based—used packaging similar in color to Cheerios. Given the number and nature of competitive cereal products in yellow packaging, the TTAB concluded that the color yellow on boxes of Cheerios served primarily as a decorative element rather than as a source identifier.[51] Even though the company established that the consuming public associates a yellow box with regular Cheerios, the TTAB said that when a color appears on products from many different sources, consumers are more likely to perceive that color as a device designed to make the package attractive and eye-catching and less likely to view it as a single source identifier. "This is especially true of a primary color, like yellow, which is used by many merchants and is not a color that in context seems unusual."[52]

False Association

While the Lanham Act is primarily associated with the exclusive right to use a registered trademark, it also prohibits a range of competitive activities regarded as unfair. These activities encompass more than the unauthorized use of a registered trademark. Under section 43(a) of the Lanham Act, for example, an **unfair competition** claim can be filed for the false impression that certain commercial activities send to consumers even though those activities do not involve a registered trademark.

This type of unfair competition claim covers conduct that is likely to create a **false association** as to who is sponsoring, endorsing, or in some way connected to a product, service, or commercial activity. Claims for false association are broader in scope than trademark infringement claims in that anyone likely to be damaged by such conduct may sue regardless of whether they hold a federally registered trademark. Through this section of the Lanham Act, protection has been extended to cover both registered and unregistered marks. This means that the total physical image conveyed by the name and product together as well as every facet of a selling program is relevant.[53]

False association claims cover a broad range of conduct, including

- Marketing a product with the physical appearance of another product. Here we see cases where the
    - Plaintiff's goods are marketed with the defendant's trademark or using a picture or sample of the defendant's goods.
    - Defendant's goods are marketed with plaintiff's trademark. This is common in the knockoff industry where cheaper goods are disguised to look like luxury goods.
    - Defendant removes the plaintiff's trademark and sells the item in an unbranded state.
- Activities that are designed to capitalize on other brand's
    - Market reputation
    - Trademark or trade name
    - Physical appearance
- Trademark infringement of unregistered marks.

Basically, any actions that imply that the plaintiff is affiliated, connected, or associated with the defendant or the defendant's business are prohibited. This restriction does not include lawfully naming a competitor while making a truthful comparison with the competitor's product.

False Association?

In 2009, Anheuser-Busch came out with twenty-seven different two-tone color versions of Bud Light. The colors used corresponded to the school colors of popular universities and colleges. No school name, mascot, or other identifying marks appeared on the can. It was just the colors. But Anheuser-Busch sold these "fan cans" near the schools on game days. The Collegiate Licensing Co., which represented about two hundred schools at the time, warned Anheuser-Busch that the use of the colors in connection with how the beer was marketed created potential trademark violations.[54]

INFRINGEMENT

The Lanham Act allows plaintiffs to bring trademark infringement suits for the unauthorized use of registered as well as unregistered marks. Moreover, the act permits plaintiffs to bring an unfair competition claim for conduct that falsely associates one business with another. Infringement suits and unfair competition claims often arise from the same set of facts. While trademark infringement and unfair competition are not identical, they both allow owners of enforceable marks to recover damages for unauthorized uses of their marks that are likely to cause consumer confusion. Thus, the key to waging a successful infringement or unfair competition suit lies in the plaintiff's ability to show that consumers are likely to be confused, misled, or deceived as to the source or sponsorship of the good or service bearing one of the marks.

Plaintiffs alleging trademark infringement and unfair competition for false association must show

1. Ownership of a valid and enforceable mark.
2. Defendant used the mark or something substantially similar to it on or in connection with goods or services.
3. Use is likely to cause confusion in the minds of consumers regarding the source or sponsorship of the goods or services.[55]

Most courts recognize two types of confusion: forward and reverse. To understand these types of confusion, it is helpful to distinguish the marks at issue in a case according to the length of time each has been registered or used in commerce. In doing so, courts refer to the mark that was registered or used first as the "senior" mark, and the succeeding mark as the "junior" mark.

Typically, when we think about consumer confusion, we think about **forward confusion**. This occurs when consumers believe that the goods or services bearing the **junior mark** came from or had some connection to the **senior mark** holder. This type of confusion allows the junior user to unjustly take advantage of the market dominance and goodwill of the senior mark. Due to this mistaken association, the senior user may lose sales and business opportunities. Moreover, if the junior user produces inferior goods, the senior user's market reputation can be damaged.

As the name suggests, **reverse confusion** involves a situation where the junior user is a larger, more powerful entity than the company holding the senior mark. Given its outsized economic advantage, the junior user saturates the market with a mark identical or similar to the senior mark on related goods or services.[56] In these situations, a larger, more prominent newcomer engages in extensive advertising to promote a product with a name taken from or similar to its smaller competitor. This strategy causes the public to mistakenly believe that the senior user's products are produced by the larger company or that the two sets of goods are somehow connected.[57] While this practice is not intended to ride on the goodwill of the senior user, it may diminish the value of the senior mark and the reputation associated with it as well as the opportunities the smaller company has to move into new markets.[58] Without the means to recover damages for reverse confusion, senior mark holders would be unable to protect their trademarks against extensive marketing efforts by well-resourced junior users.[59]

Likelihood of Confusion

Trademark law is built largely on the idea that the use of a mark is illegal if it confuses a substantial number of consumers.[60] This means that uses that are unlikely to cause consumer confusion are protected speech. And it also means that the outcome of most infringement and unfair competition suits will turn on the court's analysis of likelihood of confusion. In their analysis, courts consider more than just a likely mix-up regarding the source of the product. Uses that are likely to mislead consumers into thinking that the senior mark holder is connected to or is in some way affiliated with the defendant's goods or services are also considered.

To determine whether a defendant's use of a mark actually created a likelihood of confusion, courts rely on a variety of multifactor tests. The application of these factors differs from case to case. No single factor determines the outcome of the case, and decisions are not necessarily decided by the number of factors that weigh in favor of either party. Like the fair use defense in copyright law, the relative importance of each factor can fluctuate depending on the circumstances of the case. As a result, decisions tend to rest on the most pertinent factors to the case and may reflect other case-specific variables than those outlined in the likelihood of confusion analysis.[61] The following list of factors is used by the Ninth Circuit. Other circuits apply similar factors.

Strength of Senior Mark

The strength of a trademark is evaluated in terms of its conceptual and commercial strength. A mark's conceptual strength refers to its category of distinctiveness. Courts classify marks along a spectrum of increasing inherent distinctiveness. From weakest to strongest, marks are categorized as generic, descriptive, suggestive, arbitrary, or fanciful. As the uniqueness of the mark increases, so too does the degree of protection. *Fanciful marks*—that is, words invented for the sole purpose of identifying a good—are exceptionally strong because they convey nothing about the nature of the product. Junior uses of these marks tend to be viewed as an attempt to capitalize on the reputation of the senior mark. *Arbitrary marks*, on the other hand, use common words that have no logical relationship to the underlying goods. These marks are distinctive only within their product market and are entitled to little or no protection outside of that area.[62] *Suggestive marks* are fairly weak in that they call to mind the qualities of the underlying product. Since products share similar qualities, junior uses of these marks are easier to justify. *Descriptive marks* that have gained a *secondary meaning* are the weakest of the distinctive marks. Because these marks merely describe their underlying goods, it is more difficult to prevent others from using similar terms.

Once a mark's classification is determined, courts turn to the question of commercial strength. Commercial strength represents the degree of actual recognition the mark receives in the marketplace and is assessed by such factors as advertising expenditures, length of exclusive use, and public awareness of the brand. Relatively weak conceptual marks can be strengthened by a finding of strong commercial recognition.

Similarity of Marks

Similarity is based on the sight, sound, and meaning of the marks as they are normally encountered in the marketplace by an average consumer. The key question is whether a consumer who has a general recollection of the senior mark and comes across the junior mark in the marketplace would likely associate the junior mark with the senior mark. In their analysis, courts consider the overall impression created by the marks instead of their component parts. This means that other identifying features, such as the trade dress of the product, are also considered.[63] Within this context, more attention is paid to the dominant features of the mark or prominent elements on the packaging, with similarities weighing more heavily than differences.

While the focus of the examination is on the entirety of the mark, courts also consider whether the name of the product or service viewed in insolation of its packaging and other visual elements but as it would appear in the marketplace would confuse the public. Here, sight, sound, and meaning are important. In a case between Starbucks Coffee and a Texas beer brand trademarked as "Starbock" and "Star Bock Beer," the court found that the use of "Starbock" and "Star Bock" without the word beer or any design elements infringed the coffee giant's trademarks. Given that the words are "remarkably similar in sight and sound," it is likely that consumers would believe that a beer called "Starbock" or "Star Bock" is connected to Starbucks, the court said.[64]

In its analysis, the court discounted the category of meaning because Starbucks and Starbock are essentially coined terms that lack a standard dictionary definition. In such circumstances, "slight variations in spelling or the arrangement of letters" are often ineffective at helping consumers distinguish one brand from another.[65] That said, the use of the words "Star Bock Beer" displayed in three separate lines over a blue star on a white field in a circular logo was "very different in appearance and meaning" and more different in sound from the siren logo.[66] Additionally, the product's logo included the words "since 2003" immediately below the three words and the information "Born in Galveston—The Old Quarter Acoustic Cafe" on the outside circle of the logo. This logo, the court said, clearly differentiates the two brands as it "unequivocally indicates that the product was born in Galveston (not Seattle) in 2003 (not 1971), and is sold in only The Old Quarter Acoustic Cafe (which sells no Starbucks products whatever)."[67]

Because marks are analyzed as they appear in the marketplace, courts also factor in the degree to which a product market is crowded with similar marks. In a case involving two brands of vodka, for example, the defendant argued that the "lip" images at issue in the case were part of a "crowded field" of similar lip logos that commonly appear on alcohol products, and thus consumer confusion was less likely to occur.[68] While no other companies that sold flavored vodka used a lip mark,[69] such designs can be found on beer, wine, and nonalcoholic beverages.[70] Given that lip designs were frequently used in connection with certain alcoholic beverages and other consumer products, the court conceded that the field was crowded with such marks and agreed that this conclusion weighed against a finding of likelihood of confusion.[71]

Figure 6.3. The court found that "Star Bock Beer" did not create a likelihood of confusion with Starbucks. However, the court prohibited the use of "Starbock" and "Star Bock" and confined the use of "Star Bock Beer" to beer and promotional items sold only at local establishments owned or operated by the mark holder in the Galveston area.
Star Bock logo courtesy of Rex Bell.

Similarity is a critical factor in trademark infringement cases and is usually accorded greater weight in the analysis. In cases where the marks are virtually identical and the products or services are identical, a finding of confusion is likely to follow.[72]

Relatedness of the Goods

Relatedness focuses on the degree to which consumers are likely to think that the two products at issue are connected. In cases where the goods are related, less similarity between marks is needed to find infringement. On this point, the Sixth Circuit has provided three benchmarks:

1. If the products compete directly and the marks are sufficiently similar, confusion is likely.
2. If the products are somewhat related but not competitive, then other factors determine the likelihood of confusion.
3. If the products are totally unrelated, then confusion is unlikely.[73]

When considering relatedness, courts focus on the extent to which the public would assume that the maker of one product was the sponsor or maker of another. Direct competition is not necessary for infringement to occur. Even though two products are noncompetitive, confusion due to relatedness may be found. This is particularly probable when a plaintiff intends to expand the company's product line or marketing efforts to compete directly with the defendant, or the public assumes that such an expansion has occurred even though the plaintiff has no plans to do so.

Related goods have been defined as those that complement one another, are sold to the same class of consumer, or are similar in use and function.[74] That said, courts have been less likely to find relatedness if the "related" product was designed and used solely for publicity purposes. The powerhouse cereal producer Kellogg attempted to do just that when it argued that the use of a toucan logo and word mark "Toucan Gold" by an Ohio-based golf equipment manufacturer created a likelihood of confusion with "Toucan Sam," the Froot Loop mascot.

To show relatedness of products, Kellogg pointed to its catalog offerings of golf balls and golf shirts on which a picture of Toucan Sam is imprinted as well as a decades-old television commercial "wherein Toucan Sam is portrayed soliciting his Froot Loops on a golf course and interacting with a golf-playing bear."[75] The cereal company claimed that these materials indicate that Toucan Sam was related not only to cereal but to the golf equipment industry. The court disagreed, finding that the advertisement and novelty catalog did not make Kellogg a player in the golfing industry and that no consumer would associate the cereal company with a top-line golf equipment company based on the licensing of a cartoon character and novelty items.[76]

Evidence of Actual Confusion

Evidence that consumers have confused the junior mark for the senior mark may be the best indicator of likelihood of confusion.[77] However, proving actual confusion is very difficult, especially in cases where the two marks have coexisted for only a short time or, like with Star Bock Beer, in a different setting entirely. Moreover, if there is no evidence of actual confusion after a long period of concurrent use of marks, it is much more difficult to show that likelihood of confusion will occur in the future. Given these limitations, senior mark holders are not required to prove actual confusion. This means that likelihood of confusion may be found without any evidence of actual confusion.

To establish actual confusion, senior mark users may show that consumers contact, return products to, or purchase goods from the wrong company. In a case involving two similar eyelash extension products, Xtreme Lashes, the senior mark holder, had a sworn statement from a cosmetologist who intended to purchase Xtreme's lash kit but selected the Xtended Beauty product by mistake. The cosmetologist explained that when she saw an eyelash extension kit in a catalog that began with the letter "X," she assumed it was Xtreme Lashes and purchased it. Xtreme also presented evidence of two other similar incidents. While Xtended Beauty, the junior mark holder, argued that three isolated anecdotes of confusion were not enough to show actual confusion, the court disagreed. "The evidence shows more than a fleeting mix-up of names," the court said. "It shows actual confusion about the origin of the parties' products." The confusion, the court noted, was caused by the similarity of the two marks, and "it swayed consumer purchases."[78]

To provide stronger evidence of actual confusion, companies may also conduct surveys. Properly performed random sample surveys can be very expensive. Even convenience sample surveys where interviewers stop shoppers at shopping malls are costly to conduct and the outcome is not always valued by the court. Walmart Inc. found this out after it collected responses from more than 650 participants in shopping malls in nine cities across the country. Walmart claimed that nearly 48 percent of respondents perceived an association between Walmart and a t-shirt that included either the word "WAL*OCAUST" or "WAL-QAEDA."[79] In an extensive analysis, the court found numerous substantial flaws in the design and execution of the survey.

The court pointed out that the study targeted respondents with no potential to purchase the t-shirts in question; asked leading questions; failed to adequately replicate the shopping experience; and interviewed a nonrandom sample that was too small to link the results to the general market.[80] In the end, the court gave the survey virtually no weight and noted that surveys grounded as trustworthy evidence of actual confusion must

1. Target a properly defined population;
2. Select a representative sample from that population;
3. Frame questions in a clear, precise, and nonleading manner;
4. Conduct sound interviews by competent interviewers who have no knowledge of the litigation or purpose of the survey;
5. Accurately report the data;
6. Analyze the data in accordance with accepted statistical principles; and
7. Assure objectivity of the entire process.[81]

It is good to note that the considerable cost of a statistically valid survey may disadvantage small business owners in cases involving large corporate giants. Rex Bell, the mark holder of the Star Bock brand, confronted "an exhaustive statistical analysis" that examined consumer reaction to the brand names "Starbock" and "Star Bock."[82] The survey showed that 25 percent of respondents affiliated the words "Star Bock" with Starbucks and 48 percent connected the word "Starbock" with Starbucks. Armed with these percentages and the validity of the research method, the court afforded the survey "great weight" and concluded that a "significant level of actual confusion" existed when it came to the use of these word marks.[83]

Marketing Channels

This factor examines the degree of similarity between the primary purchasers of each party's goods and the marketing approaches employed to attract them. Every facet of the marketing approach may be examined, including

- Where products are sold—for example, geographical location, type, and location of retail outlet.
- How and where goods are advertised—for example, type of advertising used, look and feel of ads, use of spokesperson or celebrity, national, regional, or local ad campaigns.
- Type of promotional tactics used—for example, sponsorships, giveaways, coupons.
- Price ranges for products.
- Sales and distribution methods—for example, direct to consumer, business-to-business, use of an intermediary.
- Target customers—for example, demographics, psychographics, lifestyle.

The goal is to determine whether the marketing approaches employed by each party overlap. Direct competition or identical outlets or purchasers are not required for this factor to weigh in favor of the likelihood of confusion.[84] But when the products are sold under the same roof, it provides strong evidence that confusion is likely.[85] That said, courts are generally looking for some degree of overlap in the marketing channels used by each party—for example, the fact that a national marketing effort of one party overlapped with the local advertising campaign of the other party. In *Xtreme Lashes v. Xtended Beauty*, the court found several overlapping trade practices. Both companies (1) target trained professionals; (2) compete directly for the same class of buyers; and (3) use print advertisements, direct mailings, and internet promotion. Based on these tactics, the court concluded that the parties use similar marketing channels.[86]

Star Bock beer was helped by this factor given it is only offered at The Old Quarter Acoustic Cafe in Galveston, Texas, and Starbucks is not sold in similar venues or bars. The court concluded that the two trademark owners did not target the same purchaser or share a common pool of retail outlets.[87] This factor also favored TGI and its attempt to brand a golf club Toucan Gold. The court found significant differences in distribution and advertising channels as well as target customers. Kellogg distributes Froot Loops through regular wholesale and retail channels and advertises its product nationally on television and in print. Conversely, TGI distributes its golf equipment primarily at trade shows and over the internet, rather than via retail outlets. TGI does not advertise on television or radio, and its clientele is primarily corporations and wealthy golfers. The two industries are so distinct that rarely, if ever, would a consumer look for a Kellogg's product in the golf equipment market.[88]

Type of Goods versus Purchaser Care

Purchaser care recognizes that not all buyers and purchases are equal. For example, a consumer breezing through the supermarket after work exhibits a much different level of care than a person shopping for a new car. And an average person who needs to purchase a family car possesses a different level of knowledge and experience than a car dealer looking to acquire additional vehicles. Given that it is much easier to select the wrong box of facial tissues than it is to purchase a Honda when you meant to buy a Hyundai, the risk of confusion and thus the degree of acceptable market similarly between marks may vary. In circumstances involving high-end goods or items purchased by professional buyers, courts will require a greater degree of similarity to justify a claim of likelihood of confusion.

It is not only high-end goods that have careful purchasers. Courts have recognized greater consumer care when ordering alcohol products at bars or restaurants and in purchases of perfume, skincare, and other beauty products. That said, the eyelash extension case recognized both types of buyers—those professionally trained and cautious in their purchases and younger, impressionable cosmetologists who are more impulsive buyers. While the former is less likely to be confused by the similarities of two products, the same cannot be said for the latter. This was especially apparent, the court noted, given the **affidavit** of an inexperienced buyer who was seeking to broaden her expertise to include lash extensions and purchased the wrong product. In the end, the court concluded that this factor favored Xtreme and a finding of likelihood of confusion, even though the senior mark user's lash extensions were relatively pricey ($529 for the gold kit and $949 for the platinum kit) and sold only to trained professionals.[89]

Intent of Defendant in Selecting Mark

An intention to pass off goods or derive reputational benefits from the senior mark is a critical factor and may be sufficient in and of itself to establish likelihood of confusion. Because direct evidence of intent is usually unobtainable, courts accept circumstantial support that shows the contested mark was adopted with knowledge of its similarity to the protected mark. Courts have said that this knowledge provides a "sound basis for inferring an intent to deceive" and divert business away from the senior mark through consumer confusion.[90] Rex Bell, the owner of The Old Quarter Acoustic Cafe, explained how he came up with the name "Starbock" beer. The word "Starbock" blends the names of two beers brewed locally in Texas—Lone Star, a long-standing Texas-based beer and state nickname, and Shiner Bock, a type of beer brewed in Shiner, Texas. Bell borrowed "Star" from Lone Star and "Bock" from Shiner Bock to come up with Starbock. Because it was not his intention to infringe or unfairly capitalize on the coffee giant's trade name, the court concluded that he was "innocently motivated" when he came up with the name and began selling Starbock beer.[91]

Circumstantial evidence has also been used to establish an indifference to confusion. In a case involving an advertisement for a fictitious Anheuser-Busch product called "Michelob Oily," the court found that the creator of the magazine ad "had, if not an intent to confuse, at least an indifference to the possibility that some consumers might be misled" given that "no significant steps were taken to remind readers that they were viewing a parody and not an advertisement sponsored or approved by Anheuser-Busch."[92] The court came to this conclusion based on the placement of the ad on the back cover of the magazine, the little-to-no alteration of the Anheuser-Busch trademarks, a virtually undetectable disclaimer and the use of the ® symbol after the words "Michelob Oily." These facts, the court said, suggest that the parody "sought to do far more" than just poke fun at Anheuser-Bush and was likely to confuse consumers.[93]

An intent to confuse or an indifference to it also applies to reverse confusion. In such cases, courts "consider whether the defendant deliberately intended to push the plaintiff out of the market by flooding it with advertising" or disregarded the risk of reverse confusion by failing to conduct an adequate trademark search.[94] Conversely, the greater the geographic distance between where products are marketed, the less likely intent will be established. Vast differences between products also mitigate any showing of intent as does a rigorous design approach that includes an extensive search for similar marks.

Likelihood of Expansion of Product Lines

Lastly, courts take into consideration the possibility that either party will expand their business to begin competing with the other. A strong probability of direct competition through a geographic or product line expansion favors a finding of likelihood of confusion. If, on the other hand, the parties do not intend to expand their markets significantly, the factor is neutral, neither increasing nor decreasing a finding of likelihood of confusion.[95] Of course, at the time of any lawsuit, the parties may not fully appreciate the potential for an expansion. This occurred in 1981 when Apple computers settled a trademark dispute with Apple Corps, a multimedia company founded in 1968 by members of the Beatles. As a part of the settlement, the computer company agreed not to enter the music business, and the record company made a similar concession with regard to the computer business. More than twenty years later, Apple computers created iTunes Music Stores, which Apple Corps claimed was a violation of the agreement. This dispute ended in 2007 when the two reached another agreement in which Apple Inc. gained the rights to all the trademarks related to "Apple." This allowed the computer giant to continue using its name and logos on iTunes, and through licensing agreements allowed Apple Corps to continue using some of its trademarks.[96]

Celebrities

Celebrities have long used trademark law to protect the use of their name. This protection stems from section 43(a) of the Lanham Act and its protection against any false or misleading description or representation of fact that is likely to cause confusion or deceive consumers as to affiliation or association of one person with another person. The broad language contained in section 43(a) applies to uses of a celebrity's persona that falsely imply the endorsement of a product or service. Because false endorsement claims involve the unauthorized use of a person's identity, they are similar to right of publicity claims and are often viewed as the federal equivalent of a state right of publicity statute. That said, the two differ in that false endorsement claims are subject to the likelihood of confusion test. In other words, the unauthorized use of a celebrity's persona in connection with goods or services will constitute a false endorsement only if it is likely to confuse, deceive, or mislead consumers into thinking that the celebrity endorses the business, product, or service.[97] This requirement means that the likelihood of confusion factors discussed previously will be applied to the facts in a false endorsement case and only those uses of a celebrity's identity that result in a finding of likelihood of confusion are prohibited under the law.

When applying factor one (strength of mark) to a false endorsement claim, the mark is the celebrity's persona and the strength of the mark is the level of public recognition the celebrity enjoys among likely consumers of the product or service. A celebrity who is widely known, then, would have a strong mark recognized by a large segment of society. The widespread popularity of the game show *Wheel of Fortune* helped Vanna White, the game's hostess, in her case against Samsung, an electronics manufacturer who depicted White as a robot in an ad for videocassette recorders (VCRs). The court explained that if White was unknown to the segment of the public targeted by the advisement, likelihood of confusion could not occur. But because she is widely known throughout society, including the segment of the population targeted by Samsung, the court said the likelihood of confusion was possible.

Like factor one, factors two (similarity of the marks) and three (relatedness of goods) are adjusted in cases involving celebrities. When it comes to determining similarity of marks, courts examine the degree of similarly between the defendant's use of the celebrity's persona and the actual celebrity. Here, the court found that Samsung's use of White's persona as a robot both supported and contradicted a finding of likelihood of confusion. On the one hand, all the aspects of the robot personify White, but on the other hand, the robot is clearly not a human. This meant that factor two neither advanced nor detracted from a finding of likelihood of confusion.

In determining factor three, the court examined the relatedness between White's fame (i.e., her product) and Samsung's advertisement promoting VCRs. White, the court concluded, is famous for her television performances, and the ad is promoting a device that allows consumers to record television shows. Moreover, the ad reinforced this relatedness by including an appeal that indicated consumers would be taping the "longest running game show" well into the future. Given the connection between the reason for White's fame and Samsung's product and the pitch the company used to sell that product, this factor favored a finding of likelihood of confusion.

The court also found that factors five, six, and seven led toward a finding of likelihood of confusion given the following:

- Factor 5: Marketing Channels. White had appeared in the same stance as the robot in numerous magazines and the robot ad was placed in magazines.
- Factor 6: Purchaser Care. Consumers are not likely to be particularly careful in determining who endorses VCRs.
- Factor 7: Intent. Samsung intended to spoof Vanna White and *Wheel of Fortune*. The ad depicting White as a robot was one of a series of similar Samsung ads containing portrayals of other celebrities. Looking at the entire series of advertisements, the court said, a jury could reasonably conclude that beneath the surface humor lay an intent to persuade consumers that Vanna White was endorsing Samsung products. The court also noted that unlike the other celebrities used in the advertising campaign, "White neither consented to the ads nor was she paid."[98]

- White did not present any evidence of actual confusion (factor four), and the court did not find that factor eight (likelihood of product line expansion) was relevant.[99]

TRADEMARK LAW AND THE FREEDOM OF EXPRESSION

Well-known trademarks that have become elements of popular culture are ripe targets for expressive works. From works of art to humorous spoofs and ridicule, trademarks have been used in ways that conflict with their role as source identifiers and symbols of goodwill and market strength. It is not surprising, then, to find a tension between trademark law and the First Amendment. As with copyright and right of publicity law, the speech restrictive nature of trademark law needs to be reconciled with expressive freedom. How courts go about this is not always very clear or consistent.

Parody

In trademark parody cases, the mark is used in a way that builds upon its cultural popularity by adding something new for an amusing or satirical effect. The humorous effect represents an irreverent contrast to the mark's idealized image. Courts have explained that to be successful, a parody "must convey two simultaneous—and contradictory—messages: that it is the original, but also that it is *not* the original and is instead a parody."[100] This means that a trademark parody must make it abundantly clear that it is not what it parodies. To the extent that it only conveys that it is the original, "it is not only a poor parody but also vulnerable" to a finding of trademark infringement, since the consumer will be confused.[101] Samsung tried to argue that its comical adaption of Vanna White was a parody, and, therefore, the robot ad constituted protected speech. Their argument, the court said, was better addressed to noncommercial parodies, noting that the difference between a true parody and an infringing knock-off is the difference between fun and profit.[102]

Trademark parody can be a challenging area of trademark law. While parody is considered a protected form of speech, no clear-cut legal rule separates a legitimate parody from an infringing use. In cases like *White v. Samsung*, where the parodic element involves commercial speech, parody is not so much a defense but rather a claim that the mark's use is not likely to mislead consumers. In these cases, courts tend to focus only on the likelihood of confusion factors and give no special weight to the First Amendment interest. In doing so, courts use the factor analysis as a balancing mechanism to resolve the tension between expressive rights and trademark protection.

Humorous uses of a trademark that are likely to confuse are thus deemed an infringement, whereas appropriations that merely amuse rather than confuse are protected speech.

Louis Vuitton v. Chewy Vuiton

Given the flexible nature of the factor analysis, case outcomes involving parody can seem inconsistent and hard to predict. A couple of amusing takes on two famous brands makes this point. Up first is a novelty chew toy in the shape of a small handbag, aptly named "Chewy Vuiton." As the name suggests, the plush pet product pokes fun at the Paris-based design house Louis Vuitton Mattetier (LVM) and its use (or perhaps overuse) of a set of instantly recognizable design marks. The marks consist of the interlocking LV logo and a set of four-pointed flowers and stars that blanket its handbags. Haute Diggity Dog (HDD), in an attempt to successfully parody the famous couture, adorned its chew toy with caricatures of these marks that altered the "LV" to a "CV" and Louis Vuitton to Chewy Vuiton. HDD's design choices prompted the court to conclude that the fuzzy pet purses were a joking and amusing parody of the upscale handbags. The design differences immediately conjure up the famous LVM marks while also communicating to consumers that the novelty item is an inexpensive plaything for a pet that pokes fun at the elegance and expensiveness of an LVM handbag—which, the court said, "must *not* be chewed by a dog."[103]

Figure 6.4. Chewy Vuiton successfully evokes Louis Vuitton's famous design marks while differentiating itself from the luxury brand in terms of quality, cost, product type, and marketing channels. In this way, Chewy Vuiton satirizes LVM's expensive handbags and conveys the message that it is an amusing but not confusing novelty item.
Photo courtesy of Robert Whitmore.

The fact that Chewy Vuiton was found to be a successful parody was key in the court's analysis of whether the pet toy was likely to cause consumer confusion. Here, the court noted that even the strength of the mark favored HDD. It reasoned that while widespread recognition of the plaintiff's mark usually favors the plaintiff, in cases of a parody, the fame and popularity of the mark is the mechanism by which consumers figure out the joke and true target of the spoof. In performing this function, strength of mark actually works to avoid consumer confusion where parody is concerned, and thus the strength of the fashion designer's mark did not help LVM prove likelihood of confusion. The finding that Chewy Vuiton was an obvious parody helped the defendant with the other factors as well. As a successful parody, the court found that HDD appropriately mimicked the LVM marks, and at the same time, sufficiently differentiated the pet toy as its own. The crude use of the LVM marks and the fact that Chewy Vuiton is sold alongside other pet products and novelty items supported the conclusion that consumers encountering the fuzzy purse in the marketplace would not mistake it for a top-end luxury item purchased in Louis Vuitton boutiques simply on the basis of mark similarity.[104]

This conclusion was furthered by the fact that LVM does not make chew toys and does not intend to do so in the future. While the fashion designer sells accessories for pets, such as dog collars, leashes, and pet carriers, those items sell in the range of $200 to $1,600, whereas Chewy Vuiton sells its products for under $20.[105] As one might expect, the two products use different advertising channels. LVM products can be found in high-end fashion magazines while HDD primarily markets its dog toys through pet supply channels.[106] The big difference in cost, place of purchase, and advertising approach supported the conclusion that the marketing channels are sufficiently different. Not surprisingly, no evidence of actual confusion was found, and the court ruled that HDD's intent to parody was not an intent to confuse the public.[107]

Budweiser v. Buttwiper

VIP Products relied on the detailed analysis of the parody defense in the *Vuitton* case to justify its attempt to poke fun at Anheuser-Busch and its signature beer Budweiser. VIP, which creates, manufactures, and sells high-quality, durable dog toys, developed a squeeze toy dubbed "Buttwiper." The idea for Buttwiper emerged from a Stanley Steamer commercial that featured a dog scooting across the floor in a manner that suggested a carpet cleaning needed to be scheduled. After viewing the commercial, the owner and operator of the company directed a graphic designer to create a mock Budweiser label that prominently featured a dog dragging its rear end across the floor.[108] The classic Budweiser color combination of red, white, and blue was used for the Buttwiper label, and the toy itself was shaped and toned to resemble Budweiser's amber beer bottle. The Buttwiper label also mimicked the classic ribbon design over a circular graphic above the word Budweiser. In all, the Buttwiper play toy was designed to evoke the King of Beers, but its graphic features were largely a crude knock-off of the Anheuser-Busch trade dress marks.

At first take, Buttwiper appears indistinguishable from Chewy Vuiton. But several differences between the two parody products and their trademark targets left the squeeze toy vulnerable to a finding of trademark infringement and unfair competition. Product relatedness proved to be a problem for VIP because Anheuser-Busch sold various non-beer items, including dog leashes and collars branded with the word "Budweiser." The beer manufacturer also sold other branded pet items, including food/water bowls, frisbees, balls, and pet mats, but did not sell or license a doggy squeeze toy. In addition, no appreciable cost difference existed between the Budweiser branded pet items and Buttwiper. A Budweiser dog leash and collar sold for $10 each while Buttwiper sold for $11, making the products more appreciably competitive than the handbags at issue in the Vuitton case.[109]

To top it off, Anheuser-Busch produced credible survey evidence that showed a confusion rate of more than 30 percent. This meant that one in three people interviewed mistakenly believed that VIP's Buttwiper was manufactured and marketed by or with the approval of Anheuser-Busch or that some affiliation existed between the squeeze toy and the beer maker.[110] Moreover, additional evidence of actual confusion was found when Anheuser-Busch employees were conducting an internet search for a Budweiser cooler on the Sears & Roebuck website. The term "Budweiser Beer" was used and the search results included VIP's Buttwiper product.[111] Because both companies sold branded pet items at or near the same price and survey results showed that a substantial portion of consumers who purchase pet items experienced actual confusion, the court blocked VIP from distributing Buttwiper.

In the end, Chewy Vuiton was distinguished from Buttwiper given the cost differential between LVM dog collars and leashes and the under $20 play toy. This difference, the court pointed out, prevents market confusion. Moreover, the court found that the fuzzy dog purse clearly satirizes the luxury brand and its handbags that sell for thousands of dollars. The outcome of these two cases signals that when it comes to trademark parody attention needs to be paid to how closely the goods at issue are related. To be successful, a commercial parodist who wants to poke fun at a well-known trademark needs to develop an item that is clearly unrelated to any products marketed under the senior mark. The parodic item should cleverly evoke the famous mark, but it should not be taken seriously. In short, the goal is to amuse—not to confuse.

Purity of Use

The weight given to the First Amendment is stronger when the unauthorized mark is the target of an editorial or artistic work. Visual, literary, and musical compositions; protest slogans and bumper stickers; and even t-shirts that communicate ideas or express viewpoints via an unauthorized trademark are likely to garner protection as speech when their commercial aims are subordinate to their desire to convey some social, artistic, entertainment, or political message.[112] Courts have long held that "[s]peech is protected even though it is carried in a form that is sold for profit."[113] Artists who sell their work are thus entitled to full First Amendment protection rather than the lower degree of protection afforded to commercial speech. In cases involving such expressive works, courts may require a stronger showing of likelihood of confusion to outweigh the defendant's free speech rights or apply a variety of other legal approaches to resolve the conflict between the Lanham Act and the First Amendment. In all, no easily articulated or clearly defined legal principle governs this area of trademark law, but the works of one artist are illustrative here.

Artist Daniel A. Moore had been painting notable University of Alabama football plays for more than twenty-five years when the university brought suit against him for trademark infringement. The university argued that the uniforms worn by its football players were protected trade dress and that Moore violated the Lanham Act by portraying and selling football scenes which included the uniforms and their colors of crimson and white.[114] The university also contended that Moore's use of the uniforms created a likelihood of confusion as to whether the university sponsors the artwork.[115] Their contention was based largely on a survey, which the university said provided strong evidence of confusion, but which the court concluded lacked credibility given its use of leading questions and the fact that only one print was involved. As a result, the court called the evidence of actual confusion "weak," but acknowledged that it established at least some likelihood of confusion.[116] The court and the university also disagreed over the strength of the uniforms as a mark. The court said that color schemes can be protected only when the color itself is nonfunctional. Football uniform colors clearly perform the function of helping to avoid confusion as to the team members on the field and thus uniforms are descriptive at best and not inherently distinctive.[117]

On appeal, the Eleventh Circuit took up Moore's First Amendment defense and whether it should give way to the university's trademark rights. It relied on *Rogers v. Grimaldi*, a case where famed dancer Ginger Rogers argued that the film titled *Ginger and Fred* violated her right of publicity as well as falsely implied that she endorsed the motion picture. The *Rogers* case established the relatedness test and the principle that the public interest in free expression should prevail if the use of a celebrity's image has artistic relevance and is not used in such a way that it explicitly misleads as to the source of the work.[118] With regard to artistic works, the court noted that while the purchaser of such works, "like the purchaser of a can of peas, has a right not to be misled,"[119] the public interest in preventing consumer confusion must be evaluated narrowly to avoid infringing the public interest in free expression.[120]

Given the constitutional weight of the First Amendment, an artistically expressive use of a trademark will not violate the Lanham Act unless it has "no artistic relevance to the underlying work whatsoever or if it has some artistic relevance, unless it explicitly misleads as to the source or the content of the work."[121] Here the court concluded that the uniform colors and designs are artistically relevant to the realistic portrayal of famous scenes from Alabama football history. In addition, no unlicensed painting was ever marketed in such a way as to indicate or suggest that the university endorsed, sponsored, or was otherwise affiliated with the artwork. Even if some members of the public would infer that the university had some involvement with Moore's paintings, the court said, the risk of such a misunderstanding is so outweighed by the interest in artistic expression as to preclude any violation of the Lanham Act.[122]

In Moore's case, the court essentially repurposed a test that traditionally covered uses of a trademark in the *title* of an artistic work by applying it to the use of the mark in the *body* of the artwork. This means that artistic works that otherwise would have violated the Lanham Act will likely be held nonactionable if (1) the use of a trademark has some relevance to the underlying expressive work and (2) the expressive work does not explicitly mislead consumers with regard to its source or content. Without the Rogers test, the court may have found that Moore's paintings created a likelihood of confusion. Such an outcome would likely have subjected Moore to an 8 percent royalty payment to the university for both new and prior work dating back to 1979.[123] Instead, the Rogers test gave the court a mechanism to weigh the public interest in the artwork against the public interest in any consumer confusion it may have generated.

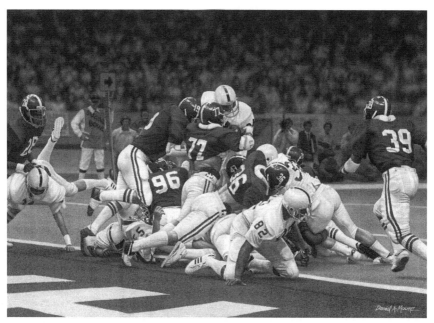

Figure 6.5. The court concluded that the interest in artistic expression outweighed any risk of confusion regarding the University's sponsorship of the artwork. The court based its decision on the fact that 1.) the uniforms are artistically relevant to the portrayal of Alabama football and 2.) Moore never explicitly misled consumers as to the source of the artwork or its sponsorship by the University.

Photo courtesy of Daniel Moore, New Life Art.

Fair Use

In addition to the straight application of the likelihood of confusion test and the Rogers test, trademark law also recognizes two types of fair use: "classic" and "nominative." A **classic fair use** defense is based on the principle that a trademark holder's rights extend only to the mark's significance as a source identifier and not to the original, descriptive meanings of the words that make up the mark. This provides defendants with an affirmative defense in situations where they used the plaintiff's mark to describe their own product. For example, under the defense, a company that specializes in selling, repairing, and maintaining BMW vehicles would be able to use the term BMW to describe their service, as in "We repair BMW vehicles." To assert a classic fair use defense, the defendant must show that the words constituting the mark were used (1) as something other than a mark; (2) fairly and in good faith; and (3) only to describe the defendant's goods and services. A classic fair use defense is exerted once the plaintiff has demonstrated the likelihood of confusion. The defendant does not need to rebut the likelihood of confusion evidence in addition to establishing the fair use defense as the Supreme Court noted that fair use can exist even if there is some degree of consumer confusion.

Harley-Davidson successfully raised a classic fair use defense in its case against a company that trademarked the term "ride hard" for use on the apparel they sold. Harley-Davidson was able to show that their use of the term as a phrase on t-shirts, bumper stickers, caps, headbands, and other such accessories described the vigor, strength, and energy consumers associate with owning Harley-Davidson branded products.[124] Oprah Winfrey, on the other hand, had trouble convincing the court that her use of the catchphrase "Own Your Power" was merely descriptive and not an attempt to build a new subbrand of her media empire.

Winfrey first used the slogan on the cover of the October 2010 issue of *O Magazine*. The magazine contained the "2010 O Power List!" of "20 Women Who Are Rocking the World." Winfrey promoted the issue on her television show, and days after the magazine dropped she held a motivational advice and self-awareness event around the slogan. The event featured various celebrities who posed for photographs in front of an "Own Your Power" backdrop and was cosponsored by national brands, such as Chico's and Clinique as well as *O Magazine*. Video clips from the event and "Own Your Power" banners and content appeared on at least seventy-five different pages on Winfrey's Harpo website, and the event was described as the "FIRST-EVER OWN YOUR POWER EVENT" in the December 2010 issue of *O Magazine*.[125]

Simone Kelly-Brown, who owns the motivational services business, Own Your Power Communication, filed a trademark infringement claim against Winfrey. Winfrey moved to dismiss the claim, asserting a classic fair use defense. The court took issue with Winfrey's repeated use of the catchphrase across various forms of media in a manner that created an association between the Oprah brand and the slogan. The court ruled that Winfrey had failed to establish that her use of the slogan was anything other than as a mark whereas the plaintiff, the court said, had plausibly alleged that Winfrey "intended to create a new line of products and services offered by Oprah under the mark 'Own Your Power.'"[126]

Nominative fair use is somewhat similar to the Rogers test in that it was created to accommodate the free expression interests at issue when a defendant deliberately uses the plaintiff's trademark or trade dress for purposes such as comparison, criticism, and point of reference.[127] The nominative fair use defense was developed by the Ninth Circuit in 1992 and used to release two newspapers from a trademark infringement claim for conducting a popularity poll of the boy band New Kids on Block. Specifically, the poll asked readers to call in and vote for their favorite New Kids band member. Because the newspapers needed to use the trademarked name New Kids on Block to identify the group, the band sued for trademark infringement.

The court noted that the group's name as represented in this case was best understood as a nontrademark use in that its treatment did not implicate the mark's source-identification function, imply sponsorship or endorsement by the group, or constitute unfair competition.[128] Instead, the newspaper accurately referred to the group's trademark in order to identify or describe the boy band. Here, the court said that the newspaper was entitled to a nominative fair use defense because the following three requirements had been met:

1. The product or service in question was one that is *not* readily identifiable without the trademark;
2. The defendant used only so much of the mark as was reasonably necessary to identify the plaintiff's product or service; and
3. The defendant did nothing to suggest sponsorship or endorsement by the trademark holder.

While the Rogers test as applied in Moore is viewed as more speech-protective than the Ninth Circuit's fair use,[129] the nominative fair use defense has been pressed into service to safeguard artistic depictions of protected marks. Self-taught photographer Thomas Forsythe was a distinctive beneficiary of the defense. In 1997 Forsythe developed a series of seventy-eight food-related photographs of cultural icon and trademark powerhouse Barbie. The series, titled *Food Chain Barbie*, was Forsythe's attempt to lambast the objectification of women and the conventional stereotype of female beauty Barbie is thought to embody.[130] To accomplish this, Forsythe placed one or more nude Barbie dolls in various absurd and often sexualized positions in or around kitchen appliances. For example, "Malted Barbie" features a nude Barbie stuffed into the mixing cup of a vintage milkshake maker as if she was an ingredient ready to be pulverized. Similarly, in "Barbie Enchiladas," five dolls are partially wrapped in tortillas covered with salsa and placed in a casserole dish in a lit oven. Forsythe explained that he chose to parody Barbie because the doll "feed[s] on the insecurities of our beauty and perfection-obsessed consumer culture."[131]

The Ninth Circuit agreed that the Barbie trade dress had transcended its identifying purpose and at least for some women, symbolizes the unattainable ideal of femininity.[132] The court noted that when a mark assumes a role outside the bounds of trademark law, First Amendment protections come into play and a constitutional balancing analysis, like the Rogers test, is warranted. Here, however, the court found that the case could be resolved on narrower grounds by applying the nominative fair use defense.[133] In doing so, the court ruled that all three elements of the defense weighed in favor of Forsythe. First, in order to create a photographic parody of Barbie, Forsythe needed to conjure up the Barbie product in the viewer's mind. Second, given that the artistic goal was to represent the issues of sexuality and body image associated with the doll, the use of Barbie's head and torso was reasonably necessary. The court said, determining what is "reasonably necessary" in order to identify the plaintiff's product will differ from case to case. Here Forsythe's parody depends on the identification of Mattel's product. "It would be very difficult," the court said, for Forsythe to "represent and describe his photographic parodies of Barbie without using the Barbie likeness."[134]

In moving to the third element of the defense, Mattel took issue with the fact that Forsythe repeatedly told galleries and friends that one of his photographs "hangs on the wall of the office of Mattel's President of Production," whom Forsythe referred to as "Joe Mattel."[135] Forsythe claimed that a client gifted the photograph to the senior executive and that he had no intention of suggesting any affiliation between *Food Chain Barbie* and Mattel. Nonetheless, Forsythe mentioned the Joe Mattel story in virtually every promotional packet for the series while the remainder of information in the packets helped to reduce confusion as to Mattel's endorsement of the series. The information included a biography that identified Forsythe as someone who was attempting to "deglamourize[] Barbie," "skewer[] the Barbie myth," and expose an "undercurrent of dissatisfaction with consumer culture."[136] Similar statements were prominently featured on Forsythe's website. In addition, the critical nature of Forsythe's work also weighed in his favor. The court noted that a perceived affiliation is much less likely to occur with such works, and thus it is highly unlikely that any reasonable consumer would have believed that Mattel sponsored or was affiliated with *Food Chain Barbie*.[137]

Because it is unlikely consumers would be confused, it has been argued that the traditional likelihood of confusion analysis or First Amendment consideration would have provided an ample defense to Forsythe's conduct. This has led to the charge that the nominative fair use defense is of "dubious value, at best."[138] The courts applying the third element of the defense have often treated it as a quick-and-dirty confusion analysis that uses more intuition and much less evidence.[139] Even the Ninth Circuit has had trouble determining whether nominative fair use is a distinct defense or "merely one type of use which is not likely to cause confusion."[140] As a result, it has yet to be widely accepted among the federal circuits.[141]

While the defense allowed Forsythe to continue to market his work, his success was quite limited. Prior to the lawsuit, he received only four or five unsolicited calls about his work, displayed his work at two art festivals, and earned a total gross income of $ 3,659 from the series. His legal fees, on the other hand, mounted to $1.8 million—a sum a federal judge instructed Mattel to pay.[142]

CHAPTER SUMMARY

Trademarks symbolize the character, cultural image, and market strength of their associated brand. As such, trademarks are viewed as important assets that go beyond a graphic element or a logo to include any word, name, symbol, or device, or any combination thereof used to identify and distinguish goods or services from those produced by others. Since almost any symbol or device is capable of conveying meaning, trademark protection has been extended to nearly every facet of a product's total physical image and selling program. Protected under the Lanham Act, federal trademark law has grown substantially in its effort to prevent consumer confusion and misinformation. Given these consumer protection goals, the success of trademark and trade dress infringement as well as false association claims are largely dependent on the court's analysis of the likelihood of confusion factors. Given the flexible nature of the factor analysis, case outcomes are often hard to predict, especially in cases where well-known trademarks have become the targets of parody, satire, or ridicule, or are used in editorial or artistic works. To resolve the tension between free expression and trademark protection goals, courts have adopted other forms of First Amendment defenses and balancing approaches, including descriptive and nominative fair use standards and a modified version of the Rogers test.

KEY TERMS

Abandonment   A mark becomes abandoned when a trademark holder stops using it and has no intent to resume its use. Three years of nonuse is considered evidence of abandonment.

Actual Confusion   Actual confusion is a factor in the likelihood of confusion analysis that considers whether there is evidence that consumers have confused the marks in question. While actual confusion may be the best indicator of the likelihood of confusion, it is difficult to establish, especially in cases where the two marks have coexisted for only a short time.

Affidavit   An affidavit is a written statement of facts made under oath. The document is signed by the person making the statement as well as by a person legally authorized to administer the oath. Affidavits are used in court proceedings and other legal matters.

Arbitrary Trademark   Marks that use common words as source identifiers for unrelated goods or services. An example is the trademarked name "Apple" for Apple computers.

Classic Fair Use   A defense based on the principle that a trademark holder's rights extend only to the mark's significance as a source identifier and not to the original, descriptive meanings of the words that make up the mark. This provides defendants with an affirmative defense in situations where they used the plaintiff's mark to describe their own product.

Commerce   To be eligible for federal trademark protection, a mark must be distinctive and used in commerce. Under the Lanham Act, the word commerce refers to the trade in goods and services that may be regulated by Congress. The US Constitution gives Congress the power to regulate commerce among the states and with other nations. This means that "used in commerce" is commonly understood as interstate commerce. Interstate commerce refers to the movement of goods across state lines but also can include services that cater to customers from out of state, such as hotels, or services offered via the internet.

Descriptive Trademark   A mark that immediately conveys at least one major underlying characteristic of the good or service. In this way, no thought or imagination is necessary to understand the nature of the product. An example of a descriptive mark is "Holiday Inn." Because descriptive marks describe the nature of the product or service, they are not considered distinctive upon inception and must acquire a secondary meaning to receive trademark protection.

Disparagement Clause   A clause in the Lanham Act that denied trademark registration to marks that "may disparage . . . persons, living or dead, institutions, beliefs, or national symbols, or bring them into contempt, or disrepute." The disparagement clause was intended to prevent demeaning messages in commercial advertising but was struck down by the US Supreme Court as an unconstitutional viewpoint-based speech restriction.

Distinctiveness   The degree to which a trademark invokes the source of the product or service in the mind of the consumer. Distinctiveness is determined by the uniqueness of the text, visuals, and other symbols companies use to identify the origin of their goods or services.

False Association   Section 43(a) of the Lanham Act prohibits conduct that is likely to create a false association as to who is sponsoring, endorsing, or in some way connected to a product, service, or commercial activity. False association claims are broader in scope than trademark infringement claims in that unregistered marks are also covered. This means that the total physical image conveyed by the name and product together as well as every facet of a selling program is relevant.

False Endorsement   Section 43(a) of the Lanham Act allows celebrities to sue for uses of their identity that falsely imply an endorsement of a product or service. Because false endorsement claims involve the unauthorized use of a person's identity, they are similar to right of publicity claims and are often viewed as the federal equivalent of a state right of publicity statute. The two differ in that false endorsement claims are subject to the likelihood of confusion test.

Fanciful Trademark   Marks that are comprised of made-up or archaic terms that are used solely to identify a good or service. Fanciful marks are considered the most distinctive category of trademarks.

Forward Confusion   A type of consumer confusion that occurs when consumers believe that the goods or services bearing the junior mark came from or were sponsored by the senior mark holder.

Generic Trademark   Terms that basically denote the product itself, such as "lite beer," are categorized as generic. Because such terms are not capable of distinguishing, for example, one source of lite beer from another, generic terms do not receive trademark protection.

Genericized   Registered trademarks can become genericized over time. This occurs when the word mark becomes so ingrained in the language that it signifies the product itself rather than the source of the product. Examples of registered trademarks that have become genericized include "elevator," "aspirin," and "teleprompter."

Immoral or Scandalous Clause   A clause in the Lanham Act that denied trademark registration to marks that contain immoral or scandalous matter. The USPTO rejects marks under this clause that the public would view as "shocking to the sense of truth, decency, or propriety." The clause was struck down by the US Supreme Court as an unconstitutional viewpoint-based speech restriction.

Intent   The intent of the defendant in selecting the mark is a critical factor in the likelihood of confusion analysis. An intention to pass off goods or derive reputational benefits from the senior mark may be sufficient in and of itself to establish the likelihood of confusion.

Junior Mark   In an infringement suit, the mark that followed the senior mark in registration or use.

Lanham Act   A federal law enacted in 1946, the Lanham Act set up a formal system of federal trademark registration and protection. Over the years, the Lanham Act has been expanded and is now the primary and most extensive source of trademark protection in the United States. The Lanham Act is based largely on the consumer protection goals of preventing market confusion and misinformation. It exists alongside state statutes and common law unfair competition.

Likelihood of Confusion   Plaintiffs bringing suit for trademark infringement or unfair competition must show that the defendant's conduct is likely to cause consumer confusion as to the source or affiliation of the goods or services. To determine whether a defendant's use of a mark actually created a likelihood of confusion, courts examine a variety of factors. No single factor determines the outcome of the case, and decisions are not necessarily decided by the number of factors that weigh in favor of either party.

Likelihood of Expansion   Likelihood of expansion of product lines is a factor in the likelihood of confusion analysis. It assesses the likelihood that either party will expand their business to begin competing with the other. A strong probability of direct competition through a geographic or product line expansion favors a finding of likelihood of confusion.

Marketing Channels   Marketing channels is a factor in the likelihood of confusion analysis. This factor examines the degree of similarity between the marketing approaches each party employs and the consumers they tend to attract.

Nominative Fair Use   A test created to accommodate the free expression interests at issue when a defendant deliberately uses the plaintiff's trademark or trade dress for comparison, criticism, and as a point of reference.

Nonfunctional   Only nonfunctional trade dress can receive trademark protection. Trade dress that is essential to the use or purpose of the product; affects the product's cost or quality; or would put competitors at a significant nonreputation-related disadvantage is considered functional and is not eligible for trade dress protection.

Purity of Use   The weight given to the First Amendment interest is often stronger when the unauthorized mark is used as a target of an editorial or an artistic work.

Registered Trademark   Trademarks can be federally registered through the US Patent and Trademark Office. Registration provides notice that the holder has the exclusive nationwide right to use the mark in commerce and that the use of substantially similar marks is prohibited by the USPTO. Registration also allows the holder to bring suit in federal court and to overcome claims by subsequent users of the mark. Registered marks have the exclusive right to use the registered symbol ® and are protected as long as they remain distinctive, are used in commerce, and registration is renewed periodically.

Relatedness of the Goods   Relatedness of the goods is a factor in the likelihood of confusion analysis. It focuses on the degree to which consumers are likely to think that the two products or services at issue are connected. When the goods are related, less similarity between marks is needed to find infringement.

Reverse Confusion   A type of consumer confusion that occurs when the junior user is a larger, more powerful entity than the company holding the senior mark and saturates the market with a mark identical or similar to the senior mark on related goods or services. This strategy causes the public to mistakenly believe that the senior user's products are produced by the junior user's company or that the two sets of goods are somehow connected.

Secondary Meaning   Descriptive marks and certain forms of trade dress are not distinctive enough when they are created to function as a source identifier for a particular brand. To receive trademark protection, the mark holder needs to show that over time consumers have come to associate the otherwise descriptive term or appealing color with a particular brand. Once an otherwise nondistinctive term, color, shape, or the like acquires a secondary meaning as a source identifier, it is eligible for trademark protection.

Senior Mark   In an infringement suit, the mark that was registered or used first.

Similarity of Marks   Similarity of marks is a factor in the likelihood of confusion analysis. It gauges the degree of similarity between the marks in terms of their sight, sound, and meaning and as they are normally encountered in the marketplace by the average consumer.

Source Designator   See Source Identifier.

Source Identifier   A trademark's main purpose is to identify the origin of a product or service. When a trademark is no longer capable of identifying or designating the source of the good, it loses its trademark protection.

Strength of the Mark   Strength of the mark is a factor in the likelihood of confusion analysis. It is assessed by the mark's distinctiveness as well as the degree of actual recognition the mark receives in the marketplace.

Suggestive Trademark   Suggestive marks allude to or evoke (rather than describe) some quality, ingredient, or characteristic of the product, and, thus, they require some imagination to determine the nature of the good. They are a favorite of marketers but can be confused with descriptive marks. Orange Crush is an example of a suggestive mark.

Surname   A person's family name or last name. Some surnames are eligible for trademark registration at the time of application. Others, however, must acquire a secondary meaning before receiving trademark protection. The deciding factor is whether the public is likely to perceive the surname as a trademark or someone's last name.

Trade Dress   Trade dress consists of the total image or appearance of a product in the marketplace, including the shapes, sizes, colors, or color combinations that make up a product's packaging; the designs and placement of words, graphics, and decorations on the product or its packaging; and even the décor, environment, or façade of the building in which a service is provided. Basically, anything that makes the presentation of the product or service distinctive.

Trademark The Lanham Act describes a trademark in the broadest of terms as "any word, name symbol or device, or any combination thereof" used to identify and distinguish goods or services from those produced or sold by others. Trademarks commonly include letters, words, logos, images, and slogans as well as sounds, smells, shapes, sizes, colors, or color combinations, and even the décor or façade of the building in which a service is provided.

Trademark Erosion Trademark erosion refers to the process by which registered trademarks become genericized.

Trademark Infringement Trademark infringement is the unauthorized use of a trademark or service mark in a manner that is likely to cause consumer confusion in the marketplace. A plaintiff bringing suit must prove ownership of a valid mark; that the defendant used the mark or something substantially similar to it on or in connection with goods or services; and that the use is likely to cause confusion in the minds of consumers about the source or sponsorship of the goods or services.

Trademark Parody Trademark parody uses the mark in a way that builds upon its cultural popularity by adding something new for an amusing or satirical effect. To be successful, a trademark parody must convey two contradictory messages: that it is the original mark and that it is not the original and is instead a parody.

Trademark Trial and Appeal Board (TTAB) The TTAB was created by the USPTO to resolve legal disputes that arise when trademark applications are denied by a USPTO examining attorney or contested by a senior trademark holder. The TTAB also hears petitions for the cancellation of registered marks. Applicants who are not happy with a TTAB ruling may sue in US District Court or appeal directly to the US Court of Appeals for the Federal Circuit.

Type of Goods versus Purchaser Care Type of goods versus purchaser care is a factor in the likelihood of confusion analysis. This factor recognizes that not all buyers and purchases are equal. In circumstances involving high-end goods or items purchased by professional buyers, courts will require a greater degree of similarity to justify a claim of likelihood of confusion.

Unfair Competition   Unfair competition is an umbrella term that refers to a variety of unjust commercial activities that damage other business interests. Some of these activities are prohibited by the Lanham Act. Trademark infringement and false association are types of unfair competition prohibited by the Lanham Act.

United States Patent and Trademark Office (USPTO)   The USPTO is the federal agency responsible for registering trademarks. The agency reviews applications and determines whether an applicant meets the requirements for federal trademark registration. USPTO examining attorneys commonly deny registration for marks that deceptively misdescribe the good; are merely descriptive or primarily a surname; or create a likelihood of confusion with a senior mark.

United States Court of Appeals for the Federal Circuit   The US Court of Appeals for the Federal Circuit was established in 1982 and given nationwide jurisdiction in a variety of subject areas, including trademarks. The Federal Circuit is located in Washington, DC, and hears direct appeals from rulings by the Trademark Trial and Appeal Board. Litigants who appeal a TTAB ruling to the Federal Circuit may not present any new evidence. The TTAB must accept the Federal Circuit's decision.

7

Dilution

Anyone who has shopped for a handbag recently has experienced the unvarnished selling power of trademarks. From Givenchy and Vuitton to Chanel and Prada, handbags from high-end fashion houses function more as external symbols of status than a carrying case for personal items. As a result, consumers are willing to shell out big bucks to cover not only the tangible worth of the bag but also the cachet of the famous brand. Perhaps the most illustrative example of this phenomenon is the ultimate luxury handbag—the Birkin. While the bag itself is a simple looking tote-like purse with two top handles and a key-lock closure, the Birkin routinely commands a five-figure selling price and months to years of wait time for those who are worthy enough to secure one from Hermès. In this way, the bag is "wildly coveted by celebrities, style insiders, and the general accessory-obsessed"[1] primarily for the magnified value of its trade dress and the Birkin trademark rather than any distinct quality guarantees associated with the source of the product.

The immense market power wielded by famous brands has long confounded federal trademark law. Since its inception, trademark law has been motivated by consumer protection goals. To achieve these goals, the law focuses on preventing unauthorized uses of marks that are likely to create consumer confusion as to the source of the product or service. A producer's interest in protecting the mark's commercial strength against uses that would likely diminish its market value but not result in consumer confusion was not covered by federal law until 1996, when an antidilution statute was added to the **Lanham Act**. This area of trademark law, known as **dilution** law, prevents unauthorized uses of **famous trademarks** that are likely to diminish the mark's selling power regardless of whether or not those uses are likely to cause consumer confusion.

DILUTION LAW

Dilution law is somewhat controversial because it seeks to protect the good-will and market strength of the brand rather than its consumers. In this way, dilution law recognizes the substantial investment the company has made in creating its brand identity and the commercial value of the mark itself.[2] In light of its producer focus, it has been viewed as a fundamental shift in the nature of trademark protection.[3] This shift took decades to complete after it was first articulated in a 1927 *Harvard Law Review* article written by Frank Schechter.

In the article, Schechter argued that a mark's selling power can be impaired by its use on related as well as nonrelated goods.[4] While uses on nonrelated goods are unlikely to trigger confusion among consumers and thus unlikely to violate trademark law, such uses, according to Schechter, weaken a mark's overall **distinctiveness** in the minds of consumers and thus diminish the commercial value of the brand's identity.[5] Schechter singled out, as an example, a 1924 case where the publisher of *Vogue* magazine filed suit against a department store for marketing a line of hats bearing labels with the name "Vogue Hats." In the case, the court refused to prohibit the use of the word "vogue" on somewhat related but noncompetitive goods. It noted that the word itself is synonymous with "style" or "fashion" and as such "all are at liberty to use [it]."[6] Schechter, on the other hand, saw real injury in these cases in that uses of a word mark on noncompeting goods could over time whittle away the brand's trademarked identity in the minds of the consuming public.[7]

Schechter's antidilution concept was first enacted into law in 1947 by the state of Massachusetts. By 1995, approximately half of the states had passed antidilution legislation. At that time, Congress enacted the first of two federal **antidilution statutes**, and thereby extended protection against trademark dilution to the entire country in an attempt to bring consistency and uniformity to this burgeoning area of law. The **Federal Trademark Dilution Act of 1995** (FTDA) protected owners of famous marks against commercial uses of a mark or trade name that "causes dilution of the distinctive quality" of the famous mark.[8] The act defined dilution as "the lessening of the capacity of a famous mark to identify and distinguish goods or services regardless of the presence or absence of (1) competition between the owner of the famous mark and other parties, or (2) **likelihood of confusion**, mistake, or deception."[9]

In 2003, the US Supreme Court weighed in to resolve splits among the lower courts on whether *causes dilution* required a showing of "actual injury to the economic value of the famous mark" or a likelihood of such injury.[10] The case, ***Moseley v. V Secret Catalogue***, involved an adult novelty and lingerie store in Elizabethtown, Kentucky, named Victor's Secret and the national retailer Victoria's Secret. Although the lower courts found in favor of the national retailer, the Supreme Court reversed, holding that the FTDA required a showing of **actual dilution**.[11] Actual dilution, the court said, could be established through direct evidence such as consumer surveys or circumstantial evidence in cases where the marks are identical.[12] In an effort to overturn *Moseley*, Congress substantially altered the FTDA with the enactment of the **Trademark Dilution Revision Act of 2006** (TDRA). In addition to the TDRA, dilution law has been enacted in a majority of states. This chapter focuses on federal dilution law as it is currently understood with the passage of the TDRA.

Famous Trademarks

The TDRA gives owners of trademarks that are both famous and distinctive the ability to bar others from using a mark that is *likely* to cause dilution. Because dilution law is extended only to holders of famous trademarks, the threshold question in a case is whether the mark at issue is truly "famous."[13] According to the statute, fame for dilution requires widespread recognition by the general consuming public.[14] This means that even marks that are considered conceptually and commercially strong under the likelihood of confusion test may not merit the degree of public recognition needed to trigger antidilution protection.[15] In addition, marks that are famous only in some niche market, small town, state, or region will most likely not be considered famous for dilution purposes. Instead, courts have largely reserved the designation for brands that have become household names[16] or "part of the collective national consciousness."[17] Since the passage of the TDRA, brands such as Nissan, Nike, Pepsi, Audi, and Victoria's Secret have been deemed famous while the Texas Longhorn logo, Coach (handbags), and Maker's Mark (bourbon whiskey) were not, even though they are inherently distinctive brand names.[18]

When considering whether a mark possesses the level of fame required for dilution law, it is good to remember that a mark's strength or **level of distinctiveness** (likelihood of confusion standard) differs from the degree to which it has attained widespread recognition (dilution law). Under the likelihood of confusion standard, marks are assessed in varying degrees of distinctiveness from very strong to very weak, whereas fame in the dilution sense either does or does not exist.[19] Moreover, establishing fame may require additional evidence beyond that which a mark holder must present to successfully show inherent or acquired distinctiveness.[20] This is why a "terrifically strong and focused brand" like Maker's Mark, for example, can fail to successfully meet the more demanding threshold required for fame.[21] To aid courts in determining fame, the following four nonexclusive factors are considered.

1. The duration, extent, and geographical reach of the advertising and publicity of the mark, and whether the mark was advertised or publicized by the owner or third parties.
2. The amount, volume, and geographic extent of the sales of goods or services offered under the mark.
3. The extent of actual recognition of the mark.
4. Whether the mark was registered on the **principal register** or under the trademark acts of 1881 or 1905.[22]

Based on these criteria, courts generally have limited famous marks to those with multimillion-dollar ad budgets, annual sales figures in the hundreds of millions of dollars, and nearly universal public recognition.[23] In short, famous marks are so distinctive that the general public associates the word with the trademark regardless of the context in which the term is encountered.[24] To establish this level of fame, courts examine the extent to which the mark has been widely and prominently featured in national, regional, and local advertising campaigns appearing across various media platforms. Ad campaigns are not limited to those conducted by the mark holder but include third-party and other cross-promotional or co-branded efforts. In addition, solicited and unsolicited publicity and other promotional and sponsorship activities may demonstrate widespread recognition as well as scores of supplementary evidence such as associations of the mark with celebrities, brand rankings, industry awards, and the mark's appearance in movies, television shows, books, museums, and the like. Consumer recognition surveys also provide persuasive evidence.[25] But whether the body of evidence presented includes articles, media references, sales figures, and the like, it needs to clearly establish that the plaintiff's mark achieved widespread recognition *before* the defendant's mark was used in commerce. Evidence of fame dated *after* the defendant's mark entered commerce will be disregarded by courts.

Trademark Dilution

Plaintiff's Trademark	Defendant's Trademark
• Famous to significant portion of general consuming public • Distinctive: either inherent or acquired	• Used on commerce *after* plaintiff's mark became famous • Use is *likely* to cause dilution to plaintiff's mark through blurring or tarnishment

Figure 7.1.

Blurring and Tarnishment

Once a distinctive mark is deemed famous, the holder possesses the right to stop uses that are likely to dilute the mark's value. Under current law, two types of dilution are recognized: (1) **dilution by blurring** and (2) **dilution by tarnishment**. Blurring and tarnishment are separate **causes of action**. But regardless of which cause of action forms the basis of the lawsuit, the plaintiff must show that the defendant's use of a mark in commerce is "likely to cause dilution" by either blurring or tarnishment. The TDRA explicitly lowered the standard of harm from a showing of actual dilution to a finding of likelihood of dilution. In demonstrating **likelihood of dilution**, plaintiffs are not required to show the presence or absence of (1) actual or likely confusion; (2) competition between parties; or (3) actual economic injury.[26]

Blurring

Of the two concepts, blurring is perhaps the most difficult to fully grasp. The TDRA defines dilution by blurring as the "association arising from the similarity between a mark or trade name and a famous mark that impairs the distinctiveness of the famous mark."[27] An "**association**" in dilution law occurs when a substantial percentage of consumers who encounter the **junior mark** in the marketplace are immediately reminded of the famous mark and associate the junior mark holder with the owner of the famous mark.[28] Such an association is established even if consumers do not believe that the goods or services sold under the junior mark come from the famous mark's owner.[29]

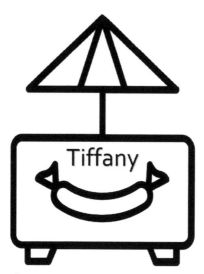

Figure 7.2.

A characteristic example from the Seventh Circuit is the use of the name "Tiffany" for a hotdog stand. The word "Tiffany" or "Tiffany's" is widely associated with the premier jeweler and retailer "Tiffany & Co." Because the retailer and the food stand sell nonrelated goods, it would be difficult to show a likelihood of confusion among the consuming public. Thus, a trademark infringement claim is most likely out of the question. A claim for dilution by blurring, however, is probable given that consumers who see the name Tiffany on the hotdog stand are likely to think of the jewelry store and the absurdity of marketing hotdogs and upscale jewelry under the same trade name. Over time, the juxtaposition in the minds of the consuming public between Tiffany jewelry and Tiffany hotdogs works to slowly whittle away the distinctiveness of the celebrated jewelry store. As its brand cachet diminishes, consumers are likely to switch their patronage to other high-end retailers, such as Cartier and Harry Winston, thus impairing the famous mark Tiffany & Co.[30]

In determining whether a junior use is likely to cause dilution by blurring, the statute lays out six nonexclusive factors for courts to consider. Courts are not required to evaluate each of the factors listed and may limit their discussion to those factors that are relevant to the case at hand. This provides courts with the flexibility to examine additional evidence relevant to resolve the dispute.[31]

1. The degree of similarity between the mark or trade name and the famous mark.
2. The degree of inherent or acquired distinctiveness of the famous mark.
3. The extent to which the owner of the famous mark is engaging in substantially exclusive use of the mark.
4. The degree of recognition of the famous mark.
5. Whether the user of the mark or trade name intended to create an association with the famous mark.
6. Any actual association between the mark or trade name and the famous mark.[32]

Of these factors, two, three, and four are intended to establish that the plaintiff holds a famous mark and is, therefore, entitled to protection against trademark dilution. For famous mark holders, these factors will most likely weigh in their favor as the famous coffee brand, Starbucks, found out in its case against a family-run coffee roastery. In *Starbucks Corp. v. Wolfe's Borough Coffee*, the coffee giant claimed that Wolfe, which operated Black

Bear Micro Roastery, diluted the Starbucks marks by selling specialty blends of coffee beans called Charbucks Blend and Mister Charbucks. In the case, Starbucks easily proved distinctiveness, recognition, and exclusivity of use. The company, at the time of the suit, operated some 8,700 stores throughout the world and spent more than $136 million on advertising, promotion, and related marketing activities over a preceding three-year period.[33] In conclusion, the **district court** noted that Starbucks is the "largest and best-known purveyor of specialty coffees and coffee products in North America."[34] While Starbucks presented strong evidence establishing itself as a famous mark holder, it still needed to address factors one, five, and six.

Factor one examines the degree to which the junior mark and the famous mark are similar. With the passage of the TDRA, courts have held that factor one does not require a showing of "substantial similarity" given that the statute does not use the words "very" or "substantial" in connection with "**degree of similarity**." This means that a successful dilution claim can be waged not only with marks that are virtually identical or substantially similar but also in circumstances where the degree of similarity between the two marks is less pronounced.[35] In *Starbucks v. Wolfe*, the district court found that the two marks were only "minimally similar." The **appeals court** agreed and noted that while "Charbucks" is similar in sound and spelling to "Starbucks," the package designs for "Mister Charbucks" and "Charbucks Blend" are different in imagery, color, and format from the marks used by the coffee giant.

According to the owners of Black Bear Micro Roastery, the labels and packaging for Charbucks Blend and Mister Charbucks were designed to highlight the roasting process rather than anything related to the Starbucks brand.[36] For example, the packaging for Charbucks Blend prominently pictures a black bear and the name "Black Bear Micro Roastery." Beneath the image of the bear and the company's name in the center of the package, the words "Charbucks Blend" appear in a large font. The lower half of the package contains the phrases "You wanted it dark . . . You've got it dark!" as well as the product descriptor "WHOLE BEAN GOURMET COFFEE" and information regarding where the coffee beans were roasted and the weight of the package. As for "Mister Charbucks," the dominant artwork on the package is a picture of a man walking above the name "Mister Charbucks," which is displayed in a large font. Again, the name of the roastery and where it is located is included on the package as well as the phrase "ROASTED TO THE EXTREME . . . FOR THOSE WHO LIKE THE EXTREME."

Figure 7.3.
Photo courtesy of Black Bear Micro Roastery

The appeals court said that neither the graphic of the bear nor the man walking are comparable to the Starbucks siren in terms of "pose, shape, art-style, gender or overall impression."[37] Moreover, the lack of evidence that "Charbucks" would ever serve as a stand-alone identifier of Black Bear's products or be presented to the public unaccompanied by the Black Bear name further supported a finding of minimal similarity.[38] On **remand**, the district court held that the marginal degree of similarity weighed in Black Bear's favor.[39]

Figure 7.4.
Photo courtesy of Black Bear Micro Roastery

Turning to factor five, the appeals court explained that an intent to associate an allegedly diluting mark with a famous mark does not require an act of bad faith on the defendant's part.[40] The statute "requires only the consideration of '[w]hether the user of the mark intended to create an association with the famous mark.'"[41] Defendants who create marks with the intent to associate them with a famous mark will violate factor five. Here the owners of Black Bear Micro Roastery admitted that the name "Charbucks" was a wordplay intended to signal that the coffee blend was a dark roast characteristic of a Starbucks product.[42] Thus, intent was plainly admitted by the defendant, and the factor favored a finding of likelihood of dilution.[43]

While a finding of intent to associate the two marks favored the plaintiff, it did not establish definitive proof that actual association occurred.[44] To prove association between the marks, Starbucks relied on a telephone survey, in which respondents were asked: "What is the FIRST THING that comes to your mind when you hear the name 'Charbucks,' spelled C-H-A-R-B-U-C-K-S." Some 30 percent of the six hundred respondents interviewed said "Starbucks" and 9 percent said "coffee." But when asked "Can you name any company or store that you think might offer a product called 'Charbucks'?" only 3.1 percent answered "Starbucks" and 1.3 percent answered "coffee house."[45] Based on the small percentage of respondents who mentally associated Charbucks with Starbucks and the fact that the survey neglected to measure reaction to the marks as they appeared in commerce, the survey was discounted.[46] Because the TDRA defines dilution as the *association* arising from the degree of *similarity* between the two marks, the decision turned on the analysis of factors one and six. In the end, the reviewing courts found a weak association between two minimally similar marks and concluded that the Charbucks mark as it was used in commerce was unlikely to impair the distinctiveness of the Starbucks mark.[47]

Tarnishment

Dilution by tarnishment also involves an association arising from a degree of similarity between a mark or trade name and a famous mark. But with a likelihood of tarnishment claim, the association is likely to degrade the positive reputation of the famous mark rather than impair its distinctiveness. While the TDRA did not provide any specific factors for evaluating a claim of dilution by tarnishment, courts have repeatedly held that tarnishment is likely to occur when a famous mark is linked to shoddy, low-quality goods, or is portrayed in an unwholesome or unsavory context. In this respect, tarnishment has been found where the defendant's use connected the famous mark to an adult entertainment exhibition;[48] a pornographic website that also included illustrations of drug use and drug paraphernalia;[49] an adult video, novelty, and lingerie store;[50] websites that advertise, link to, or are affiliated with other sites that sell pornographic images and videos;[51] and inferior counterfeit goods.[52] As these cases show, the essential element in any successful dilution by tarnishment claim is the likelihood that the famous mark "will suffer negative associations through the defendant's use."[53] In cases where the association is light-hearted and there is nothing to suggest that the famous mark will be adversely affected by the association, tarnishment is not likely. This includes uses involving harmless, clean puns that merely parody or poke fun at the famous mark[54] or, as Starbucks discovered, associations with high-quality products.

In addition to dilution by blurring, Starbucks brought a tarnishment claim against Black Bear Micro Roastery, arguing that the name "Charbucks" damaged its positive reputation. The coffee giant pointed to survey results which showed that (1) 30.5 percent of respondents immediately associated the word "Charbucks" with "Starbucks" and (2) of that group, 62 percent also conveyed an unfavorable view of a coffee named "Charbucks."[55] Some respondents, for example, described the likely flavor of "Charbucks" coffee as "charred," "burnt," "bitter," or "smoky."[56] The Second Circuit explained that "a mere association between 'Charbucks' and 'Starbucks,' coupled with a negative impression of the name 'Charbucks,' was insufficient to establish a likelihood of dilution by tarnishment."[57] Such an association, the court said, does not necessarily mean that consumers view Mister Charbucks or Charbucks Blend in a manner unfavorable to Starbucks.[58] A more important inquiry, according to the court, is the way in which the Charbucks line of products is marketed and the quality attributes of those products. In this regard, the court pointed to the fact that Black Bear Micro Roastery subjects Charbucks to rigorous quality control mechanisms[59] and markets it as a premium line of coffee. Both of these findings run counter to the concept of tarnishment.[60] In the end, the court rejected Starbuck's likelihood of tarnishment claim given that both brands produce very high-quality coffees. This finding alone undercut the principal argument that Starbucks would suffer a negative association as a result of Black Bear's continued use of Mister Charbucks or Charbucks Blend.

DILUTION AND THE FIRST AMENDMENT

The TDRA revised the Federal Trademark Dilution Act of 1995 in two ways that particularly concerned free speech advocates. First, the standard of harm was lowered from actual dilution to likelihood of dilution. This meant that plaintiffs could wage a successful case based on the mere likelihood that the defendant's use would cause dilution of the famous mark rather than a showing of actual dilution. Second, the TDRA specifically included dilution by tarnishment, which protected famous marks from uses likely to cause reputational damage. Free speech advocates pointed out that parody, satire, criticism, and other forms of protected speech were closely linked to tarnishment and that together these revisions could effectively allow plaintiffs to suppress unfavorable uses of their marks.[61] This concern led to the adoption of three separate but overlapping exceptions to the law. Together, they exempt noncommercial speech and news reporting and news commentary from liability as well as provide an expanded fair use defense.

The TDRA's fair use defense was largely intended to quell free speech concerns. To do so, it explicitly includes both nominative and descriptive fair use as well as uses in comparative advertising and for purposes of identification in connection with parody, criticism, or comment. These exceptions, while broad-based in scope, are limited and do not cover uses that function as trademarks. The statutory language expressly bars fair use protection from uses that function "as a designation of source" for the defendant's own goods or services.[62] Thus, a company that intends to poke fun at a famous mark will not be shielded from liability by the fair use exception if its parody of the senior mark is used as a product identifier. This means that Black Bear Micro Roastery, for example, was ineligible for a fair use parody exemption for Mister Charbucks and Charbucks Blend given that the word "Charbucks" was used a source identifier for Black Bear's coffee products.

Three exceptions to a claim of dilution:

1. Use of mark in all forms of news reporting and news commentary
2. Noncommercial use of a mark
3. Fair use, excluding use as source identifier for a person's own goods or services, but including uses in connection with
   a. Comparative advertising or promotion
   b. Parody, criticism, and commentary[63]

While the parody exception is limited, a plush chew toy for dogs was able to evade a dilution charge even though it was named and designed to poke fun at a famous mark. The toy, named Chewy Vuiton, crudely mimicked the design marks, trade dress, and color combinations embodied in a line of Louis Vuitton handbags. The luxury handbag designer sued for dilution by blurring. In its analysis, the Fourth Circuit rejected the fair use exception and focused instead on whether the parodic nature of the use was likely to impair the famous mark's distinctiveness. In its consideration of the six TDRA factors listed earlier, factors two, three, and four were uncontested as both parties agreed that Louis Vuitton Malletier's marks and designs are distinctive, famous, and strong. Instead, the case turned on the degree to which the marks were similar and associated. Here, the simple and unrefined imitation of the LVM design marks effectively lessened the similarly and association between the marks. In effect, the court found that Chewy Vuiton had separated itself from Louis Vuitton to the point where the two sets of marks were only partially and imperfectly related. This allowed the defendant to create a successful parody that would "not blur the distinctiveness of the famous mark." Moreover, the court noted that "a successful parody might actually enhance the famous mark's distinctiveness by making it an icon."[64]

Creating an obvious parody is central to evading a judgment of trademark dilution. For trademark purposes, courts define a parody as a "simple form of entertainment conveyed by juxtaposing the irreverent representation of the trademark with the idealized image created by the mark's owner."[65] To be successful, the parodic work must send two contradictory messages at the same time. In terms of dilution, the objectionable use needs to signal that it is the famous mark and that it is NOT the famous mark but is a parody instead. The latter message is very important in that it needs to not only differentiate the parody from the protected work, but it must also communicate some clear and coherent satirical element.[66] In this case, the court noted that the "strength of the famous mark allowed consumers to immediately perceive the target of the parody, while simultaneously . . . recogniz[ing] the changes to the mark that make the parody funny or biting."[67] Parodic uses of famous marks that may be funny but not biting or where the resemblance is "neither similar nor different enough to convey a satirical message" will fall short of protection under a parody defense.[68]

CHAPTER SUMMARY

Dilution law is not motivated by the same consumer protection goals upon which trademark law was founded. Instead, it protects the goodwill and market power of famous brands from a gradual lessening of the mark's identity in the minds of the consuming public. While only famous marks receive dilution protection, courts have largely reserved the "famous" designation for national brands that have become household names through extensive advertising, publicity, and sales efforts. Armed with the designation, a famous brand has the ability to prevent uses that are likely to impair the mark's distinctiveness through blurring or tarnishment. To wage a successful dilution claim, the owner of the famous mark must demonstrate a degree of similarity between the two marks and that the association is likely to impair the distinctiveness of the famous mark or harm its reputation. Under fair use standards, the TDRA exempts from dilution claims advertising or promotion of a comparative nature as well as parody, criticism, commentary, news reporting, news commentary, and noncommercial uses of the mark.

KEY TERMS

Actual Dilution   Before the enactment of the TDRA, federal dilution law was interpreted as requiring the plaintiff to prove that the defendant's mark actually impaired the plaintiff's mark. This meant that the plaintiff had to show through consumer surveys or circumstantial evidence that the defendant's mark actually decreased the strength and distinctiveness of the plaintiff's mark.

Antidilution Statutes   State and federal laws that allow holders of famous trademarks to sue for commercial uses of a mark or trade name that diminishes the distinctive quality of the famous mark.

Appeals Court   There are thirteen appellate courts in the federal judicial system. These courts sit below the US Supreme Court and above the US District Courts. As intermediate courts, they hear challenges to decisions from federal district courts and federal agencies.

Association   An "association" in dilution law occurs when a substantial percentage of consumers who encounter a junior mark in the marketplace are immediately reminded of the famous mark and associate the holder of the junior mark with the famous mark. An association is established even if consumers do not believe that the goods or services sold under the junior mark come from the famous mark's owner.

Cause of Action   The basis on which a lawsuit is filed. The cause of action gives the plaintiff a right to sue the defendant. The cause of action may be based on a statute, common law, constitutional law, or other sources of law.

Degree of Similarity   Dilution law does not require a high degree of similarity between the defendant's mark and the famous mark. A successful dilution claim can be waged in cases where the degree of similarity between the two marks is less pronounced.

Dilution   Dilution refers to the impairment of a famous trademark's strength and distinctiveness through the mark's use on unrelated goods.

Dilution by Blurring   Dilution by blurring is a type of dilution that occurs when the similarity between the famous mark and the defendant's mark creates an association between the two marks that is likely to impair the distinctiveness of the famous mark. Dilution by blurring can result when a famous mark like Tiffany & Co. is used on an unrelated product like a hotdog stand. The association between Tiffany jewelry and Tiffany hotdogs works to slowly whittle away the distinctiveness and strength of the jewelry brand.

Dilution by Tarnishment   Dilution by tarnishment is a type of dilution that arises when the association between the famous mark and the defendant's mark is likely to harm the positive reputation of the famous mark. Dilution by tarnishment is likely to occur when the famous mark is linked to shoddy, low-quality goods or portrayed in an unwholesome or unsavory context.

Distinctiveness   Distinctiveness refers to the degree to which a trademark evokes the source of the product or service in the mind of the consumer. Distinctiveness is determined by the uniqueness of the text, visuals, and other symbols companies use to identify the origin of their goods or services.

District Court   There are ninety-four district courts in the federal judicial system. At least one is located in each state. US District Courts are general trial courts.

Famous Trademark   Only holders of famous trademarks can sue for trademark dilution. Fame for dilution purposes requires widespread recognition of the mark by the general consuming public. Trademarks deemed famous have become household names.

Federal Trademark Dilution Act of 1995   As the first of two federal anti-dilution statutes, the Federal Trademark Dilution Act extended protection against trademark dilution to the entire country. It was amended in 2006 with the passage of the TDRA.

Junior Mark   The terms junior and senior mark refer to the length of time two trademarks have been registered or used in commerce. Senior denotes the mark that was used or registered first. The junior mark is the mark that followed the senior mark in registration or use.

Lanham Act   A federal law enacted in 1946, the Lanham Act set up a formal system of federal trademark registration and protection. Over the years, the Lanham Act has been expanded and is now the primary and most extensive source of trademark protection in the United States. The Lanham Act is based largely on the consumer protection goals of preventing market confusion and misinformation. However, in 1995, with the passage of the Federal Trademark Dilution Act, the Lanham Act was expanded to include antidilution protection. This addition to the Lanham Act is somewhat controversial in that antidilution law seeks to protect the goodwill and market strength of a brand rather than consumers.

Likelihood of Confusion Standard   Plaintiffs bringing suit for trademark infringement or unfair competition must show that the defendant's conduct is likely to cause consumer confusion as to the source or affiliation of the goods or services. To determine whether a defendant's use of a mark actually created a likelihood of confusion, courts examine a variety of factors. No single factor determines the outcome of the case, and decisions are not necessarily decided by the number of factors that weigh in favor of either party.

Likelihood of Dilution   The TDRA of 2006 altered federal dilution law by lowering the standard of harm the plaintiff needed to prove in order to prevail in a dilution claim. Prior to the passage of the TDRA, a plaintiff needed to establish actual dilution. That standard was changed to likelihood of dilution. Under the likelihood of dilution standard, the plaintiff is not required to show actual or likely confusion, competition between parties, or actual economic injury.

Level of Distinctiveness   Because not all marks are equally distinctive, trademarks are grouped into one of five levels or categories of distinctiveness—that is, generic, descriptive, suggestive, arbitrary, and fanciful. Generic marks receive no trademark protection. Descriptive marks must acquire distinctiveness through proof of secondary meaning. And suggestive, arbitrary, and fanciful marks are inherently distinctive upon inception.

Moseley v. V Secret Catalogue   A US Supreme Court decision that required plaintiffs bringing dilution claims to prove actual dilution. The decision prompted the enactment of the TDRA, which lowered the standard of proof to likelihood of dilution.

Principal Register   The USPTO, which is the federal agency responsible for registering trademarks, maintains two separate registers: the principal register and the supplemental register. Marks listed on the principal register are fully protected in that they meet all the USPTO requirements for distinctiveness. Trademarks the USPTO considers descriptive must prove acquired distinctiveness and are listed on the supplemental register. Once descriptive marks meet all the necessary requirements, they will be placed on the principal register.

Remand   When an appellate court remands a case, it sends the case back to the lower court with instructions for further action.

Trademark Dilution Revision Act of 2006 (TDRA)   The TDRA amended the Federal Trademark Dilution Act in several ways. Most notably was the reversal of the actual dilution standard imposed by the Supreme Court in *Moseley v. V Secret Catalogue*. The TDRA made it clear that plaintiffs need to prove *likelihood* of dilution rather than actual dilution. By lowering the standard of harm, the TDRA made it easier for plaintiffs to establish dilution.

8

False Advertising

In a free-market economy, competition among rivals is celebrated for the positive effects it brings to consumers. From reasonable prices to a diverse array of innovative, quality products, healthy competition is said to be the driving force behind a well-functioning economic system. While competition can create better businesses, it can also prompt rivals to engage in aggressive and deceptive advertising tactics to maintain or increase their customer base and market share. These high-stakes tactics can boil over into full-blown wars where top competitors duke it out through advertising campaigns that take on their primary opponent by name and by claim. From *Samsung v. Apple* to *Coke v. Pepsi*, ad wars are nothing new. One clever shot here, another shrewd shot there and soon an unrelenting back and forth escalates into a barrage of chess-like moves that send ad opponents onto a battlefield where the line between the fair shot and the cheap and potentially illegal shot is drawn. When rivals cross that line, they open themselves up to a charge of **false advertising** and the threat of an impending court challenge.

A BREWING BATTLE

For Anheuser-Busch, its 2019 court battle against long-time rival MillerCoors began with a humorous, but crafty ad set in a medieval world and broadcast to more than one hundred million Super Bowl viewers. The ad opened with the Bud Light King, the Bud Light Knight, and a wizard walking in front of four oversized barrels. Each barrel is labeled with one of four ingredients used in brewing Bud Light beer: "water," "rice," "hops," and" barley." The king turns to the wizard and in an apparent reference to Bud Light beer says, "And that's how you brew it." The camera then pans to a second Bud Light Knight, who enters the picture with another large barrel labeled "corn syrup," and a back and forth between the Knight and King ensues.

"My King," the Knight says, "this corn syrup was just delivered."

"That's not ours," the King replies. "We don't brew Bud Light with corn syrup."

"Miller Lite uses corn syrup," the Knight explains.

"Let's take it to them," the King responds.

And so begins the arduous journey to return the barrel of corn syrup to its rightful owner. The first stop—the Miller Lite Castle, where the Bud King announces: "Oh brewers of Miller Lite, we received your corn syrup by mistake."

"That's not our corn syrup," the Miller Lite King responds. "We received our shipment this morning. Try the Coors Light Castle. They also use corn syrup."

The party moves on and eventually ends up at the Coors Light Castle, where the Bud Light King again announces, "Oh brewers of Coors Light, is this corn syrup yours?"

"Well, well, well," the Coors Light King responds. "Looks like the corn syrup has come home to be brewed. To be clear, we brew Coors Light with corn syrup."

The commercial closes with the image of a perfectly poured glass of Bud Light and the words and accompanying voiceover statement: "Bud Light. Brewed with no Corn Syrup."[1]

In addition to its sixty-second "Special Delivery" ad, Anheuser-Busch ran two shorter but similarly themed ads during the third and fourth quarters of the game. The three ads launched Anheuser-Busch's transparency campaign against MillerCoors, which continued after the game and included additional commercials, print media ads, billboards, and packaging claims notifying consumers that Bud Light contains "no corn syrup" or has "100 percent less corn syrup than [name of either Coors Light or Miller Lite]."[2] Together, these ads conveyed the unmistakable message that Miller Lite and Coors Light use corn syrup as an ingredient in the brewing process of their beers, and Bud Light does not.

While the MillerCoors company did not dispute this fact, it did take issue with the implicit message of these ads, which the company said deceives consumers into believing that the finished Miller Lite and Coors Light products "actually contain corn syrup and thus are unhealthy and inferior to Bud Light."[3] According to MillerCoors, the corn syrup dissipates during the fermentation process. In an attempt to prevent Anheuser-Busch from running these ads, MillerCoors filed a false advertising claim that called on the court to issue an **injunction** that would prohibit its rival from mentioning "corn syrup" in its comparison ads against Miller Lite and Coors Light.

FALSE ADVERTISING LAW

The ability of a competitor to **enjoin** false or misleading advertising stems from the **Lanham Act**'s package of protections for persons engaged in commerce. In addition to its limitations on secondary uses of trademarks and trade dress, the act specifically prohibits commercial advertising or promotion that "misrepresents the nature, characteristics, qualities, or geographic origin" of one's own or another person's goods, services, or commercial activities.[4] Classic false advertising claims, like the one detailed earlier, involve allegedly false or misleading statements about either the defendant's own product or a competitor's product. To wage a successful false advertising suit, federal courts commonly require the plaintiff to establish the following:

1. Defendant made a false or misleading statement of fact about their own or another's products or services.
2. A false statement actually deceives or has the potential to deceive a substantial segment of its audience.
3. Deception is material in that it is likely to influence the purchasing decision.
4. Advertised goods or services involve **interstate commerce**.
5. Plaintiff has been or is likely to be harmed by the false statement—for example, loss of sales or lessening of goodwill.[5]

In its consideration of the MillerCoors, Anheuser-Busch dust-up, the Seventh Circuit said the case was relatively simple because the basic contention that corn syrup is used in the brewing process of Miller Lite and Coors Light is true and openly acknowledged by the Molson Coors Company. While MillerCoors took issue with the implied message conveyed by the advertisements, the court noted that Anheuser-Busch never claimed that Miller Lite and Coors Light *actually contained* corn syrup. Moreover, because MillerCoors chose to list corn syrup as an ingredient on their finished products, their own marketing may elicit the same inference from consumers. With the injunction denied, the court offered Molson Coors the following advice: If the company "does not like the sneering tone of the Anheuser-Bush's ads, it can mock Bud Light in return."[6]

Figure 8.1. The Bud Light transparency campaign prominently lists the ingredients used to brew the beer as well as its nutritional contents. The packaging provoked the ire of MillerCoors when it also featured the phrase "no corn syrup" and an icon that reinforced this message. While the appeals court lifted the restraint on the campaign, "no corn syrup" has yet to reappear on Bud Light packaging.

Photo courtesy of Robert Whitmore

False or Misleading Statements of Fact

Three types of false commercial messages are **actionable**: literally false, literally false by implication and ambiguous, or literally true but misleading. Of the three, the most obvious is a claim that the statement is **literally false on its face**.

Type 1: Literally False on Its Face

Type one statements are provably false as stated. A case in point involved the bottled juice companies Pom Wonderful and Purely Juice. According to the court's fact finding, Pom Wonderful built its reputation as a leader in the premium juice market through an investment of millions of dollars in research that documented and promoted the nutritional qualities and health benefits associated with pure 100 percent pomegranate juice. Through its investment, Pom Wonderful raised the profile of and demand for pomegranate juice. Purely Juice, a competitor of Pom Wonderful, produces a substantially lower-priced pomegranate product that it marketed and labeled as "100% pomegranate juice" with "no sugar added." Concerned with the price difference and industry allegations concerning the purity of the product, Pom Wonderful pursued independent testing of Purely Juice and found that it contained "little or no pomegranate juice," but instead consisted "primarily of cane sugar and corn sweetener." In the end, some seven independent labs, as well as one commissioned by Purely Juice, established that the juice was adulterated.[7] Given these results, the court concluded that Purely Juice's advertising was literally false.

Based on Pom Wonderful's proof of literal falsity, the court assumed that the statements actually misled consumers. This meant that Pom Wonderful did not need to introduce consumer testimonies or marketing surveys, or prove lost profits to establish deception. Moreover, the false claims pertained to the very nature of the juice and as such were deemed **material** in the purchasing decisions. According to the court, materiality was further evidenced by the routine inquiries Purely Juice received regarding the purity and health benefits of its pomegranate juice. Purely Juice's president also admitted in court testimony that the company "would lose its position in the market if it could not label or advertise its product as '100% pomegranate juice' with 'no sugar added.'"[8] These findings, coupled with the dominant wording of the false claims on the bottle and elsewhere, led the court to conclude that the false statements were indeed material.[9] In the end, the Ninth Circuit upheld the **District Court**'s ruling as well as the $2.1 million it awarded to Pom Wonderful in damages, lost profits, and attorney fees and costs.[10]

Type 2: Literally False by Implication

As the previous case denotes, an explicitly expressed false claim is the most direct form of false advertising. As such, courts typically grant **injunctive relief** without requiring the plaintiff to additionally prove that consumers were deceived or misled.[11] But not all false advertising is so obvious. For that reason, some circuits recognize a subcategory of literally false advertising in which an unmistakable false message is implied rather than explicitly stated.[12] Courts refer to this second type of literally false advertising as a false claim expressed by "necessary implication." This type of claim recognizes that consumers routinely draw inferences from ads and remember implied but unstated claims as if they were plainly expressed.[13] When deciding whether an advertisement is **literally false by implication**, courts examine the ad in its entirety. The goal of this examination is to determine the clear-cut claim the audience would easily recognize. While an ad that is literally false by implication does not explicitly express a false statement, the words or images considered in the context of the ad imply an unambiguous false message.[14] This means that advertisements where the words or images are "susceptible to more than one reasonable interpretation" cannot be literally false by implication.[15]

A case involving two television commercials—one literally false on its face and the other literally false by implication—is *Time Warner Cable v. DIRECTV*. In 2006, the satellite service provider DIRECTV aired the commercials to inform consumers that high-definition programming required more than just an HDTV. To receive a high-resolution picture, consumers also needed a service signal that provided enough bandwidth to deliver HD programming. At this time, both Time Warner Cable (TWC) and DIRECTV offered this service for a limited number of channels and, thus, provided the same picture quality when it came to HDTV. Despite these facts, DIRECTV began running two commercials that rival TWC challenged as false advertising. In the first commercial, actress Jessica Simpson, as the character Daisy Duke from the movie *The Dukes of Hazzard*, is talking to some of her customers at the local diner. In the critical lines of the commercial, Simpson says, "You're just not gonna get the best picture out of some fancy big screen TV without DIRECTV. It's broadcast in 1080i." The Second Circuit concluded that these lines made the "flatly untrue" claim "that a viewer cannot 'get the best picture' without DIRECTV." In doing so, it upheld the **lower court**'s determination that commercial one is "likely to be proven literally false."[16]

According to the Second Circuit, the second commercial was as not as straightforward and required more analysis. It opens with William Shatner, as Captain James T. Kirk from the *Star Trek* television and film series, somewhat annoyed by the ship's navigator, Mr. Chekov. Mr. Chekov asks Captain Kirk whether the Starship should raise its defense shields. Captain Kirk turns to the audience and says, "Again with the shields. I wish he'd just relax and enjoy the amazing picture clarity of the DIRECTV HD we just hooked up. With what Starfleet just ponied up for this big screen TV, settling for cable would be illogical."

Mr. Spock then clears his throat, and Captain Kirk responds, "What, I can't use that line?"

The original version ended with the voiceover: "For picture quality that beats cable, you've got to get DIRECTV." After TWC objected to the voiceover, the tag line was changed to "For an HD picture that can't be beat, get DIRECTV" in response to objections by TWC.[17]

In its analysis, the district court considered the advertisement in its entirety and called attention to three particular statements.

1. Kirk's opening comment regarding the "amazing picture quality" of DIRECTV HD;
2. The announcer's closing remark highlighting the unbeatable "HD picture" provided by DIRECTV;
3. The line in the middle that "settling for cable would be illogical."[18]

These three lines, the district court concluded, "clearly referred to cable's HD picture quality." To determine whether the ad unambiguously made the false claim that cable's HD picture quality is inferior to that of DIRECTV's, the district court examined the logic of the advertisement's explicit claims. Since it would only be "illogical" to "settle" for cable's HD picture quality if it was materially inferior to the picture quality provided by DIRECTV, the district court concluded that "TWC was likely to establish that the statement was literally false." DIRECTV took issue with the district court's analysis, arguing that the statement at issue, "settling for cable would be illogical," neither explicitly compared the picture quality of DIRECTV HD with that of cable HD, or mentioned HD at all.[19] On appeal, the Second Circuit was not convinced and pointed to the fact that the preceding line explicitly praised DIRECTV's "amazing picture quality." Taking these lines together as well as the commercial in its entirety, the Second Circuit agreed that it was likely TWC could prove that the ad was literally false by implication.[20]

Type 3: Ambiguous or Literally True but Misleading

The Lanham Act's prohibition on false advertising encompasses more than literal falsehoods. It also covers literally true or ambiguous statements that have a tendency to mislead or deceive the consumer.[21] This third category of actionable statements embraces indirect assertions and ambiguous suggestions.[22] Such claims may implicitly convey a false impression or mislead consumers given their context.[23] Plaintiffs alleging this type of falsehood are "claiming that a statement, whatever its literal truth, has left an impression on the [consumer] that conflicts with reality."[24] Therefore, when bringing a case based on statements that are either **ambiguous or literally true but misleading**, evidence of **actual deception** is critical. This evidence needs to demonstrate that a substantial portion of the audience for the advertisement was actually misled or deceived.[25] This means that plaintiffs will need to engage in the expensive task of conducting and providing consumer survey data that "show[s] how consumers have actually reacted to the challenged advertisement rather than . . . how they could have reacted."[26] Because reactions of the public are typically tested through the use of consumer surveys,[27] the quality of the research can be an issue for the court. Most courts routinely admit surveys conducted according to accepted principles; however, the weight a court affords the survey depends on its technical reliability.[28] Leading or suggestive questions that lack relevancy to the actual marketing conditions are largely disregarded. A case in point involves the "often aggressive and sometimes amusing" Burger Battles.[29]

CKE Restaurant v. Jack in the Box, which pits fast-food chains Carl's Jr. and Hardee's against Jack in the Box, is basically a beef about beef. In two humorous commercials, Jack in the Box pokes some phonetic fun at its rivals' 100 percent Angus burgers. In commercial one, Jack, the fictional, clown-headed CEO of Jack in the Box, is giving a presentation to a group of employees who are sitting around a conference table.

"Listen up," he says. "This is big. We have launched the first 100 percent sirloin burger in fast-food history. Take a look."

At this point, Jack provides the voiceover for a series of images showing the preparation, topping ingredients, and finished version of a perfectly prepared sirloin burger. "That's 100 percent ground sirloin, seasoned while it cooks," Jack says over a shot of a burger sizzling on a grill. "People can choose what kind of cheese and onions they want. But it's the sirloin that has to be tasted to be believed."

"Now for those of you not from Texas," Jack says as he points to a diagram of a cow, "that's the sirloin area."

"Jack, our competitors serve Angus burgers," an employee responds. "Could you point to the Angus area?" he asks, while tracing a small circle in the air with a pen as he says the word "area."

Jack looks behind him at the rear of the cow then turns and faces the employee.

"I'd rather not," he says.

The commercial closes with the words "Sirloin Rules" and the "Jack in the Box" logo.

In the second commercial, the same set of employees laugh every time the word "Angus" is said. Jack tells them to "settle down" and then makes essentially the same new sirloin burger pitch as in commercial one. When he finishes, he faces the group and asks, "Questions?" One employee responds.

"Are you saying that people will find our sirloin more attractive than their Angus . . . es?" he asks as laughter erupts.[30]

The fast-food companies were not amused by the intimation that their 100 percent Angus beef burgers came from the rear end of the cow. "They're not being funny," the chief executive of CKE told the Associated Press. "They need to stop misleading people about what Angus beef is."[31] To obtain an injunction that would prevent the commercials from further distribution, the restaurant group filed a false advertising action arguing that the commercials, while not literally false, were misleading. With that charge, CKE, Hardee's, and Carl's Jr. would need to show that a significant portion of the audience was deceived. To do so, the plaintiffs conducted a pilot survey in four different cities. During the survey, respondents viewed the two commercials and were asked, "Based on the commercials, does Angus beef refer to [1] where on the cow the meat comes from, [2] a type of cattle, [3] neither statement is true, [4] both statements are true, or [5] you don't know?"[32]

While no statistical results were provided, the plaintiffs said the survey showed a "statistically significant number" of respondents believed Angus beef (1) is a cut of meat, not a breed of cattle; (2) is an inferior type of meat; and (3) comes from the "rear-end and/or anus of beef cattle."[33] When it comes to the percentage needed to show that a statistically significant number of consumers are misled, courts recommend 20 percent and above[34] but have accepted 15.5 percent as sufficient.[35] A survey that showed no more than 7.5 percent of viewers were likely misled was rejected. The court in that case commented that a level significantly below 15 percent was problematic and would most likely result in an unsuccessful outcome for the plaintiff.[36]

In the CKE case, the court discounted the survey, saying that the plaintiffs used leading and suggestive questions that did not allow respondents to articulate their own impressions of the commercials. Typically, the court said, consumer perception surveys begin with open-ended questions that permit consumers to identify the primary commercial message or any source of deception. By providing consumers with the suggested response, plaintiffs unfairly framed the survey and increased the likelihood of biased results. Moreover, the wording obscured any evidence that the commercial's Angus message was negated because the consumer understood the joke. These design deficiencies, the court concluded, weakened the survey's relevance and credibility "to the point where it shed little if any light on the issue of likelihood of deceiving consumers."[37]

Deception is Material

The court also was not impressed with the survey evidence when it came to establishing materiality and injury. Here, results showed that 17 percent of consumers were less likely and 14 percent were more likely to buy hamburgers made with Angus beef. The court found these results undermined a showing that the alleged deception was likely to influence a consumer's purchasing decision and harm the two fast-food restaurants.[38]

As this case indicates, it is not uncommon for courts to equate materiality with a finding of injury given the logical connection between a consumer's purchasing decision and harm to the plaintiff. Courts will often presume materiality if the objectionable statement falsely represents the essential characteristics, nature, or quality of the advertised product or service.[39] Such statements may misrepresent an important part or characteristic that defines the product; is central to its marketability; impugns its features; or relates to its identity, desirability, or substitutability.[40] Claims relating to health, safety, and price are particularly problematic and are often "treated as virtually *per se* material because of their obvious potential effect on purchasing decisions."[41] In the same vein, courts also have held that the element of materiality may be presumed from a literally false claim.[42] In such cases, courts reason that a literally false claim is likely to affect sales given that it was made by a knowledgeable advertiser who is in a position to know the validity of the advertisement as well as its sales-related effect on the audience.[43]

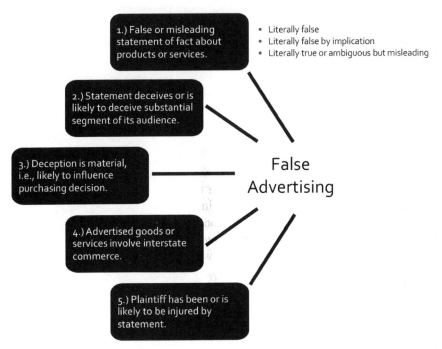

Figure 8.2.

Likelihood of Injury

The Lanham Act allows "any person who *believes* that he or she is or is likely to be damaged" by a false or misleading advertisement to file a case.[44] Courts have interpreted the word "believes" as meaning something more than the litigant's personal view of the situation. This means that a plaintiff must demonstrate more than a mere subjective belief of likely harm to establish a valid claim, but is not required to show an actual quantifiable loss to bring a case. That said, the type of evidence needed to establish injury varies depending on case facts and whether monetary damages or injunctive relief is sought.

In cases where the statements are ambiguous or literally true but misleading, plaintiffs seeking monetary damages need to prove actual deception whereas those seeking injunctive relief need to show that the statements have a tendency or **likelihood to deceive** consumers.[45]

The lower standard for injunctive relief is appropriate given that the plaintiff is arguing that the company will likely suffer irreparable harm if the advertising continues. In cases where the parties are competitors, irreparable harm may be established by showing a "logical causal connection between the alleged false advertising" and the manner in which the plaintiff's brand is positioned in the market.[46] A causal connection can be established with sales data, consumer testimony, survey evidence of consumer confusion, or the correlation between the defendant's advertising campaign and consumer use of plaintiff's product.[47] This standard may change when a statement is literally false, the parties are competitors, and the advertising claim is comparative in nature. In such cases, some courts presume harm given that a "misleading comparison to a *specific competing product* necessarily diminishes that product's value in the mind of the consumer."[48]

Puffery Defense

Preventing an allegedly false or misleading advertising statement from reaching consumers certainly inhibits both the speaker's right to engage in commercial speech and the public's right to receive information. Even so, courts rarely consider the chilling effect of such an injunction on a commercial speaker. Instead, they point to the lack of First Amendment protection for false or misleading commercial speech[49] and the narrow scope of the Lanham Act, which limits false advertising claims to false or misleading descriptions or representations of *fact*.[50] Fact-based assertions on which consumers rely to make a purchasing decision form the basis of a false advertising claim. Such statements differ from expressions of opinion in that they are specific and measurable and can be proven true or false.[51] Broad-based, subjective statements, on the other hand, are incapable of such measurement and are, thus, nonactionable. The distinction between statements of fact and expressions of opinion is important in that it allows commercial speakers to make general assertions of superiority without running afoul of the law. Courts refer to these types of opinion-laden statements as **puffery**.

Puffery is often described as either an exaggerated, boastful statement upon which no reasonable buyer would justifiably rely or a vague, generalized claim of superiority that is commonly understood as nothing more than a mere expression of opinion.[52] Consumers recognize puffery in such slogans as "America's Favorite Pasta,"[53] "The Best Beer in America"[54] or "The

Earth's Most Comfortable Shoes."[55] Puffery can also be found in vague terms such as "natural fit,"[56] "durable," "manufactured to high quality standards" and "maintenance free."[57] While puffery can be dismissed as simple sales talk, its placement within an ad campaign can turn a mere boast into an actionable statement.

A case in point involves Papa John's slogan "Better Ingredients. Better Pizza." As a stand-alone slogan, the court reasoned that the phrases "Better Ingredients" and "Better Pizza" taken separately or combined were unquantifiable, generalized statements of opinion regarding the product's perceived superiority over all others. In this form, the slogan constitutes "typical puffery." In its reasoning, the court honed in on the word "better" and the question of "what makes one food ingredient 'better' than another comparable ingredient?" Without additional information, the court said, it is "wholly a matter of individual taste or preference not subject to scientific quantification." Words like "better," "best," and "greatest" fall into a class of terms that lack a measurable definition. In its analysis of Papa John's slogan, the court found it "difficult to think of any product, or any component of any product, to which the term 'better,'" without some additional explanation, is quantifiable.[58]

In its case against Papa John's, Pizza Hut argued that the additional explanation the court needed could be found in Papa John's national marketing campaign. The campaign revolved around a series of comparative ads that made several assertions regarding the food quality of Papa John's competitors. In particular, the ads compared Papa John's sauce and dough with that of its competitors. The ads claimed that Papa John's sauce tasted better because it was made from "fresh, vine-ripened tomatoes" that were canned through a process called "fresh pack," while its competitor's sauce was made from remanufactured tomato paste. When it came to the dough, Papa John's stressed that it was made with "clear filtered water," while the "biggest chain" uses "whatever comes out of the tap." Papa John's also compared its yeast, which has "several days to work its magic," to that of its competitors who use "frozen dough or dough made the same day. Each of these ads was punctuated with the slogan "Better Ingredients. Better Pizza."[59]

While Pizza Hut did not challenge the truthfulness of these assertions, it did provide independent taste tests and other scientific evidence that showed no discernable quality difference between the two sets of ingredients. Papa John's, on the other hand, did not present any support or properly conducted taste tests that showed its ingredients and methods were superior to Pizza Hut's. Based on the evidence before it, the court concluded that the sauce and dough ads were not only misleading but also gave the otherwise nonactionable slogan a fact-based meaning. Considered in its entirety, the court found that the ads conveyed the following message: "Papa John's uses 'better ingredients,' which produce a 'better pizza' because Papa John's uses 'fresh- pack' tomatoes, fresh dough, and filtered water."[60]

Through the slogan's inclusion in the ad, Papa John's effectively gave the word "better" a definition. Used in this context, the words "better ingredients" and "better pizza" become statements of fact that could be proven true or false. Here, the evidence presented showed that the claim was in fact misleading as the difference in ingredients had no detectible effect on taste or food quality. This prompted the court to conclude that the slogan standing alone was puffery, but when used with the sauce and dough ads, it had a specific, measurable meaning that was misleading and actionable. In the end, however, Pizza Hut lost its case on the issue of materiality as it failed to establish that the misleading facts conveyed by the slogan affected the purchasing decisions of consumers.

CHAPTER SUMMARY

The Lanham Act's package of protections includes protection against false advertising by competitors. To wage a successful false advertising suit, a plaintiff typically is required to show that the defendant made a false or misleading statement in a commercial advertisement and that the statement is likely to deceive and the deception is likely to influence the purchasing decisions. Three types of false claims are actionable: advertising that is literally false; a false claim that is implied rather than explicitly stated; and advertising that is ambiguous or literally true but intends to mislead or deceive the consumer. The Lanham Act bases false advertising claims on misrepresentations of fact. Such statements differ from expressions of opinion in that they are specific and measurable and can be proven true or false. The distinction between fact and opinion is important in that it allows commercial speakers to make general assertions of superiority without running afoul of the law. Courts refer to these types of opinion-laden statements as puffery. While exaggerated claims, or puffery, may be recognized by consumers as simple sales talk, its placement in an advertising campaign can turn a mere boast into an actionable statement.

KEY TERMS

Actionable Actionable statements furnish the grounds for a legal action. In false advertising law, there are three types of statements that are actionable: literally false, literally false by implication, and ambiguous or literally true but misleading. Puffery, by contrast, is nonactionable.

Actual Deception   A standard of proof in false advertising cases that requires the plaintiff to show that a substantial portion of the audience for the advertisement was actually misled or deceived. Evidence of actual deception is critical in cases involving statements that are ambiguous or literally true but misleading. Actual deception can be established through consumer surveys that demonstrate how consumers actually perceived the advertisement.

Ambiguous or Literally True but Misleading   Ambiguous or literally true statements are a type of false commercial message that is actionable. These advertising claims have the ability to mislead or deceive the consumer with indirect assertions and ambiguous suggestions. Such claims may implicitly convey a false impression or mislead consumers given their context. When bringing a case based on statements that are either ambiguous or literally true but misleading, evidence of actual deception is critical.

District Court   US District Courts are general trial courts. As such, findings of fact and law are first determined in the district court.

Enjoin   To legally prohibit or stop a party from doing something by means of a court order.

False Advertising   False advertising is advertising that is untrue, deceptive, or misleading. The Lanham Act specifically prohibits commercial advertising or promotion that "misrepresents the nature, characteristics, qualities, or geographic origin" of one's own or another person's goods, services, or commercial activities.

Injunction   A court order that commands a party to carry out a particular act. In false advertising law, injunctions are commonly sought to prevent the defendant from disseminating an allegedly false or misleading commercial message.

Injunctive Relief   Injunctive relief is a type of legal remedy for an alleged wrongdoing. Injunctive relief is commonly sought in false advertising suits when the plaintiff wants the defendant to stop running an advertisement or ad campaign. Injunctive relief may be pursued in place of or in addition to monetary damages.

Interstate Commerce   Interstate commerce refers broadly to goods and services that move across state lines, serve customers from out of state or impact the interstate movement of goods or services. The US Constitution gives Congress the power to regulate interstate commerce in order to maintain the free flow of trade among the states.

Lanham Act   A federal law enacted in 1946, the Lanham Act set up a formal system of federal trademark registration and protection. Over the years, the Lanham Act has been expanded and is now the primary and most extensive source of trademark protection in the United States. The Lanham Act is based largely on the consumer protection goals of preventing market confusion and misinformation. It exists alongside state statutes and common law unfair competition.

Likelihood of Deception   A standard of proof in false advertising cases that requires the plaintiff to show that the advertisement has the potential to deceive a substantial portion of the audience. Survey evidence that demonstrates how consumers actually reacted to the advertisement is not required to establish likelihood of deception.

Literally False by Implication   Literally false by implication is a type of false commercial message that is actionable. Advertising claims that fall into this category unmistakably imply a false message rather than explicitly state it. Some courts recognize this type of false advertising given that consumers routinely draw inferences from ads and remember implied but unstated claims as if they were plainly expressed.

Literally False on Its Face   Literally false on its face is a type of false commercial message that is actionable. These types of messages are provably false as stated. For example, a manufacturer that falsely claims that an item was "made in America" when it was made in another country.

Lower Court   There are three levels of judicial review in the federal court system: (1) Trial or District Courts, (2) Appellate or Circuit Courts, and (3) the US Supreme Court. Cases begin at the trial level and can be appealed to the intermediate level and upon writ of certiorari to the US Supreme Court. In this way, courts are often referred to in terms of their authority to review another court's decision. The term lower court refers to the court whose decision is being reviewed.

Material   In false advertising law, material refers to the significance of the false or misleading claim on a consumer's purchasing decision. A deceptive claim that is found to be material means that it is likely to influence the purchasing decisions of consumers, whereas false claims that are immaterial will not.

Puffery   Puffery refers to exaggerated, boastful statements upon which no reasonable buyer would justifiably rely or vague, generalized claims of superiority that are commonly understood as nothing more than a mere expression of opinion. Because these broad-based, subjective statements are incapable of being proven true or false, they are nonactionable.

9

Libel and Privacy

The American idea of freedom of speech has long carved out an exalted space for wide-open debate on public issues. Public discussion, uninhibited by regulation, is highly valued in the American system for its ability to produce results that are wiser, more useful, and more desirable than outcomes generated in speech-restrictive environments. While these benefits are widely acclaimed in First Amendment law, they go hand in hand with the realization that robust debate may also produce unpleasantly sharp and inaccurate attacks on the reputations of public and private individuals. In *New York Times v. Sullivan*, the US Supreme Court tackled the collision between reputational interests and the nation's profound commitment to the vigorous exchange of ideas. What followed was a series of opinions that dramatically shifted the balance of power from one that favored reputational interests to one that provides a level of free speech protection against libel claims that is largely unmatched throughout the world.[1]

NEW YORK TIMES V. SULLIVAN

Surprisingly, one of the most consequential free speech decisions in modern times began with a paid editorial advertisement placed in the *New York Times* on March 29, 1960. The ad, titled "Heed Their Rising Voices," described the alleged mistreatment of civil rights protesters by government authorities in Montgomery, Alabama, as it sought financial support for student activists, right-to-vote efforts, and a legal defense fund for Dr. Martin Luther King Jr.[2] Even though no government official was named in the advertisement, L. B. Sullivan, an elected commissioner in Montgomery who supervised the police department, brought a defamation suit against the *Times* in state court, seeking $500,000 in damages.

In the United States, **defamation** refers to a false statement of fact that harms a person's reputation. A written or published form of defamation is called **libel**. With the right to file a lawsuit for defamation in state court, four other officials, including the governor of Alabama, also charged the *Times* with libel, which brought the total amount of damages for running the advertisement to $3 million.[3] More libel suits were generated by the paper's reporting on the civil rights movement. In total, the paper was facing $5.6 million in damages from eleven suits filed by Alabama officials for the paper's news coverage. These suits prompted the distinct possibility that the *New York Times*, which was emerging from a labor dispute, would not survive.[4] Alarmingly, the *Times* was not alone. By the time the Sullivan case reached the US Supreme Court, multiple news organizations were at risk from the nearly $300 million in libel actions brought by Southern officials against the press.[5]

These suits were particularly ominous because libel law, at the time, was thought to lie outside the boundary of First Amendment protection. Instead, the law was fashioned by each state through legislation or **common law**. Under Alabama law, Sullivan was set to win. Even his attorney acknowledged the long shot of a loss, claiming that "'[e]ither I will win the case or they will change the law of the land.'"[6] The long odds stemmed from the ease of which plaintiffs could prove their case. At this time, individuals bringing suit were required to show that the defendant published a defamatory statement about the plaintiff. Sullivan pointed to two particular paragraphs in the ad. One denoted the truckloads of armed police that ringed the Alabama State College and the other referenced the arrests of Dr. King. Sullivan contended that as a city commissioner he was identified by these statements, and that the statements tended to lower his reputation in the community. Sullivan argued that the advertisement defamed him even though he admitted during the trial that he had not been ridiculed or shunned by anyone as a result of the ad. In the end, Sullivan's lack of proof of reputational harm did not dissuade the judge from declaring that the statements were indeed libelous. Under Alabama law, statements judged to be libelous per se were also presumed to be false and injurious, and since the advertisement contained factual errors, the *Times* could not raise the defense of truth.[7] As a result, the jury brought forth a verdict for Sullivan, which the Alabama Supreme Court affirmed on appeal.

The outcome of the US Supreme Court case *New York Times v. Sullivan* was stunning. In a 9-0 opinion, the High Court set in motion one of the most seismic shifts in First Amendment law by bringing the weight of the US Constitution to bear on a state's judgment in a libel suit. In doing so, the decision overturned two hundred years of libel law and knocked down the argument that the Constitution does not protect libelous publications. Specifically, the court took on the idea that false statements of fact that tend to injure a public official's reputation were beyond the reach of the First Amendment. In the opinion, the court viewed injury to an official's reputation as an outgrowth of the public's right to criticize official conduct. The court noted that criticism of "official conduct does not lose its constitutional protection merely because it is effective" at diminishing one's reputation. As for falsehoods, the court found that errors are inevitable in free debate and must be protected in order to provide a safe space that gives individuals the assurances they require to actively engage in the national discussion. Based on the conclusion that both injury to reputation and factual error lie within the confines of the First Amendment, the court reasoned that the combination of the two also receives constitutional protection.[8]

Fortified with the constitutional strength of the First Amendment, the court severely curtailed a public official's ability to win a libel suit. In doing so, the court mandated that to recover damages for a defamatory falsehood relating to official conduct, a public official must prove that the statement was made with "actual malice"—that is, with knowledge that the statement was false or with reckless disregard of the truth. This demanding standard effectively requires a plaintiff to show that the defendant knew a story was false or had serious doubts about its accuracy and chose to publish it anyway. In applying this standard to the facts of the case, the court concluded that the evidence did not support a finding of actual malice even though the *Times* published the advertisement without checking it against its own news stories. According to the court, the mere presence of stories that would have exposed the inaccuracy of the ad did not establish that the *Times* knew the advertisement was false.[9]

In the end, the court held that Alabama's state law of defamation was constitutionally deficient in that it failed to provide safeguards for freedom of speech and freedom of the press. Going forward, the court would bring the First Amendment to bear on other elements of defamation law and, thereby, reshape state law. Despite the court's efforts, differences still exist among the states with regard to defamation, and, thus, it is important for communication professionals to review state law. This chapter focuses on the basic elements of a libel claim that largely transcend state borders.

ELEMENTS OF A LIBEL CLAIM

Defamation is an all-encompassing legal term that denotes the communication of a false statement of fact about the plaintiff that inflicts reputational harm. The transmission of a defamatory statement to a person who is neither the defendant nor plaintiff can be categorized as either **slander** or libel. In general, slander refers to spoken, interpersonal conversation whereas libel is much broader and includes multiple forms of published material, such as audio, video, film, radio, or television, in addition to traditional written or printed communication.

Who can sue? Any living person can bring a claim for libel. Libel litigation is also available to corporations and nonprofit organizations. However, individuals who are deceased at the time of publication as well as governments and government agencies cannot bring a suit. When bringing a suit, the burden of proof lies with the plaintiff, who needs to establish the basic elements of a libel claim listed next.

1. Publication
2. Identification
3. Defamation
4. Falsity
5. Fault
6. Injury

Publication

The distribution of an allegedly defamatory statement does not need to be widespread to establish publication. In fact, it usually takes only a single person—a so-called **third party**—to constitute an audience large enough for publication to occur. As one might expect, publication is rarely at issue in cases involving the media. That said, publication is important in establishing reputational injury, which, generally, can be traced to a discrete statement that occurred at an identifiable moment in time.[10] Even in cases where the allegedly defamatory statement is publicly accessible for a lengthy period of time, reputational injury needs to be linked to a distinct publication.[11] Thus the date of publication is an important factor in setting the time frame in which a plaintiff can bring a lawsuit. While states may vary in how they calculate the exact date of publication, in general **publication** occurs when the statement is made available to its intended audience. Depending on the state, a plaintiff may have from one to three years to bring a suit.

Tracing a reputational harm back to a particular statement in a discrete publication raises the question of how many lawsuits may arise when the publication containing the statement is widely distributed. In most states, the answer is one. To avoid excessive damage awards and unnecessary strain on the judicial system, the **single publication rule** was adopted. This rule limits damages based on any single issue of a widely circulated publication to one **cause of action**. This means that the plaintiff must recover the totality of the injuries arising out of the discrete publication in one claim. This rule applies to television and radio broadcasts as well as online content. That said, the **republication** of the defamatory statement opens the defendant up to a separate lawsuit with a new time frame under which a claim may be filed.

Republication

Because a defamatory statement is published when it is first made available to the public, it is generally considered to be republished when it is repeated or recirculated to a new audience. Examples include a statement that is rebroadcast later the same day, reprinted in a new edition of a book, or repackaged years later in a "remember when" series. In determining republication, courts also examine whether

1. The subsequent publication is distinct from the original.
2. Modifications were made to the form or content of the statement.
3. The defendant controlled the decision to republish.[12]

Applying these factors to online platforms can be difficult, and questions have emerged whether a republication occurs each time a web page is viewed. In an approach that has been followed by other jurisdictions, a New York appellate court ruled that a defamatory statement published on a website is not republished every time a user accesses it via a hyperlink.[13] While case law is still evolving with regard to online publications, courts have held that providing easy access to already published content through hyperlinks and "share" buttons is not considered republication.[14] The same conclusion has been reached for minor modifications to a website that do not significantly alter or add to the defamatory statement.[15] However, substantive changes or updates to hosted content are likely to trigger a republication as is the redirection of the published statement to a new audience.[16]

Under the republication rule, a person who repeats a defamatory statement is responsible for the reputational damage it causes. This means that when media publish defamatory quotes, letters to the editor, or advertisements, they are legally responsible even if the statement is attributed to the original source and expressly refuted in the publication.[17] That said, the extent to which users of social media who retweet or share content created by a third party are liable remains to be determined. Some legal experts have argued that **Section 230** of the **Communications Decency Act** of 1996 (CDA) provides at least some protection in these cases given that the act shields **online service providers** from **liability** for **user-generated content**. Specifically, the act states that "[n]o provider or user of an interactive computer service shall be treated as the publisher or speaker of any information provided by another information content provider."[18] Under Section 230, social media sites, websites, and blogs are immune from liability for defamatory content unless they are "responsible, in whole or in part, for the creation or development of [that] information."[19] Although Section 230 promises broad protection for online content, the full extent of its reach is unclear. This is especially notable with regard to retweeting, sharing, and the republication of user comments and social media posts in stories.[20]

In *La Liberte v. Reid*, the defendant relied on Section 230 in her motion to dismiss a defamation complaint stemming from her social media activity. The complaint involved a photo taken during a session break at a city council meeting. The plaintiff was prominently pictured in what looked like a confrontation between her and a fourteen-year-old boy. Three days after it was taken, the photo appeared in a tweet above the following description:

> "You are going to be the first deported" [and] "dirty Mexican" [w]ere some of the things they yelled they yelled [sic] at this 14-year-old boy. He was defending immigrants at a rally and was shouted down. Spread this far and wide this woman needs to be put on blast.

A day later, MSNBC host Joy Reid retweeted it to her approximately 1.24 million followers, and the tweet went viral. She also posted the photograph to her Instagram account with a caption that attributed the racial slurs to the plaintiff. Reid wrote:

> He showed up to rally to defend immigrants. . . . She showed up too, in her MAGA hat, and screamed, "You are going to be the first departed" . . . "dirty Mexican!" He is 14 years old. She is an adult. Make the picture black and white and it could be the 1950s and the desegregation of a school. Hate is real y'all. It hasn't even really gone away.

That same day, the fourteen-year-old boy disputed the notion that the plaintiff was shouting at him. In an interview on a local news program, the youth said that he felt like the plaintiff was "trying to keep" the interaction "civil," which he appreciated.[21] Two days later Reid published a second post with a similar theme about La Liberte but deleted both posts and apologized to the plaintiff on social media the following day upon learning of the inaccuracy.[22] Despite the apology, a lawsuit ensued.

Reid argued that she was immune from liability under Section 230 for the subsequent posts on Instagram. The court disagreed. Section 230's immunity applies only if the user is not also responsible in some way for the creation or development of the content at issue in the case. Courts applying the CDA consider whether the

1. Defendant is a provider or user of an interactive computer service.
2. Claim is based on information provided by another content provider.
3. Claim treats the defendant as the publisher or creator of the information.

Even though Reid's use of Instagram makes her a user of an interactive computer service, the fact that she authored the information was problematic. According to the court, the altered content in the Instagram post changes Reid's status to an **information content provider** rather than a user of an online service. As a content creator, the court ruled that Reid was not shielded from liability by the CDA.[23] Although this case did not address the question of whether a user who simply retweeted a post would be protected by Section 230, it does provide caution to online users who routinely alter social media content when retweeting and sharing it.

Anonymous Sources

Some of the most vile and hateful online comments come from anonymous speakers. For those targeted by such content, a defamation claim may provide some relief if the unknown poster of the information can be identified. Unmasking a speaker, however, presents its own legal hurdles. First is Section 230. Since the CDA provides social media sites, blog hosting companies, and other online service providers broad immunity from liability for user-generated content, the very companies that can identify the poster or remove the damaging material are under no obligation to do so. The second roadblock is the freedom to publish anonymously. The idea that one has the right to engage in anonymous speech dates back to the **Federalist Papers**—a set of nameless essays that advanced the ratification of the US Constitution.[24] Given the prominent role this freedom has played in the formation of the United States, the right to publish anonymously has been highly extolled and presents a significant barrier to **unmasking** the identity of a speaker.

While the weight of the First Amendment interest in such a scenario is significant, it is not insurmountable. A plaintiff who is willing to aggressively pursue the case may take advantage of a variety of court-created tests designed to balance the reputational interests of the plaintiff against the speech rights of the defendant. While the exact approach will differ among states, the elements listed next are followed by most states.

Notification:

- The plaintiff is required to make a reasonable effort to alert the anonymous poster that he, she, or they is the subject of a **subpoena** or application for disclosure. With regard to online speech, this may include sending a private message to the poster's account and publicly posting a message to the internet service or message board hosting the objectionable statements.
- Courts may also require the plaintiff to delay further action in order to give the poster a reasonable amount of time to respond. This allows the defendant to seek representation and formally oppose the motion in court while remaining anonymous.

Establishing a Valid Claim:

- The plaintiff is required to provide sufficient evidence to support each element of a libel claim.[25] In *Doe v. Cahill*, for example, the Supreme Court of Delaware explained that a public figure plaintiff must prove that the

  1. Defendant made a defamatory statement;
  2. Statement concerned the plaintiff;
  3. Statement was published;
  4. Character of the statement would be understood by a third party as defamatory;
  5. Statement is false; and
  6. Defendant made the statement with actual malice.

To compel disclosure, the *Cahill* court recognized that a plaintiff need only prove facts that are within his or her control. Because it would be "difficult, if not impossible," to show that an unknown defendant made the statements with actual malice, the court held that a public figure must only offer evidence on elements one through five.[26]

- An additional step may be required by some courts in establishing a valid claim for disclosure. This step requires the plaintiff to first identify the exact statements made by the anonymous poster that are alleged to be defamatory.[27] Other courts consider this unnecessary given that the plaintiff must also produce evidence to support all the essential elements of the claim.[28] Regardless of whether this extra step is required, the goal here is to determine whether the plaintiff has a strong case.

Balancing the Results:

- Courts may also take the additional step of balancing the First Amendment implications of unmasking the defendant against the strength of the plaintiff's evidence and the need for disclosure to properly proceed with the libel claim.[29] In doing so, some courts have considered the level of protection the speech actually receives under the First Amendment.[30] Other courts, however, contend that the steps outlined above are sufficient to balance the two interests.[31]

In 2009, fashion model Liskula Cohen brought a successful disclosure action against Google that forced the tech giant to identify a blogger who attacked Cohen on a website under the company's control. The site, http://skanksnyc.blogspot.com, displayed photos of Cohen along with captions and commentary that described her as "skanky" and a "ho," and included other such "malicious and untrue" characterizations that disparaged her "appearance, hygiene and sexual conduct." Cohen argued that the blog impugned her chastity and shed a damaging light on her professional career. As a result, she intended to bring a libel claim but needed the identity of the blogger to do so.

The blogger in turn argued that the words "skank" and "ho" constituted loose and vague insults that are commonly used on the internet and network television as "trash talk." As such, no reasonable online user would view the expressions as a statement of fact referring to Cohen, and, thus, the court should consider these words protected opinion or hyperbole. For its part, the court turned to the *American Heritage Dictionary*, which defines "skank" as "one who is disgustingly foul or filthy and often considered sexually promiscuous" and "ho" as slang for prostitute.[32] Based on these definitions as well as the context in which they appeared, the court ruled that the words were capable of a defamatory meaning and ordered Google to provide Cohen with the name of the blogger. As it turned out, Cohen knew the blogger and eventually filed a $3 million libel suit against the blogger before dropping it.[33]

Identification

At the heart of defamation is the claim that a false statement lowered an individual's reputational standing in the community. As a result, individuals bringing libel suits must be clearly identifiable in the statement to pass this threshold element. In cases where the plaintiff is clearly named or pictured, identification is relatively easy to prove. It becomes more challenging, however, when the statement refers to a particular group of which the plaintiff is a member, and the plaintiff claims identification is based on that reference.

Group Libel

In cases of **group libel**, courts tend to favor claims where the group consists of twenty-five or fewer members, but have allowed claims involving fifty-three members to proceed. In addition to size, courts also consider the degree to which the "statement impugns the character of all or only some of the group's members."[34] For example, a report that falsely indicates that one or two members of a sizable group are corrupt would not directly implicate each individual member of that group. On the other hand, a report that indicates that all but one of the members are corrupt may well negatively implicate each member of the group. Lastly, the prominence of the group in relation to the size of the community may also come into play. A case that illustrates these points is *Elias v. Rolling Stone.*

At issue in *Elias v. Rolling Stone* is whether members of the Phi Kappa Psi (PKP) fraternity at the University of Virginia can plausibly show that alleged defamatory statements in the article "A Rape on Campus: A Brutal Assault and Struggle for Justice at UVA" were "of and concerning" the plaintiffs. The article, which was published in November 2014, described the violent sexual assault of a first-year student named Jackie by seven members of the PKP fraternity in fall 2012. While the article did not directly identify Jackie's attackers, it did indicate that they were PKP members who graduated in 2013. Moreover, the article identified Jackie's date the night of the alleged attack by the pseudonym "Drew." Drew allegedly escorted Jackie to a party at the fraternity and invited her to a large upstairs bedroom where the attack took place.

The story also revealed that Jackie and Drew met while working as lifeguards at the university pool. Plaintiffs George Elias and Ross Fowler, who were PKP members at the time and graduated in 2013, argued that these facts linked them directly to the defamatory allegations. Elias pointed to the fact that in fall 2012 he lived in the only upstairs bedroom that fit the article's description of the room where the alleged rape took place. Fowler, who was active in the rush process during 2011–2012, regularly swam at the

UVA aquatic center where Jackie was purported to have met and encountered Drew on multiple occasions.[35] Together, they argued that readers could plausibly identify them by the specific statements concerning these facts, and the court agreed.

Moreover, the plaintiffs argued that the article defamed each member of PKP, which at the time totaled fifty-three, in that it implied or expressly stated that fraternity members committed rape as a condition of initiation or knew that others did so.[36] The court noted that given the sufficiently small number of PKP members coupled with the allegations in the article, a "reader could plausibly conclude that many or all fraternity members participated in alleged gang rape as an initiation ritual and all members knowingly turned a blind eye to the brutal crimes."[37] This conclusion was furthered by the small size of the university community and PKP's prominence on campus. According to the court, "a plaintiff is more likely to succeed under a theory of small group defamation in small communities where individual members are readily associated with the defamed group."[38]

Libel in Fiction

Identification is also a key element in cases involving a fictional character that is based on and closely resembles an actual person. These cases arise when the fictional character is depicted in a manner that is both very similar to and very different from the plaintiff. In the case *Greene v. Paramount Pictures*, Andrew Greene, a former employee at the "notorious" brokerage house Stratton Oakmont, claimed that he was identified in the movie *The Wolf of Wall Street* through the character Nicky "Rugrat" Koskoff.[39] Greene argued that the likeness, image, and portrayal of Koskoff is so similar to Greene that people watching the movie would recognize Koskoff as Greene.[40] The movie, which is based on a memoir by Jordan Belfort, the firm's co-founder, provides a lurid account of the degenerate behavior and criminal activity that Belfort claims occurred at Stratton Oakmont during the 1990s.

While the screenplay closely tracks the storyline of the memoir, the film also contains dramatized elements and invented "characters, characterizations, incidents, locations and dialogue."[41] One composite character is Koskoff, who is depicted as a close friend of Belfort who went to law school and was involved in corporate finance at Stratton Oakmont.[42] In the movie, Koskoff is repeatedly mocked and called "Rugrat" for the "piece of shit hairpiece" he wears.[43] Greene argued that these descriptors fit him as well. In the memoir, Greene "is described as Stratton's lawyer and Belfort's 'old and trusted friend.'"[44] Like Koskoff, Greene is incessantly ridiculed and called "Wigwam" for what Belfort referred to as "the worst toupee this side of the

Iron Curtain."[45] Given these similarities, individuals who saw the movie and knew Greene testified that they believed Koskoff was Greene.

In **libel in fiction** cases, identification may be established when a reasonable person who knows the plaintiff would have no difficulty linking the character to the plaintiff.[46] Courts have noted that mere superficial similarities like name, occupation, age, and vague physical characteristics, such as "attractive" or "athletic," are insufficient to prove identification. Instead, courts look for distinct characteristics like a special birthmark, specific fashion accessory or hairstyle, or unique manner of performing work,[47] and consider the degree to which the plaintiff and character are dissimilar. In cases where the dissimilarities are profound, even a host of resemblances, such as "name, physical height, weight, build, incidental grooming habits and recreational activities," have been viewed as insufficient to prove identification.[48] That said, the sheer number of shared details can also be a factor in identification.

In *Smith v. Stewart*, the fictional character shared at least twenty-six biographical details with the plaintiff, including "going to the same high school, having daughters, having their first husbands die from a car accident, becoming engaged to men who owned nursing homes in Florida and were engaged to other women, and being awarded $750,000 in divorces from their second husbands."[49] In addition, they were both chain-smoking redheads with a smoker's cough and a timeliness problem.[50] These similarities, the court concluded, immediately linked the plaintiff to the fictional character.[51]

As for *The Wolf of Wall Street*, the defendants argued that even if Greene shares some superficial similarities with Koskoff, Koskoff is a fictional character who incorporates elements of Elliott Loewenstern, another childhood friend of Belfort's and one of the first people to work at Stratton Oakmont, and Gary Kaminsky, a toupee-wearing chief financial officer who worked for a company that used Stratton Oakmont's corporate finance services, as well as Greene.[52] Because Koskoff is a composite character, the defendants said readers of the memoir would not immediately connect him to Greene.[53] The problem for the court, however, was that the movie is based on a true story and, thus, it was plausible that individuals familiar with the fraudulent activity at the firm and Greene's association with the company could reasonably connect the Koskoff character with the plaintiff.[54] The defendants took steps to disassociate actual associates of the firm with the composite characters by running a disclaimer with the closing credits. The disclaimer acknowledged that the film was based on actual events but that certain characters and aspects of the movie were fictionalized for dramatic purposes and "not intended to reflect on an actual character, history, product or entity."[55]

While a disclaimer will not shield a defendant from a libel claim or prevent individuals from linking the character to a real person, it is recommended in fictional works based on actual events and people. Here, the court cited the disclaimer as one of five factors that showed the defendants neither knew nor acted with reckless disregard for whether their portrayal of Koskoff would be viewed as "of and concerning" Greene. In addition to the disclaimer, the court pointed to the fictionalized nature of the film; the dissimilarities between Koskoff and Greene, which included a different name and nickname as well as distinctions in their employment; personal and criminal histories; and a good faith belief among the defendants that viewers would not perceive Koskoff as depicting any real person. Given the lack of evidence to the contrary, Greene's libel claim failed.[56]

Defamation

At the core of every libel claim is a word or a set of words that form a statement about the plaintiff. To be actionable and thus constitute the grounds of a libel suit, the communication at issue must be capable of conveying a **defamatory meaning**. Statements that fall into this category tend to expose an individual to public ridicule, hatred, or contempt, or otherwise injure a person's reputation in the minds of a considerable and respectable segment of the community. Determining whether a statement is actually defamatory involves both the judge and jury. The judge initially decides whether the statement *could* reasonably be interpreted as conveying a defamatory meaning. This is the court's first attempt to separate **actionable** from **nonactionable** statements. In doing so, the statement is evaluated in context as a reader or viewer would experience it. The goal here is to discern the statement's natural effect on the audience rather than any isolated meaning the words may have. Claims that fail this step are dismissed, whereas those that survive are viewed as potentially defamatory and eventually presented to the jury. It is then up to the jury to ultimately decide whether the statement actually conveys a defamatory meaning.

Nonactionable Statements

In addition to reputational injury, a defamatory communication must state actual facts about the plaintiff that can be proven false. This means that (1) truthful statements; (2) statements that do not damage the reputation of the plaintiff; and (3) statements that no reasonable person would interpret as stating actual facts about the plaintiff are nonactionable. Statements that fall into the last category lack a readily understandable meaning and may contain exaggerated language, name calling, imaginative expression, and other types of **rhetorical hyperbole**. Phrases such as "creepazoid attorney," "loser wannabe lawyer,"[57] "snake oil job," "lazy, stupid, crap-shooting, chicken-stealing idiot," and "he's dealing with a half deck"[58] were found to be nondefamatory because they could not reasonably be interpreted as stating actual facts.[59] When determining whether a statement is an expression of fact or rhetorical hyperbole, courts examine the words used and the context in which they were published. Because the totality of the statement is evaluated, exaggerated language delivered in the context of a heated debate may be interpreted as nonactionable even if it could be verified as true or false. A case in point is *Clifford v. Trump.*

The factual roots of this case began in 2011 when Stephanie Clifford allegedly agreed to speak to a magazine about her intimate relationship with Donald J. Trump. A few weeks later, an unknown man purportedly approached and threatened her and told her to "Leave Trump alone" and "Forget the story." In 2018, after Trump was elected president of the United States, she publicly disclosed the threat along with a sketch of the unknown man. In response, Trump tweeted: "A sketch years later about a nonexistent man. A total con job, playing the Fake News Media for Fools (but they know it)!"[60] Clifford claimed and the court agreed that the tweet contained two verifiably true/false statements. First, that the unknown man does not exist, and, thus, Clifford is lying about her encounter with him. Second, that Clifford is engaging in a "con job," which the court clarified as Clifford "is lying to Mr. Trump, the public and the media about the threat (and by implication her affair with Mr. Trump)." The court noted that if the man does exist or if Clifford is not lying about the threats and the affair, then the tweet would be verifiable as false.

In its analysis, the court labeled the tweet "rhetorical hyperbole" based on its incredulous tone, the politically adversarial nature of Clifford's actions, and the fact that the tweet was a one-off comment and not a sustained attack on Clifford and her claims. The court ruled that President Trump is entitled to respond in a strongly worded fashion against a political adversary. To rule otherwise, the court noted, would hamper the president's ability to respond aggressively to Clifford and other political adversaries without triggering a libel action.[61]

Because the tweet was deemed rhetorical hyperbole, it constituted a form of nonactionable expression protected by the First Amendment even though it contained factual assertions. By focusing on the hyperbolic language and tone and the context in which the statement was made, the court brought the tweet into the protected realm of opinion-filled exchanges. In this realm, statements of **pure opinion** are protected by the First Amendment and generally immune from liability in libel cases. The thinking here is that pure opinion cannot be proven true or false. It's simply an opinion. For example, referring to someone as a "real tool" was considered pure opinion by a Minnesota court because the phrase could not be interpreted as a statement of fact that could be proven true or false.[62]

In addition to rhetorical hyperbole and pure opinion, courts recognize a third category of opinion-based statements. Sometimes referred to as a mixed expression of opinion, this category recognizes statements of opinion based on an implied knowledge of undisclosed facts. Take, for example, the statement that "Jane Doe is an alcoholic." If this opinion is based entirely on disclosed or otherwise known nondefamatory facts, reasonable readers of the statement are able to decide for themselves whether the opinion is justified. In such a case, the opinion is seen as "pure" and protected no matter how unjustified or unreasonable it is.[63] However, if the basis for this opinion is not stated or otherwise presumed, reasonable readers may conclude that the allegation is based on undisclosed defamatory facts.[64]

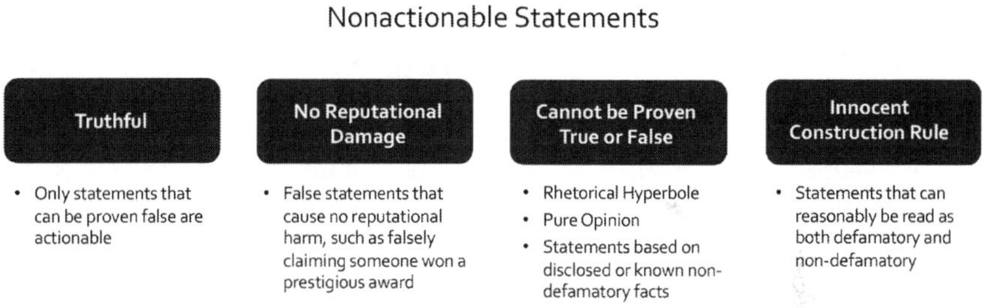

Nonactionable Statements

Truthful	No Reputational Damage	Cannot be Proven True or False	Innocent Construction Rule
• Only statements that can be proven false are actionable	• False statements that cause no reputational harm, such as falsely claiming someone won a prestigious award	• Rhetorical Hyperbole • Pure Opinion • Statements based on disclosed or known non-defamatory facts	• Statements that can reasonably be read as both defamatory and non-defamatory

Figure 9.1.

Depending on the context, this statement may now imply that the author knows of and based the opinion on a set of unidentified facts that could be proven true or false. In this type of situation, the opinionate statement becomes actionable. Whether such a statement actually implies a factual allegation is a matter for the courts. Given the complexity of language and the varying contexts in which these statements can be presented, it's a difficult task for courts to distinguish between assertions of fact and the expressions of opinion.[65] In 1984, the DC Circuit Court grappled with this complexity in *Ollman v. Evans* and outlined the four-part **Ollman test** to assist courts in evaluating whether a reasonable person would view a mixed expression as fact or protected opinion.[66] The factors, while not universally applied, have been adopted by many courts.

The Ollman Test

Courts may consider the following four factors when distinguishing a statement of fact from opinion:

Factor 1—Specific Language Used: *Does the common usage or meaning of the specific words used in the allegedly defamatory statement have a precise, commonly understood meaning or are the words indefinite and ambiguous?* In most contexts, vague or loosely definable statements are unable to support a libel claim.

Factor 2—Verifiability: *To what degree is the statement capable of proof or disproof?* As indicated earlier, an unverifiable statement cannot rationally be viewed as conveying actual facts and is thus nonactionable.

Factor 3—General Context: *How does the full context of the statement inform its meaning?* This may well include, for example, the entire article, blog, or Twitter thread. In distinguishing opinion from fact, reasonable readers are influenced by the totality of the work in which the statement is presented. That said, it is good to remember that opinion does not receive a blanket exemption from libel law. This means that a communicator will not avoid liability for a false assertion simply by using the words "I think" or "In my opinion" or labeling the piece "opinion."[67]

Factor 4—Social Context: *How does the broader social context or setting in which the statement appears inform its meaning?* The thinking here is that different types of communication have widely varying social conventions and customs that signal to the media consumer that what is being consumed is likely to be opinion and not fact.[68]

The four-factor Ollman test does not always provide a clear answer to the question of whether a statement is an actionable fact or nonactionable opinion. The Sixth Circuit wrestled with this problem in a case involving a tweet by actor James Woods and a photograph of a woman at a rally for Republican presidential candidate Donald Trump. In the photograph, the woman was wearing a Trump t-shirt and giving a Nazi salute with her right hand. Woods tweeted the photograph alongside a photograph of Portia Boulger, a supporter of Democratic presidential candidate Bernie Sanders. Woods's tweet included a short biography of Boulger and the following question: "So-called #Trump 'Nazi' is a #BernieSanders agitator/operative?" In response to the tweet, Boulger received death threats, obscene messages, and numerous phone calls. Woods eventually deleted the tweet after receiving a letter from Boulger's attorney and posted three subsequent tweets clarifying that the woman at the rally was not Boulger and asked his followers to stop harassing her.[69]

Despite the retraction, Boulger filed suit. Woods argued that the tweet was a question and, thus, could not constitute a false statement of fact. The court, however, was unwilling to hold that words stated in the form of a question are in and of themselves nonactionable opinion. Instead, the evaluation centered on the interpretation of the statement by a reasonable reader. Here, the court found that that the tweet could be read as both an actionable insinuation that the woman was Boulger and as a nonactionable question. This conclusion rendered factors one and two inconclusive. Moving to the context factors, the court found that Woods's use of Twitter showed that he posted news articles that were frequently accompanied by colorful commentary, and, thus, the general context could lead reasonable readers to conclude the tweet was not a statement of fact. But, when it came to the broader context and how the medium was likely to influence the reader's viewpoint, the court found that because Twitter is both a medium to express opinions and disseminate news, factors three and four did not clearly favor either party.[70]

The deciding factor for the court was the **innocent construction rule**. This rule covers statements that can reasonably be read as conveying both a defamatory and an innocent meaning. In such cases, the rule mandates that the innocent construction prevails. Because Woods's tweet could reasonably be read as an assertion that Boulger was the woman giving the Nazi salute as well as a question to his followers, the innocent meaning won out, and the tweet was ruled nonactionable opinion.[71]

Actionable Statements

Because not all false statements of fact are equally as damaging to the plaintiff, many states recognize two types of defamation. The first type is **libel *per se***. Libel *per se* consists of words that are inherently damaging to an individual's reputation. For example, describing someone as a "drug dealer," "slumlord," or "rapist" is considered by many states to be libelous on its face given the obvious reputational harm such words would cause. To qualify as libel *per se*, the published statement traditionally falls into one of the following four categories:

1. Illegal Behavior.
2. Loathsome Disease. While the term "loathsome" is outdated and disfavored by some courts, the category remains relevant in that portions of society lack the understanding of certain diseases, and, as a result, may shun or discriminate against those who suffer from a contagious condition.[72]

3. Professional Incompetence. This category includes statements indicating that a person acted improperly, engaged in misconduct, exhibited
incompetence, or lacked integrity in relation to one's official duties,
occupation, trade, profession, or business.
4. Sexual Misconduct or Unchaste Behavior.

False assertions that fall within these categories warrant particular care
among communicators as they are assumed to harm a person's reputation.
This means that damages may be awarded in cases of libel per se without
proof of actual injury.

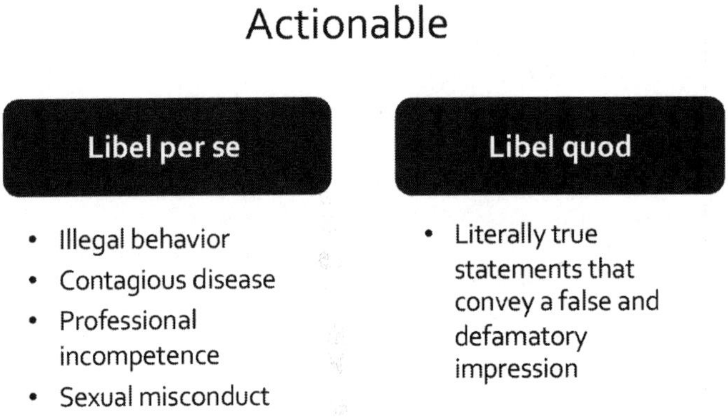

Actionable

Libel per se	Libel quod
• Illegal behavior • Contagious disease • Professional incompetence • Sexual misconduct	• Literally true statements that convey a false and defamatory impression

Figure 9.2.

Not all defamatory statements are noticeably damaging on their face. As
a result, some states recognize a second type of defamation called **libel *per
quod***. Libel *per quod* or libel by implication covers statements that, while
literally true on their face, convey a false and defamatory impression. These
statements may be actionable if given the surrounding circumstances, they
communicate a defamatory inference to others. A case in point involves a
school system's response to the heartbreaking death of a seven-year-old girl
with a severe peanut allergy. After ingesting a single peanut during recess,
the child developed hives and shortness of breath and eventually stopped
breathing while a clinic aide was trying to help her.[73] The tragic death
received widespread local, national, and international media coverage that
included several statements by school officials. Those statements served as
the basis of a defamation suit filed by Laura Pendleton, the child's mother.

In the lawsuit, Pendleton claimed that school officials falsely implied and
insinuated that she failed to provide proper emergency medical information

and medication for her daughter. Pendleton said she not only informed school staff of her daughter's medical condition but also filled out a confidential school emergency health plan that was signed by the girl's pediatrician. The plan directed the school to administer Benadryl and an auto-injection of Epinephrine if the child came in contact with certain allergens, including nuts. Pendleton also said that she attempted to provide the school with an EpiPen Jr. for use in an emergency, but the school's clinic assistant told her to keep the injectable at home.

Contrary to Pendleton's efforts, the official school response stressed the parent's responsibility in "provid[ing] the school with accurate, timely information; a health emergency plan . . . and the medicine necessary to execute the plan." In media interviews, school staff emphasized the role of the parent in "keeping their child safe at school" and linked the execution of the emergency plan to "the parent's ability to inform the school of needs and to provide the appropriate resources." In an email message to concerned parents, the assistant superintendent of schools said that when these "resources are not available, execution of the plan cannot be continued." He added that the school "welcomes medication" and that EpiPens "are not prohibited." In another response to a worried parent, the chair of the school board wrote that the school system "relies on our parents to follow through and provide whatever is prescribed by the doctor." And that while trained professionals at the school "have the best interests of [the] students in mind," they "can only be effective if a parent provides information, doctor-prescribed health plans and the medicines necessary to carry out those plans. Unfortunately," she said, "this does not always occur." In a final article, the director of community relations was quoted as describing the first grader's death as a "wake up call" for parents.[74]

On appeal, the Virginia Supreme Court was tasked with determining whether the statements could reasonably be interpreted as insinuating that Pendleton failed to inform school authorities of her daughter's condition and furnish them with an emergency plan and medications. In cases involving libel *per quod*, the defamatory meaning is not apparent from a literal reading of the statements at issue. Therefore, to establish a valid claim, the plaintiff needs to show that the "circumstances surrounding the making and publication of the statement . . . would reasonably cause the statement to convey a defamatory meaning to its recipients."[75]

Here, the court noted that the statements were published as part of extensive news coverage in which Pendleton was widely identified and, thus, publicly known. In this environment, school officials were asked to comment on Pendleton's side of the story. In doing so, school officials described their response as an effort to "correct misinformation." This effort, they added, was hampered by privacy laws. In this context, the court said, "a fair and just inference would be drawn" that Pendleton's version of the story was "misinformation" and that school authorities were unable to fully express the true version given their obedience to privacy laws. For their part, the school officials argued that their statements were true and that "truth is a defense to a defamation claim." The court took issue with this argument. The statements, the court said, "may be true if taken out of context." Under the circumstances in which they were published, however, the court found that the statements were "capable of conveying the defamatory innuendo" that Pendleton was responsible for her child's death.[76]

Falsity

In addition to proving that the speech at issue is capable of conveying a defamatory meaning, the plaintiff also shoulders the burden of showing that the damaging statements are false. This burden is particularly weighty for public figures. In libel law, the term "public figure" refers to politicians and government officials who exert control over public affairs; celebrities and media personalities; business leaders; and others who have placed themselves in the public sphere and actively court media attention. Plaintiffs who fall into the public figure category have the extra burden of proving falsity in all libel cases. In contrast, plaintiffs who have not thrust themselves into the public eye and are, thus, considered private figures are required to show falsity only in cases where the speech at issue is of a "public concern." Although "public concern" is not a well-defined concept, courts have recognized speech relating to legitimate news issues or topics of political, social, or community interest as matters of public concern.[77] Courts have extended the falsity requirement to private figure plaintiffs in these cases given the long-held belief that the public must be free to engage in robust debate on local and national issues without fear of reprisal.[78]

When proving falsity, plaintiffs must present clear and convincing evidence establishing that the defamatory statement is false. That said, an alleged defamatory statement does not need to be literally true in every detail to be nonactionable truth. It only needs to be substantially true. **Substantial truth** is a defense in libel law that allows the defendant to argue that while errors did occur, the gist of the statement is true. Under this defense, minor factual errors will be ignored as long as the facts conveying the "sting" of the defamation are justified. For example, the false report that an animal trainer beat his orangutans with a *steel* rod when in fact he beat them with a *wooden* rod was ruled to be substantially true. The court found that the composition of the rod was immaterial because the damage to the trainer's reputation came from the accurate fact that he beats his animals with a rod, not that he beats his animals with a *steel* rod.[79]

The substantial truth defense acknowledges that reputational damage is the crux of a libel action. A claim for libel, therefore, is not valid unless injury to reputation is established. This means that if the inaccuracies in the alleged defamatory statement do not inflict harm on the plaintiff's reputation, the libel claim will fail. In this vein, the substantial truth defense also acknowledges that an alleged defamatory statement is no more damaging to the plaintiff's reputation in the minds of the average person than the truth. In the case of the animal trainer, the truthful statement (that he beat the orangutans with a wooden rod) is just as damaging to the trainer's reputation as the false statement (that he beat the orangutans with a steel rod).

Because substantial truth takes into account the reputation a plaintiff has merited, courts have recognized that a person, whose reputation is so diminished at the time the allegedly defamatory material is published, may not be capable of sustaining further reputational injury. Such individuals are deemed **libel proof** as a matter of law. Whether a plaintiff is considered libel proof depends on the nature and extent of their antisocial or illegitimate conduct and the degree and range of publicity they have received as a result. In general, plaintiffs viewed as libel proof have reached the point where their reputation for a particular behavior or honest and fair dealing is so low in the minds of the public that they are basically unable to incur any meaningful reputational damage.[80] In these circumstances, burdening a defendant with a libel claim seems pointless.[81]

Deputy General Counsel of the *New York Times*, David E. McCraw, evoked this area of libel law in his response to a letter from lawyers representing presidential candidate Donald J. Trump. On behalf of candidate Trump, the attorneys demanded a retraction for a *Times* story titled "Two Women Say Donald Trump Touched Them Inappropriately." McCraw responded with his own sharply worded letter in which he called to mind the libel-proof plaintiff doctrine. The pointed part of the letter began by stating the obvious—that a libel claim rests on the contention that a published statement actually "lowers the good reputation of another in the eyes of his community." McCraw continued by citing a set of publicly known facts regarding Trump's behavior toward women, including his boastings about "non-consensual sexual touching of women" and "intruding on naked beauty pageant contestants in their dressing rooms." The paragraph ended with a summation of what it means to be libel proof. "Nothing in our article," McCraw wrote, "has had the slightest effect on the reputation that Mr. Trump, through his owns words and actions, has already created for himself." He closed by reminding those to whom it was addressed of the principles upon which libel law is built.

"It would have been a disservice," he wrote, "not just to our readers but to democracy itself" if the *Times* would have silenced the voices of the women who were quoted in the story. "We did what the law allows: We published newsworthy information about a subject of deep public concern." In the end, the matter was dropped.[82]

Fault

No other element of libel is more difficult to prove than the **actual malice fault standard**. The **fault** standard was added to the elements by the land-mark case *New York Times v. Sullivan* and has since created an imbalance in law that distinctly favors the interests of news organizations over the efforts of the individuals who want to sue them. By all accounts, the actual malice rule is an extraordinary legal standard that has both its devotees and its detractors. For their part, media interests praise the safeguards it confers on journalists in their quest to pursue tough and, at times, contentious investigations,[83] while plaintiff attorneys decry the stamp of approval it bestows on sloppy, inaccu-rate, and negligent reporting.[84] Regardless of where one stands, actual malice imposes a barrier that is hard for a plaintiff to scale.

As defined in *Sullivan*, the actual malice standard requires plaintiffs to pro-duce clear and convincing evidence that shows that the defendant published the defamatory material (1) knowing it was false or (2) acting with reckless disregard for the statement's truth or falsity. In this regard, the standard focuses on the defendant's actual state of mind at the time of publication, and thus takes into consideration the reporting, editing, and fact-checking phases of a story's development. While plaintiffs may use circumstantial evi-dence to establish actual malice, past cases show that a mere finding that the defendant failed to investigate a claim or departed from journalistic standards does not rise to the level of reckless disregard for the truth. Likewise, ill will or an intent to injure in and of itself is insufficient to prove actual malice.[85] Reckless disregard requires more than a departure from reasonably pru-dent conduct.[86] Instead, the plaintiff must present convincing evidence that the defendant entertained serious doubts as to the truth of the publication.[87] Serious doubts may be established, however, where the reliance on anony-mous or unreliable sources is coupled with a failure to investigate further.[88] Similarly, actual malice may be found in situations where there are obvious reasons to question an informant's veracity or where the defendant set out to conform the evidence to a preconceived storyline.[89]

Given the obstacles to proving actual malice, the Supreme Court has ruled that only public figures are saddled with this burden. This means that states are left to decide the fault standard for private figures, which may vary from negligence to actual malice. In states that recognize a lower fault standard for private figures, the categorization of the plaintiff is critical and may mean the difference between proving that the defendant actually had a high degree of awareness that the statement was false or that the defendant failed to exercise a reasonable level of care in publishing the statement. The latter is the **negligence standard**, and while no definitive list of what constitutes negligence exists, the standard typically measures the defendant's conduct against what a reasonable person would or would not have done under the same or similar circumstances.[90]

Under the negligence standard, a libel defendant is expected to make a good faith effort to verify the truth or falsity of the communication before publishing it. Some factors that may be considered in determining whether a defendant was negligent include

- Number of identifiable sources
- Credibility of those sources
- Whether the plaintiff was given an opportunity to respond
- Efforts to check and recheck incriminating allegations
- Accuracy and care exhibited in the reporting and verification process
- Degree to which professional standards and practices were followed

Public Figure Status

The status of the plaintiff is determined by the court, and involves a choice between a **private figure** and three general categories of public figures: public officials, all-purpose public figures, and limited-purpose public figures.

A **public official** is a government employee who holds a position of authority and whose qualifications and performance are of interest to the public. Individuals who are elected to public office are considered public officials as well as those who have a "substantial responsibility for or control over the conduct of governmental affairs."[91]

All-purpose public figures are those whose fame or pervasive power and influence reach widely throughout society. Their status as an all-purpose public figure means that the actual malice standard will be applied to virtually any libel claim they initiate.

Limited-purpose public figures are individuals who either voluntarily thrust themselves into the forefront of a pre-existing public controversy in an attempt to influence the outcome or were drawn into such a controversy and became a public figure for a limited range of issues. These individuals are required to prove actual malice given their heightened access to the media and their voluntary exposure to injury from media coverage.[92]

In determining whether a plaintiff is a private person or a limited-purpose public figure, courts consider whether the public controversy existed prior to the publication of the statement, and the plaintiff voluntarily assumed a prominent role in the controversy; sought to influence its outcome or resolution; had access to effective channels of communication; and retained public-figure status at the time of the alleged defamation.[93] In a high-profile libel suit between an associate dean of students at the University of Virginia and *Rolling Stone* magazine, the court applied these factors and concluded that Associate Dean Nicole Eramo warranted the limited-purpose public figure status.

Eramo's case began with the publication of the article: "A Rape on Campus: A Brutal Assault and Struggle for Justice at UVA." The 2014 article centered on the false narrative of an alleged gang-rape of a UVA student the story referred to as "Jackie" and the university's response to Jackie's allegations. According to the complaint, the article cast Eramo as the "chief villain of the story" by claiming that she was indifferent to Jackie's allegations, discouraged Jackie from sharing or reporting the alleged incident, and told Jackie that UVA withholds rape statistics "because nobody wants to send their daughter to the rape school."[94]

In determining Eramo's public figure status, the court first defined the scope of the controversy. Through a "fair reading" of the entire article, the court concluded that the controversy focused on the university's response to the allegation of sexual assault. Eramo, the court said, warranted public figure status in this regard given her past and present access to and use of student-run and local broadcast media, which was greater than that of a private individual and included numerous, and at times in-depth appearances. Moreover, Eramo used this access to discuss such topics as the university's process for handling sexual assault complaints, thereby indicating that the university's response to such allegations was a part of a controversy that existed prior to the publication of the *Rolling Stone* article.[95]

Encumbered with the public figure status, Eramo faced the challenge of proving actual malice. At a minimum, actual malice requires plaintiffs to show by clear and convincing evidence that the defendant made the statements with reckless disregard for the truth. *Rolling Stone* argued that the circumstantial evidence Eramo presented was insufficient to do so. The court, however, was not convinced. Instead, it found that the evidence Eramo offered suggested that Sabrina Rubin Erdely, the article's author, pursued a preconceived storyline and may have consciously disregarded contradictory evidence; had reasons to doubt Jackie's credibility but failed to further investigate her allegations; disregarded claims from at least three individuals who countered the story's portrayal of Eramo; and harbored ill will for Eramo or was intent on injuring the administration.[96] In addition, this evidence was bolstered by an editor's note appended to the article three weeks after it was published. The note publicly acknowledged that the story's allegations had been questioned[97] and that after subsequent internal conversations and discussions with outside sources the magazine's trust in Jackie was misplaced. Taken as whole, the court said, a jury could conclude that the statements concerning Eramo were made with actual malice.[98]

As the case headed to trial, a 2015 report by the Columbia University Graduate School of Journalism was entered into evidence.[99] The report was commissioned by *Rolling Stone* in an attempt to find out what went wrong with the story and to publicly acknowledge any mistakes. To do so, the magazine cooperated fully with the trio of scholars who were assigned to "investigate any lapses in reporting, editing and fact-checking behind the story."[100] The reviewers—all experts in the field of journalism—had access to a 405-page record of interview and research notes as well as original audio recordings and various drafts of the nine-thousand-word story.[101] Moreover, they were given the freedom to "investigate and write about any subject related" to the story that they thought was "germane and in the public interest."[102]

The report that resulted was damning. The investigators labeled the story a "journalistic failure that was avoidable." "Basic, even routine journalistic practices" involving "reporting, editing, editorial supervision and fact-checking" were compromised as the "magazine set aside or rationalized as unnecessary essential practices" of information gathering, including verification, source identification and diversification, and editorial scrutiny and skepticism.[103] While the investigation cleared Erdely of any charges of fabrication, it found that she relied heavily on the narrative Jackie weaved, failed to independently vet its accuracy, and declined to pursue important reporting paths.[104] Shortly after its release, the magazine retracted the story.

The details unearthed by the report were referenced multiple times in Eramo's complaint and used to establish the fact that Erdely had "serious doubts about Jackie's credibility" during a follow-up conversation with Jackie one week after the article was published. According to the complaint, "Erdely admitted to being continuously bothered by Jackie's refusal to identify" the ringleader of her assault, and "admitted to being 'worried about the integrity of her story.' She also knew she needed to do additional investigation because of these concerns. Erdely discussed her loss of confidence in the integrity of her story with her editors at *Rolling Stone*, who thus also had serious doubts as to the truth of the article."[105]

At trial, the judge instructed the jury that reckless disregard of the truth could be established if the defendants "entertained serious doubts as to the truth of the publication" and then failed to investigate. Given the evidence, which included the Columbia School of Journalism report, the jury found that the defendants' actions were egregious enough to constitute actual malice with regard to statements alleging that Eramo was unresponsive to Jackie's claims.[106] As a result, the jury awarded Eramo $3 million in damages. The parties eventually reached a confidential settlement that headed off an appeal.[107] Interestingly, the judge and jury found that the editor's note appended to the story three weeks after it was initially published constituted a republication. Jury result forms showed that the jurors did not find the magazine liable for the initial publication but determined that it operated with actual malice in the republication.[108]

Scholars contend that Eramo's ability to scale the largely insurmountable actual malice standard was likely aided by the transparent public accounting of *Rolling Stone*'s editorial and reporting failures.[109] In this regard, the Columbia report, which laid bare the magazine's disregard for even basic journalistic standards as well as the editor's note posted months earlier may have been a gift to Eramo. That said, the level of transparency and public accountability that *Rolling Stone* was willing to endure through its commission of the report was laudable. It is unfortunate that an investigation, which was intended to shed light on why the editorial process failed and what could be learned from it, was, in the end, used to scale the high barrier of the *Sullivan* standard.

INVASION OF PRIVACY

Unlike libel law, which protects an individual's reputation against false assertions of fact, privacy rights are intended to protect a person's dignity. As a dignity-based law, invasion of privacy only applies to living persons. While privacy is a broad-based concept, this chapter covers two areas of privacy that are triggered at different stages of the communication process. One, intrusion upon seclusion covers information-gathering techniques and two, publishing private facts involves the publication of truthful information. Both of these laws came together in a documentary television show, titled *On Scene: Emergency Response.*

The case, *Shulman v. Group W. Productions*, involves an automobile accident in which a mother and her son were injured when the car in which they were riding flew off the highway, tumbled down an embankment into a drainage ditch, and came to rest upside down. Ruth and Wayne Shulman were pinned under the car when a rescue helicopter arrived with a medic, flight nurse, and camera operator. While the camera operator roamed the scene filming the rescue efforts, Laura Carnahan, the nurse, recorded her conversations with Shulman and others through a wireless microphone she was wearing. The video and audio recordings were eventually edited into a nine-minute segment that aired on a reality television show.

In the segment, Shulman appeared several times. Each time her features were blocked by others or obscured by an oxygen mask or only brief shots of a limb or her torso were shown. In the broadcast, Carnahan refers to Shulman by first name and picks up audio of her as she is being freed from underneath the vehicle. Carnahan explains to Shulman that she will be airlifted to the hospital. "Are you teasing?" Shulman responds, adding, "This is terrible. Am I dreaming?" Later, as Shulman is being loaded into the aircraft, she says, "I just want to die." Although Carnahan reassures her that she is "going to do real well," Shulman repeats, "I just want to die. I don't want to go through this."[110]

Once the helicopter door is closed, a voiceover narration explains that in flight, the medical crew will "update the patients' vital signs and establish communications with the waiting trauma teams" at the hospital. Carnahan is then heard transmitting some of Shulman's vitals and explaining that she "cannot move her feet and has no sensation." Video footage inside the helicopter shows a few seconds of Shulman's face covered by an oxygen mask. After the aircraft lands on the roof of the hospital, Shulman can be heard saying, "My upper back hurts" and "I don't feel that great." As she is moved into the hospital, a voiceover tells viewers that Shulman will be evaluated further and may receive emergency surgery if need be, ending with, "Thanks to the efforts of the crew of Mercy Air, the firefighters, medics and police who responded, patients' lives were saved." The segment then concludes with the following written epilogue: "Laura's patient spent months in the hospital. She suffered severe back injuries. The others were all released much sooner."[111]

Shulman, who was left a paraplegic by the accident, was shocked when she saw the broadcast and filed a lawsuit against the production company for **intrusion upon seclusion** and **public disclosure of private facts**.

Intrusion Upon Seclusion

Intrusion punishes an unwarranted and intentional encroachment into a private place, conversation, or matter in a manner that is highly offensive to a reasonable person. Activities include an unconsented physical intrusion into a home, hospital room, or other place of privacy. Gathering information from an individual's private records or computer or with the use of highly sensitive, powerful audio/visual equipment may also constitute intrusion. To establish an intrusion case, the plaintiff must first establish that a reasonable expectation of privacy in a place or activity exists and that an intrusion into that privacy occurred.

The privacy one expects can vary greatly depending on the physical place occupied and the activities in which a person is engaged. Normally, for example, a limited expectation of privacy exists in public places. In such a space, it is reasonable to conclude that one's privacy is impacted by what others can see and hear. The degree of privacy may also vary within a fairly secluded space, like a locker room, depending on one's activities within that space or may be necessary only for a specific undertaking. In one case, a performer expected privacy in a curtained backstage area in order to discipline his orangutans before bringing them out on stage.[112] In this way, the extent to which a person's privacy can be protected is limited under intrusion laws.

In Shulman's case, she would have two contrasting expectations of privacy depending on whether she was at the accident site or in the helicopter. At the accident scene, one would expect journalists to be present, gathering information, shooting photographs, and capturing the scene through standard audio/video equipment. In this regard, Shulman's privacy expectation is limited. The same does not hold true for her time in the helicopter, her conversation with Carnahan, and her medical information. Here, the expectation of privacy is much greater. In the helicopter, Shulman could reasonably expect that a member of the media would not be physically present. She could also expect that her conversations with Carnahan at the accident site and after landing and her medical information would not be amplified, recorded, and accessed by the defendants. According to the court, Shulman's conversation with an emergency medical provider in the course of treatment "carries a traditional and legally well-established expectation of privacy."[113]

To present a valid intrusion upon seclusion claim, the plaintiff must show

1. A reasonable expectation of privacy or seclusion in a place, activity, or information
   a. Courts assess the degree of privacy expected in the place, activity, or information
   b. For example, what a passerby can see and hear
2. Defendant intentionally intruded into plaintiff's privacy in a way a reasonable person would find highly offensive or beyond the limits of decency.

After establishing that an intrusion into a private affair occurred, the plaintiff needs to show that a reasonable person would find the defendant's action highly offensive. In determining offensiveness, courts may consider the following factors:

- Context and setting of intrusion
  - *Where did the intrusion take place?*
  - *How private was the place?*
  - *Could bystanders observe what the defendant observed?*
- Conduct and circumstances surrounding the intrusion
  - *How intrusive was the defendant's action?*
  - *Did the intrusion involve force or disruptive conduct by the defendant?*
  - *Did the defendant's conduct violate law?*
- Intruder's motives and objectives
  - *Why did the alleged intrusion take place?*
- Expectations of those whose privacy is invaded
  - *Why was privacy expected?*

In Shulman's case, the court took issue with the setting and conduct surrounding the intrusion. Particularly, the act of placing a microphone on an emergency treatment nurse to intercept a private conversation between a "distressed, disoriented, and severely injured patient" and the medical personnel who were trying to care for her. In that setting, the court found that a reasonable person could rationally conclude that the defendants took deliberate advantage of the patient's "vulnerability and confusion." Arguably, the court said, the last thing an accident victim should need "to worry about while being pried from her wrecked car is that a television producer may be recording everything she says to medical personnel for the possible edification and entertainment of casual television viewers." While the defendants pointed to their newsgathering motives to validate their behavior, the court concluded that the pursuit of the "real sights and sounds of a difficult rescue" did not justify the use of these extreme reporting techniques.[114]

In the end, the newsworthiness of the information was no match for the depth of the intrusion. The court reminded the defendants that newsgathering activities generally receive no special degree of First Amendment protection or immunity from generally applicable laws. However, when it comes to the publication of truthful information, even truthful private information, the tables are turned. Here, the critical element is the presence or absence of a legitimate public interest in the facts disclosed. In cases where the published material is of legitimate public concern, a private fact claim will most likely fail.

Public Disclosure of Private Facts

A private fact case involves widespread publicity of an intimate or highly personal matter. The truthful information at issue in a case is more than

just embarrassing. It is truly private and has not been revealed publicly
by the plaintiff or through public documents. This means that the plaintiff
must show that the information was private before its public disclosure.
Information disclosed to only a few close friends or family members is likely
to be considered private. Private facts typically relate to financial matters,
medical information, domestic difficulties, sexual activities, or similar intimate facts. In addition to the privacy of the matter, the plaintiff must demonstrate that third parties would link the offending disclosure to the plaintiff.
Use of the plaintiff's full name, clear photograph or first name, and some
detailed personality traits will usually fulfill this requirement. Identification
most likely will not be established by a mere reference to a personal item or
prior name, a description of a past event the plaintiff attended, or alterations
to the plaintiff's name, description, or conduct.

To present a valid private facts claim, the plaintiff must show that the defendant

1. Publicly disclosed a highly personal private fact regarding the plaintiff.
2. Publicity given to the private fact is highly offensive and objectionable to a
   reasonable person.
3. Private fact is not of legitimate public concern.

Only disclosures of private facts that are particularly harmful are illegal.
This means that the publicity given to the private information by the defendant must be highly offensive and objectionable to a person of ordinary
sensibilities and not of legitimate public concern. Publicity that outrages a
community's sense of decency or constitutes "morbid or sensational prying"
for its own sake falls into this category.[115] California courts, for example,
have found that photographs taken at an accident scene of the decapitated
remains of a young woman and distributed on the internet were offensive and
objectionable[116] but that the publication of photos and an accompanying story
about US soldiers abusing war prisoners were not.[117]

In the former case, the court noted that the family had a right of privacy in
the autopsy photographs of their daughter and that while the decapitation was
newsworthy, the graphic details of the deceased body were not and served
no legitimate public interest.[118] In deciding whether the facts are of public
concern, courts look for a logical connection between the news event and
the private facts. The connection should be clear and directed at the news
value of the material published. Courts may also consider how deeply the
publicity intruded into the private affair and the level of details disclosed by

the defendant in relation to the public interest value associated with the private fact.

While in most states the lack of newsworthiness is an element for the plaintiff to prove, the news value of the disclosed information also serves as a defense for the publication of truthful private information. In *Shulman*, the television production company argued, and the court agreed, that the subject matter of the broadcast was of legitimate public concern. The coverage of automobile accidents, rescues, and medical treatment of accident victims, as well as Schulman's particular story, provides not only valuable information to the public but also sheds light on the challenges emergency workers face. Here, in particular, the segment conveyed the difficultly Carnahan faced in administering medical treatment to a victim who was severely traumatized, confused, and injured. For this reason, the court found that the "video depicting Ruth's injured physical state . . . and audio showing her disorientation and despair were substantially relevant to the segment's newsworthy subject matter."[119]

Shulman, on the other hand, argued that it was unnecessary to broadcast her "intimate private, medical facts and her suffering" in order to illustrate the significance of the accident and the rescue. The court, however, took issue with this argument, explaining that neither courts nor juries are in the position to second guess the news judgment of editors. Instead, the court pointed to the fact that the challenged material was substantially relevant to the news event and did not outstrip the bounds of legitimate public interest. In the end, Shulman's injured state was not luridly shown, sensationalized, or intensely personal in relation to its relevance as a legitimate news event.[120]

CHAPTER SUMMARY

While free speech benefits are widely acclaimed in First Amendment law, they go hand in hand with the realization that robust debate may also produce unpleasantly sharp and inaccurate attacks on the reputations of public and private individuals. In *New York Times v Sullivan*, the US Supreme Court severely curtailed a public official's ability to win a libel suit, creating the "actual malice" standard that requires a public official to prove that a libelous statement was made with the knowledge that it was false or with reckless disregard for the truth. While libel law differs among states, cases are largely established based on six elements: publication, identification, defamation, falsity, fault, and injury.

At the heart of a claim is a false statement that lowered the plaintiff's reputation in the community. To constitute defamation, the communication must state facts about the plaintiff that can be proven false. The complexity of determining whether the statement is an actionable expression of fact or nonactionable opinion can be challenging for courts, especially when the statement can read as both fact and opinion. For the plaintiff, however, no other element of libel is more difficult to establish than actual malice. But while actual malice is constitutionally mandated across jurisdictions for public figures, the fault standard for private figures varies from negligence to actual malice depending on state law.

Unlike libel law, which protects an individual's reputation against false assertions of fact, privacy rights are intended to protect a person's dignity. While privacy is a broad-based concept, two areas—intrusion upon seclusion and private facts—are central to communication professionals. Intrusion comes into play during the information gathering phase, whereas a private facts claim may be triggered by the publication of truthful private information.

KEY TERMS

Actionable   Actionable statements furnish the grounds for a legal action. To be actionable in libel law, a statement must state actual facts about the plaintiff that can be proven false and tend to injure the plaintiff's reputation.

Actual Malice Fault Standard   The fault standard plaintiffs classified as public figures must prove is actual malice. This standard requires the plaintiff to show that the defendant published the defamatory material (1) knowing it was false or (2) acting with reckless disregard for the statement's truth or falsity.

All-Purpose Public Figure   An all-purpose public figure refers to individuals whose fame or pervasive power and influence reaches widely throughout society.

Cause of Action   The basis on which a lawsuit is filed. The cause of action gives the plaintiff a right to sue the defendant. The cause of action may be based on a statute, common law, constitutional law, or another source of law.

Common Law   Common law is derived from case law. Case law is created when a judge renders a decision, writes an opinion detailing the reason for the decision, and publishes the opinion. Because common law stems from case law, it is referred to as a judge-made law and contrasts with statutory law, which is enacted by a lawmaking body, and constitutional law, which develops from federal and state constitutions.

Communications Decency Act See Section 230.

Defamation Defamation is an all-encompassing legal term that denotes the communication of a false statement of fact about the plaintiff that inflicts reputational harm.

Defamatory Meaning For a statement to be actionable in a libel suit, it must be capable of conveying a defamatory meaning. Statements that convey a defamatory meaning tend to expose an individual to public ridicule, hatred, or contempt, or otherwise injure a person's reputation in the minds of a considerable and respectable segment of the community.

Fault To win a libel case, a plaintiff must show that the defendant was at fault. As a general concept, fault relates to a defendant's intentional or negligent failure to use care and the resulting harm the defendant's conduct caused the plaintiff.

Federalist Papers The Federalist Papers are a series of nameless essays written to create support for the adoption of the US Constitution. Given the prominent role these documents played in the formation of the United States, courts have interpreted the First Amendment as protecting the right to publish anonymously.

Group Libel Group libel refers to cases where the allegedly defamatory statement refers to a particular group of which the plaintiff is a member and the plaintiff claims identification based on that reference. In cases of group libel, courts tend to favor claims where the group consists of twenty-five or fewer members, although claims involving fifty-three members have been allowed.

Information Content Provider Section 230 of the Communications Decency Act defines an information content provider as "any person or entity that is responsible, in whole or in part, for the creation or development of information provided through the internet or any other interactive computer service."

Innocent Construction Rule The innocent construction rule applies to statements that can reasonably be read as conveying both a defamatory and an innocent meaning. In such cases, the rule mandates that the innocent construction prevails.

Intrusion Upon Seclusion   Intrusion upon seclusion is a type of invasion of privacy that involves the unwarranted and intentional encroachment into one's personal activities. An unconsented physical intrusion into a home, hospital room, or other place of privacy as well as the gathering of information from an individual's private records or computer or with the use of highly sensitive, powerful audiovisual equipment may constitute intrusion. To establish an intrusion case, the plaintiff must show that a reasonable expectation of privacy in a place or activity exists and that the defendant intentionally intruded into that privacy in a manner highly offensive to a reasonable person.

Liability   Liability refers to the condition of being legally accountable for one's actions. For example, a person who posts a statement to a social media site is legally liable for the contents of that statement. By contrast, the social media site is immune from liability for the poster's statement.

Libel   Libel is a form of defamation that is published in a fixed medium, including written or printed communication as well as audio, video, film, radio, or television.

Libel in Fiction   Libel in fiction refers to libel claims that result from the fictional portrayal of a character that closely resembles an actual person. These cases arise when the fictional character is depicted in a manner that is both very similar to and very different from the plaintiff. In libel in fiction cases, identification is a key element and may be established when a reasonable person who knows the plaintiff would have no difficulty linking the character to the plaintiff.

Libel per quod   Libel *per quod* refers to statements that convey a false and defamatory impression but are literally true on their face. These statements may be actionable if, given the surrounding circumstances, they infer a defamatory message to others.

Libel per se   Libel *per se* refers to libelous statements that are inherently damaging to an individual's reputation. To qualify as libel *per se*, the published statement will traditionally fall into one of the following four categories: illegal behavior, loathsome disease, professional incompetence, or sexual misconduct or unchaste behavior. False assertions that fall within these categories warrant particular care among communicators as they are assumed to harm a person's reputation. This means that damages may be awarded in cases of libel per se without proof of actual injury.

Libel Proof   Libel proof refers to individuals whose reputations are so diminished that they are not capable of sustaining further reputational injury. Plaintiffs viewed as libel proof have reached the point where their reputation for a particular behavior or honest and fair dealing is so low in the minds of the public that they are basically unable to incur any meaningful reputational damage. In these circumstances, burdening a defendant with a libel claim would be pointless.

Limited-Purpose Public Figure   A limited-purpose public figure refers to individuals who either thrust themselves into the forefront of a public controversy or are drawn into a controversy and become a public figure for a limited range of issues.

Negligence Fault Standard   In some states, private figure plaintiffs are required to prove negligence on the part of the defendant. The negligence fault standard is easier than the actual malice fault standard for a plaintiff to establish. While no definitive list of what constitutes negligence exists, the standard typically measures the defendant's conduct against what a reasonable person would or would not have done under the same or similar circumstances. A plaintiff would likely establish negligence if the defendant failed to make a good faith effort to verify the truth or falsity of the information before publishing it.

Nonactionable   Nonactionable statements are not grounds for a legal action. In libel law, nonactionable statements include truthful statements, statements that do not damage the reputation of the plaintiff, and statements that no reasonable person would interpret as stating actual facts about the plaintiff.

Ollman Test   A four-part test used by courts to determine whether a reasonable person would view a mixed expression as fact or protected opinion.

Online Service Providers   An online service provider refers broadly to providers or users of interactive computer services. The Communications Decency Act provides online service providers broad immunity from legal liability for objectionable content posted by others.

Private Figure   A private figure is an ordinary individual who has not sought the limelight or been involved in a public controversy or matter of public interest.

Public Disclosure of Private Facts The public disclosure of private facts is a type of invasion of privacy that involves the widespread publicity of an intimate or highly personal matter. To establish a private facts case, the plaintiff must show that the defendant disclosed a highly personal private fact regarding the plaintiff that is not of legitimate public concern and whose disclosure would be highly offensive and objectionable to a reasonable person.

Public Official A public official is a government employee who holds a position of authority and whose qualifications and performance are of interest to the public. Elected officials and those with substantial responsibility for the conduct of governmental affairs are considered public officials.

Publication In libel law, publication refers to the distribution of an allegedly defamatory statement to a third party. Publication generally occurs when the statement is made available to its intended audience. Publication is an important element in establishing the reputational injury that resulted from a discrete statement that occurred at an identifiable moment in time.

Pure Opinion Pure opinion is a type of statement protected by the First Amendment and generally immune from liability in libel cases. A statement of pure opinion cannot be proven true or false. In determining whether a statement is pure opinion, courts consider the general tenor, tone, and context of the statement along with the language used.

Republication A defamatory statement is published when it is first made available to the public. It is generally considered to be republished when it is repeated or recirculated to a new audience. The republication of the defamatory statement opens the defendant up to a separate lawsuit with a new time frame under which a claim may be filed.

Rhetorical Hyperbole Rhetorical hyperbole refers to statements that no reasonable person would interpret as stating actual facts about the plaintiff. These statements may contain exaggerated language, name-calling, and imaginative expression. To determine whether a statement is an expression of fact or rhetorical hyperbole, courts examine the words used and the context in which they were published.

Section 230 Section 230 of the Communications Decency Act shields online service providers from liability for user-generated content. Under Section 230, social media sites, websites, and blogs are immune from liability for defamatory content unless they are responsible for creating or developing the content. Although Section 230 promises broad protection for online content, the full extent of its reach is unclear.

Single Publication Rule   The single publication rule limits to one the number of lawsuits a plaintiff may bring for any single issue of a widely circulated publication. This means that the plaintiff must recover the totality of injuries arising out of the discrete publication in one claim. The single publication rule is designed to avoid excessive damage awards and unnecessary strain on the judicial system.

Slander   Defamatory statements that are spoken, interpersonal conversations rather than written or published, as with libel.

Substantial Truth   A defense in libel law that allows the defendant to argue that, while errors did occur, the inaccuracies did not inflict harm on the plaintiff's reputation. Under this defense, minor factual errors unrelated to the plaintiff's reputation are ignored as well as alleged defamatory statements that are no more damaging to the plaintiff's reputation than the truth.

Third Party   A person who is neither the plaintiff nor the defendant but is somehow linked to the lawsuit. In libel cases, for example, the defamatory statement needs to be distributed to a person who is neither the plaintiff nor defendant for publication to occur.

Unmasking   Unmasking refers to the process of securing a court order that compels an ISP to identify an anonymous poster of allegedly defamatory information. Unmasking is necessary for plaintiffs who want to bring a libel suit against an anonymous speaker. But because the anonymous speaker is protected by the First Amendment, the court must balance the reputational interests of the plaintiff against the speech rights of the defendant. This usually means that the plaintiff will need to provide sufficient evidence to establish a valid libel claim before a judge will order an internet service provider to unmask an anonymous speaker.

User-Generated Content   User-generated content refers to any form of content that has been posted to social media sites, websites, blogs, and other online platforms by individuals who are users of those platforms rather than providers of those platforms. User-generated content is also referred to as customer-generated content or audience-generated content.

Notes

CHAPTER 1

1. David M. Rabban, "The First Amendment in Its Forgotten Years," *Yale Law Journal* 90 (1981): 523.

2. *Abrams v. United States*, 250 U.S. 616, 630 (1919).

3. *Heller v. Doe*, 509 U.S. 312, 320 (1993).

4. *Texas v. Johnson*, 491 U.S. 397, 404 (1986).

5. *Clark v. Community for Creative Non-Violence*, 468 U.S. 288 (1984).

6. *McCullen v. Coakley*, 134 S. Ct. 2518, 2531 (2014).

7. *Johnson*, 491 U.S. at 399.

8. Ibid., 406.

9. Ibid., 420.

10. *Ward v. Rock Against Racism*, 491 U.S. 781, 799 (1989).

11. *McCullen v. Coakley*, 134 S. Ct. 2518, 2535 (2014).

12. Ibid., 2540.

13. Ibid., 2541.

14. *Smith v. Goguen*, 415 U.S. 566 (1974).

15. *Coates v. Cincinnati*, 402 U.S. 611 (1971).

16. *Board of Airport Commissioners v. Jews for Jesus*, 482 U.S. 569 (1987).

17. *Doe v. University of Michigan*, 721 F. Supp. 852, 867 (E.D. Mich. 1989).

18. Ibid., 866.

19. *Minnesota Voters Alliance v. Mansky*, 136 S. Ct. 1876 (2018).

20. Ibid., 1888.

21. *Berger v. City of Seattle*, 569 F.3d 1029, 1037–38 (9th Cir. 2009).

22. *Walker v. Texas Division, Sons of Confederate Veterans, Inc.*, 135 S. Ct. 2239, 2250 (2016).

23. Ibid., 2246.

24. *Packingham v. North Carolina*, 137 S. Ct. 1730, 1735 (2017).

25. John Herrman and Charlie Savage, "Trump's Blocking of Twitter Users Is Unconstitutional, Judge Says," *New York Times*, May 23, 2018, https://www .nytimes.com/2018/05/23/business/media/trump-twitter-block.html; Michael Dresser, "Maryland, ACLU Settle Lawsuit over Deleted Comments on Gov. Hogan's Facebook Page," *Baltimore Sun*, April 2, 2018, http://www.baltimoresun.com/news/maryland /politics/bs-md-aclu-hogan-facebook-20180402-story.html; "ACLU of Maine Sues LePage over Facebook Censorship," *ACLU*, August 8, 2017, https://www.aclu.org /news/aclu-maine-sues-lepage-over-facebook-censorship.

26. See, e.g., *Knight First Amendment Institute v. Trump*, 928 F.3d 226 (2d.Cir. 2019); *Davison v. Loudoun County Board of Supervisors et al.*, 207 F. Supp. 3d 702 (E.D. Va. 2017).

27. *Knight First Amendment Institute*, 928 F.3d at 235–36.

28. Ibid., 238.

CHAPTER 2

1. See *Valentine v. Chrestensen*, 316 U.S. 52, 54–55 (1942).

2. 376 U.S. 254, 266, 271 (1964).

3. Ibid., 266, 269–70.

4. The ad was placed by the Committee to Defend Martin Luther King and the Struggle for Freedom in the South.

5. Ibid., 266 (quoting *Associated Press v. United States*, 326 U.S. 1, 20 (1945)).

6. Nancy Whitmore, "Facing the Fear: A Free Market Approach for Economic Expression," *Communication Law and Policy* 17 (2012): 33, 35.

7. Ibid.

8. *Virginia State Board of Pharmacy v. Virginia Citizens Consumer Council*, 425 U.S. 748, 762, 765 (1976).

9. Ibid., 770.

10. Ibid., 771 n.24.

11. This standard is referred to as rational basis review.

12. *Central Hudson Gas & Electric Corp. v. Public Service Commission*, 447 U.S. 557, 564 (1980).

13. Ibid., 568–69.

14. Ibid., 570.

15. Ibid., 566, n. 9.

16. *Educational Media at Virginia Tech v. Insley*, 731 F.3d 291, 299 (4th Cir. 2013).

17. Ibid., 299–300.

18. Ibid., 300.

19. Ibid., 301.

20. *Zauderer v. Office of Disciplinary Counsel of the Supreme Court of Ohio*, 471 U.S. 626, 650 (1985).

21. *New York State Restaurant Association. v. New York City Board of Health*, 556 F.3d 114, 132 (2d. Cir. 2009).

22. *Board of Trustees of the State University of New York v. Fox*, 492 U.S. 469, 480 (1989).

23. *Restaurant Association*, 556 F.3d at 134.

24. *Zauderer*, 471 U.S. at 651.

25. For background information in *R.J. Reynolds v. FDA*, see 696 F.3d 1205, 1208–09 (D.C. Cir. 2012).

26. Ibid., 1212.

27. For information regarding the court's analysis in *R.J. Reynolds*, see ibid., 1214–17.

28. For information regarding the court's application of the Central Hudson standard in *R.J. Reynolds*, see ibid., 1218–19.

29. Ibid., 1222.

30. *National Institute of Family & Life Advocates v. Becerra*, 138 S. Ct. 2361, 2372 (2018).

31. For information regarding the court's application of the intermediate scrutiny standard in *Becerra*, see ibid., 2375–76.

32. 463 U.S. 60, 66–67 (1983).

33. 45 P.3d 243, 256 (Cal. 2002).

34. Ibid., 257.

35. See ibid., 247–48.

36. Ibid., 260.

37. Ibid., 258.

38. "PRSA 'Devastated' That Supreme Court Fails to Clarify 'Free Speech' in Nike Case," *Business Wire*, June 26, 2003, https://www.businesswire.com/news/home/20030626005840/en/PRSA-Devastated-Supreme-Court-Fails-Clarify-Free.

39. *Kasky*, 45 P.3d at 260.

40. *Bank of Boston v. Bellotti*, 435 U.S. 765, 768–69 (1978).

41. Ibid., 770, n. 4.

42. For information on the court's corporate speaker analysis in *Bellotti*, see ibid., 777.

43. Ibid., 783.

44. For information on the court's application of strict scrutiny review in *Belliotti*, see ibid., 787–95.

45. 424 U.S. 1, 19 (1976) (per curiam).

46. Ibid., 44–45.

47. Ibid., 19.

48. *Citizens United v. Federal Election Commission*, 558 U.S. 310, 320–21 (2010).

49. Ibid., 357.

50. *Buckley*, 424 U.S. at 45.

51. Ibid., 46.

52. For the court's discussion on favoritism in *Citizens United*, see 558 U.S. at 359.

53. For the court's discussion on disclosure requirements in *Citizens United*, see 558 U.S. at 366–71.

CHAPTER 3

1. *Harper & Row, Publishers v. National Enterprises*, 471 U.S. 539, 558 (1985).

2. The information in this paragraph is taken from *Feist Publication v. Rural Telephone Service Co.*, 499 U.S. 340, 345 (1991).

3. 17 U.S.C. §101.

4. Ibid.

5. See *ABC v. Aereo*, 573 U.S. 431, 446–47 (2014).

6. *Campbell v. Acuff-Rose Music*, 510 U.S. 569, 575 (1994) (quoting *Emerson v. Davies*, 8 F. Cas. 615, 619 (No. 4,436) (CCD Mass. 1845)).

7. Ibid.

8. *Feist*, 499 U.S. at 345.

9. See *Eldred v. Ashcroft*, 537 U.S. 186, 219 (2003).

10. Alfred C. Yen, "Eldred, The First Amendment, and Aggressive Copyright Claims," *Houston Law Review* 40 (2003): 677.

11. The information in this paragraph and the following paragraph is taken from *Feist*, 499 U.S. at 347–49.

12. Ibid., 363–64.

13. Ibid., 358.

14. Ibid., 359.

15. Ibid., 363.

16. *Rentmeester v. Nike*, Inc., 883 F.3d 1111, 1120 (9th Cir. 2018).

17. Ibid., 1119.

18. *Ets-Hokin v. Skyy Spirits*, 323 F.3d 763, 766 (9th Cir. 2003).

19. *BUC Int'l Corp. v. Int'l Yacht Council Ltd.*, 489 F. 3d 1129, 1143 (11th Cir. 2007).

20. *Innovation Ventures, LLC v. Ultimate One Distributing Corp.*, 176 F. Supp. 3d 137, 157 (E.D.N.Y. 2016).

21. *Satava v. Lowry*, 323 F. 3d 805, 810 (9th Cir. 2003).

22. Ibid.

23. *Stromback v. New Line Cinema*, 384 F.3d 283, 296 (6th Cir. 2004).

24. See *Satava*, 323 F.3d at 811–12 for a discussion on the merger doctrine and its application to the glass-in-glass jellyfish sculpture that is at issue in the case.

25. *Shaw v. Lindheim*, 919 F.2d 1353, 1359 (9th Cir. 1990).

26. *Arnstein v. Porter*, 154 F. 2d 464, 468 (9th Cir. 1946).

27. Katherine Lippman, "The Beginning of the End: Preliminary Results of an Empirical Study of Copyright Substantial Similarity Opinions in the U.S. Circuit Courts," *Michigan State Law Review* (2013): 524.

28. *Rentmeester v. Nike*, 883 F.3d 1111, 1115 (9th Cir. 2018).

29. Ibid., 1115–16.

30. Ibid., 1118.

31. See, e.g., Gabriel Godoy-Dalmau, "Substantial Similarity: Kolus Got It Right," *Michigan Business and Entrepreneurial Law Review* 6 (2017): 241–42.

32. *Rentmeester*, 883 F.3d at 1121–23.

33. *Mattel, Inc. v. MGA Entertainment*, 616 F.3d 904, 916–17 (9th Cir. 2010) (internal quotation marks omitted).

34. Some courts refer to total concept and feel of the work.

35. See *Peter Pan Fabrics v. Martin Weiner Corp.*, 274 F.2d 487, 489 (2d. Cir. 1960).

36. Some courts use the intended audience instead of the ordinary observer. Because the intended audience in most factual scenarios is commonly the general public, this distinction is largely inconsequential. However, this distinction is important in cases where the intended audience possesses a specialized expertise or attribute (such as age). See *Dawson v. Hinshaw Music*, 905 F.2d 731, 735 (4th Cir. 1990).

37. *Arnstein v. Porter*, 154 F.2d 464, 473 (2d Cir. 1946).

38. *Rentmeester*, 883 F.3d at 1122.

39. See, e.g., Godoy-Dalmau, "Substantial Similarity," 243–49; Lippman, "The Beginning of the End," 525–25; Pamela Samuelson, "A Fresh Look at Test for Nonliteral Copyright Infringement," *Northwestern University Law Review* 107 (2013): 1823–40.

40. Godoy-Dalmau, "Substantial Similarity," 251.

41. Jason E. Sloan, "An Overview of the Elements of a Copyright Infringement Cause of Action—Part II: Improper Appropriation," *American Bar Association*, August 27, 2013, https://www.americanbar.org/groups/young_lawyers/publications /the_101_201_practice_series/part_2_elements_of_a_copyright/.

42. Ibid.

43. *Rogers v. Koons*, 960 F.2d 301, 307 (2d. Cir. 1992).

44. *Leigh v. Warner Bros.*, 212 F.3d 1210, 1215 (11th Cir. 2000).

45. Petition for a Writ of Certiorari at 39, *Rentmeester v. Nike*, 139 S. Ct. 1375 (2019).

46. Ibid., 40.

47. Information on the Contours of Copyright Law was taken from the US Copyright Office Registration Portal, https://www.copyright.gov/registration/; US Copyright Office, Compendium of US Copyright Office Practices § 310.3 (3rd ed. 2017), https://www.copyright.gov/comp3/docs/compendium.pdf; US Copyright Office, Works Not Protected by Copyright, Circular 33, https://www.copyright.gov /circs/circ33.pdf; and 17 U.S.C. §101.

48. 17 U.S.C. § 102(b).

49. US Copyright Office, Compendium of US Copyright Office Practices § 313.3(A) (3rd ed. 2017), https://www.copyright.gov/comp3/docs/compendium.pdf.

50. See US Copyright Office, Compendium of US Copyright Office Practices § 906.4 (3rd ed. 2017), https://www.copyright.gov/comp3/docs/compendium.pdf.

51. Information on Format and Layout Design, Uncopyrightable Elements, and Names, Titles, Short Phrases was taken from US Copyright Office, Compendium of US Copyright Office Practices § 313.

52. US Copyright Office, Works Not Protected by Copyright, Circular 33, https:// www.copyright.gov/circs/circ33.pdf.

53. *Star Athletica v. Varsity Brands*, 137 S. Ct. 1002, 1011 (2017).

54. 17 U.S.C. § 101.

55. Lyle Denniston, "Useful or Creative: A Look at Design Protection," *SCOTUSblog*, May 2, 2016, http://www.scotusblog.com/2016/05/useful-or-creative-a-look-at-design-protection/.

56. Ibid.

57. The information and quotations on separability in this paragraph and the following paragraph were taken from *Star Athletica*, 137 S. Ct. at 1010.

58. Ronald Mann, "Justices Worry about 'Killing Knockoffs with Copyright,'" *SCOTUSblog*, November 1, 2016, http://www.scotusblog.com/2016/11/argument-analysis-justices-worry-about-killing-knockoffs-with-copyright/.

59. Ibid.

60. *DC Comics v. Towle*, 802 F.3d 1012, 1019 (9th Cir. 2015).

61. *Rice v. Fox Broadcasting Co.*, 330 F.3d 1170, 1175 (9th Cir. 2003).

62. For a discussion on the difference between fictional and graphic characters, see "Protection of Fictional Characters," *Findlaw*, July 3, 2017, https://corporate.findlaw.com/intellectual-property/protection-of-fictional-characters.html.

63. *Metro-Goldwyn-Mayer v. American Honda Motor Co.*, 900 F. Supp. 1287, 1292 (C.D. Cal. 1995). In the case, MGM contended that the use of a male protagonist possessing Bond's unique character traits as developed in the films infringed its copyright in the character of Bond as expressed and delineated in MGM's films. Ibid., 1294. For a list of Bond's character traits, see ibid., 1296.

64. See *Halicki Films, LLC v. Sanderson Sales & Marketing*, 547 F.3d 1213, 1224–25 (9th Cir. 2008).

65. *DC Comics*, 802 F.3d at 1021. The application of these factors to the Batmobile is discussed in the next paragraph. See ibid., 1021–22. Note: Courts have not extended copyright protection to stock characters, such as a magician "dressed in standard magician garb" (*Rice v. Fox Broadcasting Co.*, 330 F.3d 1170, 1175 (9th Cir. 2003)) or an "unexpectedly knowledgeable old wino" (*Gaiman v. McFarlane*, 360 F.3d 644, 660 (7th Cir. 2004)).

66. *Klinger v. Conan Doyle Estate, Ltd.*, 755 F.3d 496, 500 (7th Cir. 2014).

67. Ibid., 503.

68. US Copyright Office, Compendium of US Copyright Office Practices § 507.2 (3rd ed. 2017) (internal quotation marks omitted), https://www.copyright.gov/comp3/docs/compendium.pdf.

69. *Klinger*, 988 F. Supp. 2d at 892–93.

70. These are works that are prepared by an employee within the scope of employment or contracted work. See US Copyright Office, Works Made for Hire, Circular 9, https://www.copyright.gov/circs/circ09.pdf.

CHAPTER 4

1. *Campbell v. Acuff-Rose Music*, 510 U.S. 569, 575 (1994) (quoting *Emerson v. Davies*, 8 F. Cas. 615, 619 (C.C.D. Mass. 1845)) (internal quotation marks omitted).

2. Pierre N. Leval, "Nimmer Lecture: Fair Use Rescued," *UCLA Law Review* 44 (1997): 1450.

3. "More Information on Fair Use," *U.S. Copyright Office,* https://www.copy
right.gov/fair-use/more-info.html.

4. The information in this paragraph concerning Judge Leval's critique of the fair use defense was taken from Pierre N. Leval, "Toward a Fair Use Standard," *Harvard Law Review* 103 (1990): 1106–107.

5. Leval, "Toward a Fair Use," 1109.

6. Ibid., 1110.

7. Ibid., 1111.

8. Ibid.

9. Ibid.

10. *Campbell v. Acuff-Rose Music,* 510 U.S. 569, 588 (1994).

11. *Acuff-Rose v. Campbell,* 754 F. Supp. 1150, 1155 (M.D. Tenn. 1991).

12. *Acuff-Rose v. Campbell,* 972 F.2d 1429, 1438–39 (6th Cir. 1992).

13. *Campbell,* 510 U.S. at 578.

14. Ibid., 583.

15. Ibid., 579.

16. Ibid., 582.

17. Ibid., 583 n17.

18. Ibid., 582 (internal quotation marks omitted).

19. Ibid.

20. Ibid., 584.

21. *MCA v. Wilson,* 677 F.2d 180, 182 (2d Cir. 1981).

22. *Campbell,* 510 U.S. at 586.

23. The information in this paragraph on the court's factor three analysis was taken from *Campbell,* 510 U.S. at 587–88.

24. Ibid., 589.

25. Ibid. Note: The court expressed no opinion on whether the repetition of the bass riff was excessive and remanded for an evaluation on this question.

26. The information in this paragraph on the court's factor three analysis was taken from *Campbell,* 510 U.S. at 589.

27. The information in this paragraph on the court's factor four analysis was taken from *Campbell,* 510 U.S. at 591–92.

28. *Campbell,* 510 U.S. at 580.

29. *Dr. Seuss Enterprises v. Penguin Books USA,* 109 F.3d 1394, 1400 (9th Cir. 1997).

30. See, e.g., *Dr. Seuss Enterprises v. Penguin Book USA,* 924 F. Supp. 1559, 1576 (S.D. Cal. 1996).

31. *Seuss Enterprises,* 109 F.3d at 1401.

32. *Campbell,* 510 U.S. at 580.

33. *Blanch v. Koons,* 467 F.3d 244, 255 (2d. Cir 2006) [hereafter *Blanch 2*].

34. Ibid., 247.

35. Ibid., 253.

36. *Castle Rock Entertainment v. Carol Publishing Group,* 150 F.3d 132, 142 (2d. Cir. 1998).

37. *Ringgold v. Black Entertainment Television,* 126 F.3d 70, 79 (2d Cir. 1997).

38. *Blanch 2*, 467 F.3d at 252.

39. *Blanch v. Koons*, 396 F. Supp. 2d 476, 478 (S.D.N.Y. 2005) [hereafter *Blanch 1*].

40. *Blanch 2*, 467 F.3d at 252.

41. Ibid.

42. Ibid., 253–55.

43. Ibid., 255.

44. Ibid.

45. Ibid.

46. *Rogers v. Koons*, 960 F.2d 301, 305 (2d. Cir. 1992).

47. Ibid.

48. Ibid.

49. Ibid., 310.

50. The information in this paragraph on the court's analysis involving Koons's parody claim was taken from *Rogers*, 960 F.2d at 309–10.

51. *Bill Graham Archives v. Dorling Kindersley*, 448 F.3d 605, 609 (2d. Cir. 2006).

52. The information in this paragraph on the court's analysis of the Grateful Dead posters was taken from *Bill Graham Archives*, 448 F.3d at 609–10.

53. Ibid., 611.

54. Ibid., 610 (quoting *Elvis Presley Entertainment v. Passport Video*, 349 F.3d 622, 628–29 (9th Cir. 2003)).

55. Ibid., 613.

56. See ibid., 614–15.

57. *Cariou v. Prince*, 714 F.3d 694, 704 (2d Cir. 2013).

58. The court's observations regarding the two works were taken from *Cariou*, 714 F.3d at 706 and *Cariou v. Prince* 784 F. Supp. 2d 337, 343 (S.D.N.Y. 2011). Background information can be found at *Cariou*, 714 F.3d at 699-704.

59. *Cariou*, 714 F.3d at 707.

60. The court's analysis regarding the two works was taken from *Cariou*, 714 F.3d at 707–708.

61. The court's factor two analysis was taken from *Cariou*, 714 F.3d at 709–10.

62. The court's factor three analysis was taken from *Cariou*, 714 F.3d at 710.

63. Ibid., 709.

64. The court's factor four analysis was taken from *Cariou*, 714 F.3d at 708–709.

65. *Lenz v. Universal Music Corp.*, 815 F.3d 1145, 1157 (9th Cir. 2016).

66. See Stephen Carlisle, "DMCA 'Takedown' Notices: Why 'Takedown' Should Become 'Take Down and Stay Down' and Why It's Good for Everyone," *NOVA Southeastern University*, July 23, 2014, http://copyright.nova.edu/dmca-takedown-notices/.

67. Ibid.

68. *Lenz*, 815 F.3d at 1148.

69. Ibid., 1154.

70. Jose Sariego, "High Court Won't Take on Lenz DMCA Case—What Now?," *BilzinSumberg*, July 27, 2017 (reprinted with permission from *LAW360*), https://www.bilzin.com/we-think-big/insights/publications/2017/07/high-court-wont-take-on-lenz.

71. Steve Schlackman, "How to Submit a Copyright Takedown Notice," *Art Law Journal*, January 29, 2014, https://alj.artrepreneur.com/submit-takedown-notice/.

72. *Ringgold v. Black Entertainment T.V.*, 126 F.3d 70, 74 (9th Cir. 1997). The court in *Ringgold* stated that *de minimis* can also mean that the technical violation of the copyright is too trivial to impose legal penalties. However, this meaning is rarely at issue in litigation given that it usually involves "questions that never need to be answered," such as posting a photocopy of a cartoon on a refrigerator. Ibid. (internal quotation marks omitted).

73. Andrew Inesi, "A Theory of De Minimis and a Proposal for Its Application in Copyright," *Berkeley Technology Law Journal* 21 (2006): 961.

74. *Ringgold*, 126 F.3d at 75.

75. *Hirsch v. CBS Broadcasting*, 2017 U.S. Dist. LEXIS 123468, *2.

76. "Stalked," *48 Hours*, February 25, 2017, https://www.cbsnews.com/news/stalked-48-hours-investigates-pauley-perrette-fights-to-change-stalking-laws/.

77. *Hirsch*, *4.

78. David Kluft, "A Copyright Fable: Debunking The 'Seven-Second Rule,'" *Foley Hoag, LLP*, August 30, 2017, http://www.trademarkandcopyrightlawblog.com/2017/08/a-copyright-fable-debunking-the-seven-second-rule/.

79. *Hirsch*, *12.

80. Ibid.

81. Ibid., *13.

82. *Gayle v. HBO*, 2018 U.S. Dist. LEXIS 73254, *7.

83. Ibid.

84. Lee S. Brenner and Allison S. Rohrer, "The De Minimis Doctrine: How Much Copying Is Too Much?," *Communication Lawyer* 24 (2006): 13.

CHAPTER 5

1. The information in this paragraph on Abigail Roberson's case was taken from *Roberson v. Rochester Folding-Box Co.*, 32 Misc. 344, 345–46 (Sup. Ct. N.Y. 1900).

2. *Roberson v. Rochester Folding-Box Co.*, 171 N.Y. 538, 556–57 (N.Y. 1902).

3. Jennifer E. Rothman, *The Right of Publicity* (Cambridge, MA: Harvard University Press, 2018), 24–25.

4. Ibid., 45.

5. See "Rothman's Road Map to the Right of Publicity," https://www.rightofpublicityroadmap.com/ [hereinafter *Road Map*]. For example, compare Indiana and Tennessee to New Mexico and North Carolina.

6. See ibid., Oklahoma and California.

7. See ibid., North Dakota, Wyoming, and Alaska.

8. Rothman, *Right of Publicity*, 96.

9. Ibid.

10. *Road Map*. See, e.g., Oklahoma, California, and Hawaii.

11. Ibid., Nebraska.

12. Ibid., Indiana and Ohio.

13. Ibid., Indiana.

14. Ibid., Indiana.

15. See *White v. Samsung*, 989 F.2d 1512, 1514 (Kozinski, J. dissenting).

16. *Midler v. Ford Motor Co.*, 949 F.2d 460, 461 (9th Cir. 1988).

17. *Motschenbacher v. R. J. Reynolds Tobacco Co.*, 498 F.2d 821, 822 (9th Cir. 1974).

18. *Wendt v. Host International*, 125 F.3d 806, 809 (9th Cir. 1997).

19. *White v. Samsung*, 971 F.2d 1395, 1396 (9th Cir. 1992).

20. *Carson v. Here's Johnny Portable Toilets*, 698 F.2d 831, 836 (6th Cir. 1983).

21. *Henley v. Dillard Department Stores*, 46 F. Supp. 2d 587, 591 (N.D. Tex. 1999).

22. Ibid., 595.

23. Gonzalo E. Mon, "Don Henley Settles Right of Publicity Suit with Retailer," *Ad Law Access*, April 17, 2015, https://www.adlawaccess.com/2015/04/articles /don-henley-settles-right-of-publicity-suit-with-retailer/.

24. Niraj Chokshi, "Chris Farley's Family Settles with Bike Maker Over 'Fat Guy' Brand," *New York Times*, June 7, 2018, https://www.nytimes.com/2018/06/07/arts /chris-farley-wisconsin-bicycle-fat-guy.html?action=click&module=In%20 Other%20News&pgtype=Homepage&action=click&module=Latest&pgtype=Home page&login=email&auth=login-email; Ed Treleven, "Chris Farley's Family and Trek Bicycle Settle Lawsuit over Farley Name," *Wisconsin State Journal*, June 7, 2018, https://madison.com/wsj/news/local/courts/chris-farley-s-family-and-trek-bicycle -settle-lawsuit-over/article_7ab33619-7627-5090-a2c2-1b4cfef22d95.html.

25. The dichotomy between right of publicity and right to privacy misappropriation is not precise as economic, dignity, and emotional harms can all occur from the same act of misappropriation. See Rothman, *Right of Publicity*, 110. Rothman notes that many states recognize this and "allow the recovery of both economic and non-economic damages (including emotional distress) under their right of publicity laws, even if the plaintiff is a celebrity." Ibid.

26. *Road Map*. See, e.g., Indiana, Massachusetts, and Michigan.

27. Ibid.; See, e.g., Illinois, North Carolina, and Nevada.

28. *Fraley v. Facebook*, 830 F. Supp. 2d 785, 791–92 (N.D. Calif. 2011).

29. The information in this paragraph was taken from *Fraley*, 830 F. Supp. 2d at 806–809.

30. Ibid., 809.

31. Neal S. Dongre, "The Right to Control the Use of Your Image and Likeness," *Gorman & Williams*, November 22, 2010, https://www.gw-law.com/blog /news-publications.

32. *Fraley*, 830 F. Supp. 2d at 807 (quoting *Motschenbacher v. R.J. Reynolds*, 498 F.2d 821, 825 n. 11) (internal quotation marks omitted).

33. See Rothman, *Right of Publicity*, 75–86, for a full discussion on the evolution of right of publicity and postmortem rights during this time.

34. *Zacchini v. Scripps-Howard Broadcasting Co.*, 433 U.S. 562, 573 (1977).

35. *Tenn. ex rel. Elvis Presley International Memorial Foundation. v. Crowell*, 733 S.W. 2d 89, 97 (Tenn. Ct. App. 1987).

36. Rothman, *Right of Publicity*, 84.

37. Ibid., 97.

38. Ibid., 98.

39. See *Road Map*.

40. See, e.g., Kevin L. Vick and Jean-Paul Jassy, "Why a Federal Right of Publicity Statute is Necessary," *Communication Lawyer* 28 (August 2011): 14.

41. *Zacchini*, 433 U.S. at 564, 573.

42. Ibid., 576.

43. The information in this paragraph was taken from *Zacchini*, 433 U.S. at 573, 575–76. Note: Additional justifications have been proposed for why right of publicity laws exist. For a full discussion on this topic, see Rothman, *Right of Publicity*, 98–112.

44. See Joshua L. Simmons and Miranda D. Means, "Split Personality: Constructing a Coherent Right of Publicity Statute," *Landside*, May 18, 2018, https://www.americanbar.org/groups/intellectual_property_law/publications/landslide/2017-18/may-june/split-personality/ [hereinafter *Split Personality*]; and *Road Map*.

45. *Tyne v. Time Warner Entertainment Co.*, 901 So. 2d 802, 808 (Fla. 2005).

46. Stacey L. Dogan, "Haelan Laboratories v. Topps Chewing Gum: Publicity as a Legal Right," in *Intellectual Property at the Edge: The Contested Contours of IP* (Rochelle C. Dreyfuss & Jane C. Ginsburg ed., 2014), 24.

47. See *Tyne*, 901 So. 2d at 806–808.

48. *Comedy III Productions v. Gary Saderup*, 25 Cal. 4th 387, 395 (Cal. 2001).

49. *Hilton v. Hallmark Cards*, 599 F.3d 894, 909 (9th Cir. 2010).

50. See *De Havilland v. FX Networks*, 21 Cal. App. 5th 845, 857 (Cal. Ct. App. 2018).

51. Ibid., 857–58 (Declining to decide the question of whether a docudrama is a product or merchandise within the meaning of the state's right of publicity statute); *Sarver v. Hurt Locker*, 813 F.3d 891, 903 (9th Cir. 2016) (Assuming for the sake of argument that the use of plaintiff's identity in the motion picture *The Hurt Locker* establishes an appropriation to the defendant's advantage, commercial or otherwise).

52. *De Havilland*, 21 Cal. App. 5th at 857.

53. See Simmons and Means, *Split Personality*.

54. See Brief of 31 Constitutional Law and Intellectual Property Law Professors as Amici Curiae in Support of Petitioner, *Electronic Arts v. Davis*, 136 S. Ct. 1448 (2016) (No. 15-424) [hereinafter *Brief of 31 Professors*].

55. *Rogers v. Grimaldi*, 875 F.2d 994, 1004 (2d Cir. 1989).

56. Eric E. Johnson, "Disentangling the Right of Publicity," *Northwestern University Law Review* 111 (2017): 911.

57. *Brief of 31 Professors*.

58. See, e.g., Diane Leenheer Zimmerman, "Money as a Thumb on the Constitutional Scale," *Boston College Law Review* 50 (2009): 1505; Mary-Rose Papandrea, "Where Intellectual Property and Free Speech Collide," *Boston College Law Review* 50 (2009): 1307; Eugene Volokh, "Freedom of Speech and the Right of Publicity," *Houston Law Review* 40 (2003): 909–13.

59. Stacey Dogan, "Stirring the Pot: A Response to Rothman's Right of Publicity," *Columbia Journal of Law and the Arts* 42 (2019): 327.

60. See *Comedy III Productions v. Gary Saderup*, 25 Cal. 4th 387, 398–400 (Cal. 2001).

61. Ibid., 407.

62. Ibid., 405.

63. *Keller v. Electronic Arts*, 724 F.3d 1268, 1273 (9th Cir. 2013).

64. See *Comedy III*, 25 Cal. 4th at 406–407 for a discussion of the transformative use test.

65. *Hilton v. Hallmark Cards*, 599 F.3d 894, 910 (9th Cir. 2010) (citing *Winter v. DC Comics*, 30 Cal. 4th 881, 891 (Cal. 2003)).

66. *Comedy III*, 25 Cal. 4th at 407.

67. Ibid., 408.

68. Ibid., 408–409.

69. Ibid., 409.

70. Ibid.

71. Ibid.

72. See *Davis v. Electronic Arts*, 775 F.3d 1172, 1177 (9th Cir. 2015); *Keller v. Electronic Arts*, 724 F.3d 1268, 1273–74 (9th Cir. 2013); *Hart v. Electronic Arts*, 717 F.3d 141, 163–64 (3rd Cir. 2013).

73. *Hart*, 717 F.3d at 166.

74. The Third Circuit's analysis discussed in this paragraph was taken from *Hart*, 717 F.3d at 166, 168.

75. *No Doubt v. Activision Publishing*, 192 Cal. App. 4th 1018, 1034 (Cal. App. 2011).

76. *Winter v. DC Comics*, 30 Cal. 4th 881, 890 (Cal. 2003).

77. Ibid.

78. The Sixth Circuit's analysis discussed in this paragraph was taken from *ETW Corp. v. Jireh Publishing*, 332 F.3d 915, 937–38 (6th Cir. 2003).

79. *Hilton v. Hallmark Cards*, 599 F.3d 894, 911 (9th Cir. 2010).

80. The Ninth Circuit's analysis discussed in this paragraph was taken from *Hilton*, 599 F.3d at 910–11.

81. *Rogers v. Grimaldi*, 875 F.2d 994, 1004 (2d Cir. 1989).

82. Ibid., 997.

83. The Second Circuit's analysis discussed in this paragraph was taken from *Rogers*, 875 F.2d at 1001, 1004–05.

84. *Parks v. LaFace Records*, 329 F.3d 437, 452–53 (6th Cir. 2003).

85. Ibid., 454.

86. The information in this paragraph was taken from *Doe v. TCI Cablevision*, 110 S.W. 3d 363, 373–74 (Mo. 2003) (en banc).

87. Ibid., 367.

88. Ibid.

89. Ibid., 374.

90. *Hart v. Electronic Arts*, 717 F.3d 141, 154 (3rd Cir. 2013).

91. Ibid.

92. *C.B.C. Distribution & Marketing v. Major League Baseball Advanced*, 505 F.3d 818, 823 (8th Cir. 2007).

93. Ibid., 824.

94. *Brief of 31 Professors.*

95. *Montana v. San Jose Mercury News*, 34 Cal. App. 4th 790, 794 (Cal. App. 1995).

96. *Hilton v. Hallmark Cards*, 599 F.3d 894, 907 (9th Cir. 2010).

97. Ibid., 912.

98. The information in this paragraph was taken from *Browne v. McCain*, 611 F. Supp. 2d 1062, 1069–73 (C.D. Cal. 2009).

99. *Hill v. Public Advocate of the United States*, 35 F. Supp. 3d 1347, 1357 (D. Colo. 2014).

100. *Zacchini v. Scripps-Howard Broadcasting Co.*, 433 U.S. 562, 576 (1977).

101. Dogan, "Publicity as a Legal Right," 18.

102. See ibid., 19.

CHAPTER 6

1. "Best Global Brands 2020," *Interbrand*, https://interbrand.com/best-global-brands/starbucks/.

2. *Qualitex v. Jacobson Prods.*, 514 U.S. 159, 164 (1995).

3. Ibid.

4. See *Elliot v. Google*, 45 F. Supp. 3d 1156, 1173–75 (D. Ariz. 2014).

5. See "A Guide to Proper Trademark use," *International Trademark Association*, 2012, http://inta.org/Media/Documents/2012_TMUseMediaInternetPublishing.pdf.

6. "Generic Trademark: Everything You Need to Know," *Upcounsel*, https://www.upcounsel.com/generic-trademark.

7. *Sara Lee v. Kayser-Roth*, 81 F.3d 455, 464 (4th Cir. 1995).

8. *Custom Vehicles v. Forest River*, 476 F.3d 481, 483 (7th Cir. 2007).

9. *Xtreme Lashes v. Xtended Beauty*, 576 F.3d 221, 232 (5th Cir. 2009).

10. *Custom Vehicles*, 476 F. 3d at 483.

11. The USPTO administers two separate registers: Supplemental and Principal. Descriptive marks may be placed on the Supplemental Register if the examining attorney believes the mark has the potential to be distinctive in the future. The Supplemental Register offers some protection to descriptive marks—for example, it bars registration of subsequent confusingly similar marks. David M. Gurfinkel, "The U.S. Trademark Registers: Supplemental vs. Principal," *The International Trademark Association Bulletin*, May 1, 2012, http://www.inta.org/INTABulletin/Pages/TheUS TrademarkRegistersSupplementalvsPrincipal.aspx.

12. *OBX-Stock v. Bicast*, 558 F. 3d 334, 340 (4th Cir. 2009).

13. *E.T. Browne v. Cococare Prods.*, 538 F.3d 185, 199 (3rd Cir. 2008).

14. Edward J. Heath and John M. Tanski, "Drawing the Line Between Descriptive and Suggestive Trademarks," *Commercial & Business Litigation* 12 (Fall 2010),

http://www.rc.com/upload/ARTICLE-Drawing-the-Line-Between-Descriptive-and
-Suggestive-Trademarks-Heath-Fall-2010.pdf.

15. See In re P.J. Fitzpatrick, 95 U.S.P.Q.2d 1412 (TTAB 2010). However, under common law trademark, it is generally held that first names, last names, and the combination of the two are not protected until they acquire secondary meaning. *Peaceable Planet v. Ty*, 362 F.3d 986, 990 (7th Cir. 2004).

16. *Trademark Manual of Examining Procedure* §1301.02(b).

17. Lilsa M. Thomas, "Creating and Protecting Rights in Personal Names," *INTA Bulletin* (July 15, 2011), http://www.inta.org/INTABulletin/Pages/CreatingandProtec tingRightsinPersonalNames.aspx.

18. See *Tana v. Dantanna's*, 611 F.3d 767, 774 (11th Cir. 2010); *Perini Corp. v. Perini Construction*, 915 F.2d 121, 125 (4th Cir. 1990); 815 *Tonawanda St. Corp. v. Fay's Drug Co.*, 842 F.2d 643, 648 (2d Cir. 1988).

19. *Sara Lee v. Kayser-Roth*, 81 F.3d 455, 464–65 (4th Cir. 1996).

20. *Xtreme*, 576 F.3d at 233.

21. *Custom Vehicles*, 476 F.3d at 483.

22. *Playtex v. Georgia-Pacific*, 390 F.3d 158, 163–64 (2d Cir. 2004).

23. Steve Rivkin, "How Did Apple Computers Get Its Brand Name," *Branding Strategy Insider*, November 17, 2011, https://www.brandingstrategyinsider.com /2011/11/how-did-apple-computer-get-its-brand-name.html#.XQKg9nspDq1 (internal quotation marks omitted).

24. "Fanciful Trademark," *Upcounsel*, https://www.upcounsel.com/fanciful -trademark.

25. *Trademark Manual of Examining Procedure* §1204.

26. *Matal v. Tam*, 137 S. Ct. 1744, 1753–54 (2017).

27. Ibid., 1764 (internal quotation marks omitted).

28. Ian Shapira, "A Brief History of the Word 'Redskin' and How It Became a Source of Controversy," *Washington Post*, May 19, 2016, https://www.washingtonpost .com/local/a-brief-history-of-the-word-redskin-and-how-it-became-a-source-of -controversy/2016/05/19/062cd618-187f-11e6-9e16-2e5a123aac62_story.html.

29. Ian Shapira and Ann E. Marimow, "Washington Redskins Win Trademark Fight over the Team's Name," *Washington Post*, June 29, 2017, https://www .washingtonpost.com/local/public-safety/2017/06/29/a26f52f0-5cf6-11e7-9fc6-c7 ef4bc58d13_story.html.

30. *Matal*, 137 S. Ct. at 1764. Only eight members of the court took part in the decision. While the ruling was unanimous, the court divided evenly between two opinions and could not agree on the overall framework for deciding the case.

31. Ibid., 1763 (internal quotation marks omitted).

32 ."Examination Guidance for Section 2(a)'s Disparagement Provision after *Matal v. Tam* and Examination for Compliance with Section 2(a)'s Scandalousness Provision while Constitutionality Remains in Question," June 26, 2017, https://www .uspto.gov/sites/default/files/documents/Exam guide 01–17.docx, *United States Patent and Trademark Office: Trademark Examination Guides*, https://www.uspto .gov/trademark/guides-and-manuals/trademark-examination-guides.

33. See Gillian R. Brassill, Giulia McDonnell Nieto del Rio, Billy Witz, and David Waldstein, "In Campaign Against Racism, Team Names Get New Scrutiny," *New York Times*, July 12, 2020, https://www.nytimes.com/2020/07/10/sports/football /washington-redskins-name-change-mascots.html.

34. Andrew Chung, "F-words and T-shirts: U.S. Supreme Court Weighs Foul Language Trademarks," *Reuters*, April 12, 2019, https://www.reuters.com/article /us-usa-court-profanity-idUSKCN1RO18W.

35. *Iancu v. Brunetti*, 139 S. Ct. 2294, 2298 (2019) (internal quotation marks omitted).

36. Ibid., (internal quotation marks omitted).

37. Ibid., 2300.

38. Ibid., 2299.

39. Ibid., 2308.

40. Anderson Duff, "4 Common Reasons for a Trademark Registration Refusal," *Revision Legal*, June 22, 2017, https://revisionlegal.com/ip/trademark -registration-refusal/.

41. 15 U.S.C. § 1127.

42. "The History of the Coca-Cola Contour Bottle," *The Coca-Cola Company*, https://www.coca-colacompany.com/stories/the-story-of-the-coca-cola-bottle (internal quotation marks omitted).

43. Ibid.

44. The information in this paragraph was taken from *Maker's Mark Distillery v. Diegeo North America*, 679 F.3d 410, 417–19 (6th Cir. 2012).

45. *Christian Louboutin S.A. v. Yves Saint Laurent Am. Holding*, 696 F.3d 206, 227 (2d. Cir. 2012).

46. Ibid., 222.

47. Ibid., 225 (emphasis in original).

48. *Qualitex Co. v. Jacobson Prods. Co.*, 514 U.S. 159, 165 (1995).

49. *Louboutin*, 696 F.3d at 216.

50. *Brunswick Corp. v. British Seagull Ltd.*, 35 F.3d 1527, 1530 (Fed. Cir. 1994).

51. In re *General Mills IP Holdings II, LLC*, Serial No. 86757390 at 19 (TTAB Aug. 22, 2017).

52. Ibid., 21.

53. *Elvis Presley Enterprises v. Capece*, 950 F. Supp. 783, 790 (S.D. Tex. 1996) (quoting Thomas McCarthy, *McCarthy on Trademarks and Unfair Competition*, §2.02 (3d. ed. 1992)).

54. John Hechinger, "Team-Color Bud Cans Leave Colleges Flat," *Wall Street Journal*, August 21, 2009, https://www.wsj.com/articles/SB125081310939148053.

55. See, e.g., *Lamparello v. Falwell*, 420 F.3d 309, 313 (4th Cir. 2005).

56. In re *Shell Oil Co.*, 992 F.2d 1204, 1208 (Fed. Cir. 1993).

57. *Freedom Card v. JP Morgan Chase & Co.*, 432 F.3d 463, 471 (3rd Cir. 2005).

58. Ibid.; In re *Shell*, 992 F.2d at 1209.

59. *Freedom Card*, 432 F.3d at 471.

60. Mark A. Lemley and Mark McKenna, "Irrelevant Confusion," *Stanford Law Review* 62 (2010): 414.

61. *Rearden v. Rearden Commerce*, 683 F.3d 1190, 1209 (9th Cir. 2012).

62. *Kellogg Co. v. Toucan Golf*, 337 F.3d 616, 626 (6th Cir. 2003).

63. *JL Beverages v. Jim Beam*, 318 F. Supp. 3d 1188, 1207 (D. Nev. 2018).

64. *Bell v. Starbucks*, 389 F. Supp. 2d 766, 771, 777 (S.D. Tex. 2005).

65. Ibid., 775.

66. Ibid., 774–75.

67. Ibid., 772.

68. *JL Beverages v. Jim Beam*, 828 F.3d 1098, 1108 (9th Cir. 2016).

69. *JL Beverages*, 318 F. Supp. 3d at 1210.

70. *JL Beverages*, 828 F.3d at 1108.

71. *JL Beverages*, 318 F. Supp. 3d at 1210.

72. *Stone Creek v. Omnia Italian Design*, 875 F.3d 426, 432 (9th Cir. 2017).

73. *Kellogg*, 337 F.3d at 624.

74. *AMF v. Sleekcraft Boats*, 599 F.2d 341, 350 (9th Cir. 1979).

75. *Kellogg*, 337 F.3d at 624–25.

76. Ibid., 625.

77. *Board of Supervisors for Louisiana State University Agriculture and Mechanical College v. Smack Apparel*, 550 F.3d 465, 484 (5th Cir. 2008).

78. The information and quotations in this paragraph were taken from *Xtreme Lashes v. Xtended Beauty,* 576 F.3d 221, 230 (5th Cir. 2009).

79. *Smith v. Wal-Mart Stores*, 537 F. Supp. 2d 1302, 1320–21 (N.D. Ga. 2008).

80. Ibid., 1334.

81. Ibid., 1322.

82. *Bell v. Starbucks*, 389 F. Supp. 2d 766, 772 (S.D. Tex. 2005).

83. Ibid., 776.

84. *Glow Industries v. Lopez*, 252 F. Supp. 2d 962, 1000 (C.D. Calif. 2002).

85. *Frehling Enterprises v. International Select Group*, 192 F.3d 1330, 1339 (11th Cir. 1999).

86. *Xtreme*, 576 F.3d at 229.

87. *Bell,* 389 F. Supp. 2d at 771.

88. *Kellogg*, 337 F.3d at 627.

89. *Xtreme*, 576 F.3d at 231.

90. *Glow Industries*, 252 F. Supp. 2d at 1002.

91. *Bell*, 389 F. Supp. 2d at 771.

92. *Anheuser-Busch v. Balducci*, 28 F.3d 769, 774 (8th Cir. 1994).

93. Ibid., 774–75.

94. *JL Beverages v. Jim Beam*, 318 F. Supp. 3d 1188, 1210 (D. Nev. 2018) (internal quotation marks omitted).

95. *Daddy's Junky Music Stores v. Big Daddy's Family Music Ctr.*, 109 F.3d 275, 287 (6th Cir. 1997).

96. "Apple Inc. and The Beatles' Apple Corps Ltd. Enter into New Agreement," *Apple Newsroom*, February 5, 2007, http://www.apple.com/pr/library/2007/02/05apple .html.

97. *ETW Corp. v. Jireh Publishing*, 332 F.3d 915, 925 (6th Cir. 2003).

98. *White v. Samsung*, 971 F.2d 1395, 1396 (9th Cir. 1992).

99. The information pertaining to the court's likelihood of confusion factor analysis in the *White v. Samsung* case was taken from *White*, 971 F.2d at 1400–01.

100. *Cliffs Notes v. Bantam Doubleday Dell Publ. Group*, 886 F. 2d 490, 494 (2d. Cir. 1989).

101. Ibid.

102. *White*, 971 F.2d at 1401.

103. *Louis Vuitton Malletier S.A. v. Haute Diggity Dog, LLC*, 507 F.3d 252, 261 (4th Cir. 2007).

104. The information in this paragraph was take from *Malletier*, 507 F.3d at 261–62.

105. Ibid., 258.

106. Ibid., 263.

107. Ibid.

108. *Anheuser-Busch v. VIP Prods.*, 666 F. Supp. 2d 974, 980 (E.D. Mo. 2008).

109. Ibid., 985.

110. Ibid., 980.

111. Ibid., 984.

112. Susan Progoff & Alexandra J. Roberts, "The Art of Parody," *New York Law Journal*, January 20, 2009.

113. *ETW Corp. v. Jireh Publishing*, 332 F.3d 915, 924 (6th Cir. 2003).

114. *University of Alabama Board of Trustees v. New Life Art*, 677 F. Supp. 2d 1238, 1244 (N.D. Ala. 2009).

115. Ibid., 1249.

116. Ibid., 1247.

117. Ibid., 1249.

118. *ETW Corp.*, 332 F.3d at 928.

119. *University of Alabama Board of Trustees v. New Life Art*, 683 F.3d 1266, 1277 (11th Cir. 2012) (quoting *Rogers v. Grimaldi*, 875 F.2d 994, 997–98 (2d. Cir. 1989)). (internal quotation marks omitted).

120. Ibid., 1278.

121. Ibid. (quoting *ESS Entertainment 2000 v. Rock Star Videos*, 547 F.3d 1095, 1099 (9th Cir. 2008)) (internal quotation marks omitted).

122. The information in this paragraph was take from *Univ. of Ala.*, 683 F.3d at 1278–79.

123. Daniel Grant, "Free Speech vs. Infringement in Suit on Alabama Artwork," *New York Times*, January 30, 2012, https://www.nytimes.com/2012/01/31/sports/ncaafootball/artist-still-fighting-alabama-over-football-paintings.html.

124. See *Bell v. Harley Davidson Motor Co.*, 539 F. Supp. 2d 1249 (S.D. Cal. 2008).

125. The information in this paragraph came from *Kelly-Brown v. Winfrey*, 717 F.3d 295, 300–02 (2d Cir. 2013).

126. *Kelly-Brown*, 717 F.3d at 311.

127. *ESS Entertainment 2000 v. Rock Star Videos*, 547 F.3d 1095, 1098 (9th Cir. 2008).

128. *New Kids on the Block v. News America Publishing*, 971 F.2d 302, 307–08 (9th Cir. 1992).

129. Matthew D. Bunker, "Mired in Confusion: Nominative Fair Use in Trademark Law and Freedom of Expression," *Communication Law & Policy* 20 (Spring 2015): 192.

130. *Mattel v. Walking Mountain Productions*, 353 F.3d 792, 796 (9th Cir. 2003).

131. Ibid.

132. Ibid., 808.

133. Ibid.

134. Ibid., 811.

135. Ibid.

136. Ibid.

137. The information pertaining to the court's nominative fair use analysis was taken from *Mattel*, 353 F.3d at 810–12.

138. Rollin Ransom, "Nominative Fair Use for TMs: An Idea Whose Time Has Gone," *Law360*, June 16, 2015, https://www.sidley.com/-/media/publications/law 360nominative-fair-use-for-tmsan-idea-whose-time-has-gone.pdf.

139. Rebecca Tushnet, "Make Me Walk, Make Me Talk, Do Whatever You Please: Barbie and Exceptions," in *Intellectual Property at the Edge: The Contested Contours of IP* 423 (Rochelle Cooper Dreyfus & Jane C. Ginsburg eds., 2014).

140. *Brother Records v. Jardine*, 318 F.3d 900, 908 n.5 (9th Cir. 2003) (quoting J. Thomas McCarthy, *Trademarks and Unfair Competition* § 11:47 (4th ed. 2001)) (internal quotation marks omitted).

141. Ransom, "Nominative Fair Use."

142. Bill Werde, "Barbie's Manufacturer Is Ordered to Pay $1.8 Million in Legal Fees to Artist," *New York Times*, June 28, 2004, https://www.nytimes.com/2004/06/28 /us/barbie-s-manufacturer-is-ordered-to-pay-1.8-million-in-legal-fees-to-artist.html.

CHAPTER 7

1. Sarah Lindig, "How to Get a Hermès Birkin Bag: It's Not as Easy as Dropping $20,000," *Harper's Bazaar*, August 26, 2018, https://www.harpersbazaar.com.au /fashion/how-to-get-an-hermes-birkin-bag-3326.

2. H.R. Rep. No. 104-374, at 3 (1995), reprinted in 1995 U.S.C.C.A.N. 1029, 1030.

3. Mark A. Lemley, "The Modern Lanham Act and the Death of Common Sense," *Yale Law Journal* 108 (1999): 1698.

4. Frank Schechter, "The Rational Basis of Trademark Protection," *Harvard Law Review* 40 (1927): 831.

5. Ibid., 825.

6. *Vogue Co. v. Thompson-Hudson Co.*, 300 F. 509, 511 (6th Cir. 1924).

7. Schechter, "Rational Basis," 825.

8. *Moseley v. V Secret Catalogue*, 537 U.S. 418, 432–33 (2003).

9. Ibid., 421, n.1.

10. Ibid., 422.

11. Ibid., 433.

12. Ibid., 434.

13. *Coach Services v. Triumph Learning*, 668 F.3d 1356, 1372 (Fed. Cir. 2012).

14. 15 U.S.C. § 1125(c)(2)(A).

15. *Coach Services*, 668 F.3d at 1373.

16. Ibid.

17. *Thane International v. Trek Bicycle Corp.*, 305 F.3d 894, 912 (9th Cir. 2002).

18. *Maker's Mark Distillery v. Diageo North America*, 703 F. Supp. 2d 671, 698–700 (W.D. Ky. 2010).

19. *Coach Services*, 668 F.3d at 1373.

20. See ibid., 1373–76.

21. *Maker's Mark Distillery*, 703 F. Supp. 2d at 699.

22. *Coach Services*, 668 F.3d at 1372–73.

23. *Schutte Bagclosures v. Kwik Lok Corp.* 48 F. Supp 3d 675, 702 (S.D.N.Y. 2014).

24. *Chanel v. Makarczyk*, 110 U.S.P.Q. 2d 2013 (TTAB 2014).

25. The information in this paragraph on establishing fame was taken from Roberta Jacobs-Meadway, "Providing Fame for Trademark Dilution Claims," *Lexis Practice Adviser Journal*, August 25, 2019, https://www.lexisnexis.com/lexis-practice-advisor/the-journal/b/lpa/posts/proving-fame-for-trademark-dilution-claims.

26. 15 U.S.C. § 1125(c)(1).

27. 15 U.S.C. § 1125(c)(2)(B).

28. *New York Yankees Partnership v. IET Products and Services*, 114 USPQ2d 1497, 1506 (TTAB 2015).

29. Ibid.

30. This example was taken from *Hugunin v. Land O' Lakes Tackle Co.*, 815 F.3d 1064, 1067 (7th Cir. 2016).

31. *Starbucks Corp. v. Wolfe's Borough Coffee*, 736 F.3d 198, 207 (2d Cir. 2013).

32. 15 U.S.C. § 1125(c)(2)(B).

33. *Starbucks Corp. v. Wolfe's Borough Coffee*, 559 F. Supp. 2d 472, 477 (S.D.N.Y. 2008).

34. Ibid., 478.

35. Mark A. Finkelstein and Michell Stover, "Recent U.S. Case Law Rejects Requirement That Marks Must Be 'Identical' or 'Substantially Similar,'" *INTA Bulletin*, September 1, 2012, https://www.inta.org/INTABulletin/Pages/TrademarkDilutionRecentUSCaseLawRejectsRequirementThatMarksMustBe%E2%80%9CIdentical%E2%80%9Dor%E2%80%9CSubstantiallySimilar%E2%80%9D.aspx.

36. Sean Melvin, "Case Study of a Coffee War: Using the *Starbucks v. Charbucks* Dispute to Teach Trademark Dilution, Business Ethics, and the Value of Legal Acumen," https://mafiadoc.com/case-study-of-a-coffee-war-using-the-starbucks-v-charbucks-_5a0b8a151723dd009f77a385.html.

37. *Starbucks Corp. v. Wolfe's Borough Coffee*, 588 F.3d 97, 106 (2d Cir. 2009).

38. Ibid., 107.

39. *Starbucks Corp. v. Wolfe's Borough Coffee*, 2011 U.S. Dist. LEXIS 148081, *9 (S.D.N.Y. 2011).

40. *Wolfe's*, 588 F.3d at 109.

41. Ibid., (quoting 15 U.S.C. § 1125(c)(2)(B)(v)) (internal quotation marks omitted).

42. *Wolfe's*, 559 F. Supp. 2d at 478.

43. *Wolfe's*, 588 F.3d at 109.

44. *Starbucks Corp. v. Wolfe's Borough Coffee*, 536 F.3d 198, 208-09 (2d Cir. 2013).

45. See Ibid., 210–11 for information on the survey.

46. See Ibid., 211; *Wolfe's*, 2011 U.S. Dist. LEXIS 148081 at *10.

47. See Ibid., 213; *Wolfe's*, 2011 U.S. Dist. LEXIS 148081 at *15.

48. *Pfizer v. Sachs*, 652 F. Supp. 2d 512, 525 (S.D.N.Y. 2009).

49. *Kraft Foods Holdings v. Helm*, 205 F. Supp. 2d 942, 949 (N.D. Ill. 2002).

50. *V Secret Catalogue v. Moseley*, 605 F.3d 382, 384 (6th Cir. 2010).

51. *Williams-Sonoma v. Friendfinder*, 2007 U.S. Dist. LEXIS 98118, *2 (N.D. Cal. 2007).

52. *Lorillard Tobacco Co. v. Ahmad's Pizza*, 866 F. Supp. 2d 872, 879 (N.D. Ohio 2012).

53. *Hormel Foods Corp. v. Jim Henson Productions*, 73 F.3d 497, 507 (2d Cir. 1996).

54. *Tommy Hilfiger Licensing v. Nature Labs*, 221 F. Supp. 2d 410, 423 (S.D.N.Y. 2002).

55. *Wolfe's*, 588 F.3d at 110.

56. *Starbucks Corp. v. Wolfe's Borough Coffee*, 2005 U.S. Dist. LEXIS 35578, *28 (S.D.N.Y. 2005).

57. *Wolfe's*, 588 F.3d at 110.

58. Ibid.

59. *Wolfe's*, 559 F. Supp. 2d at 480.

60. *Wolfe's*, 588 F.3d at 111.

61. Jennifer Files Beerline, "Note: Anti-Dilution Law, New and Improved: The Trademark Dilution Revision Act of 2006," *Berkley Technology Law Journal* 23 (2008): 530.

62. 15 U.S.C. § 1125(c)(3)(A).

63. 15 U.S.C. § 1125(c)(3).

64. The Fourth Circuit's analysis was taken from *Louis Vuitton Malletier v. Haute Diggity Dog*, 507 F.3d 252, 267–68 (4th Cir. 2007). The quotes can be found on 267.

65. Ibid., 260 (quoting *People for the Ethical Treatment of Animals v. Doughney*, 263 F.3d 359, 366 (4th Cir. 2001)) (internal quotation marks omitted).

66. Ibid.

67. Ibid., 261.

68. *Hershey Co. v. Art Van Furniture*, 2008 U.S. Dist. LEXIS 87509, *41–*42.

CHAPTER 8

1. "The Bud Light kingdom travels to make a corn syrup delivery," 2019 Super Bowl LIII Commercials, https://www.nfl.com/videos/the-bud-light-kingdom-travels -to-make-a-corn-syrup-delivery-403490.

2. See *MillerCoors v. Anheuser-Busch*, 385 F. Supp. 3d 730, 735–39 (W.D. Wisc. 2019).

3. Ibid., 746.

4. 15 U.S.C. § 1125(a)(1)(B).

5. See, e.g., *Clorox Co. Puerto Rico v. Procter & Gamble Commercial Co.*, 228 F.3d 24, 33 n.6 (1st Cir. 2000); *Hot Wax v. Turtle Wax*, 191 F.3d 813, 819 (7th Cir. 1999); *Southland Sod Farms v. Stover Seed Co.*, 108 F.3d 1134, 1139 (9th Cir. 1997).

6. The information in this paragraph came from *Molson Coors Bev. Co. USA v. Anheuser-Busch Cos.*, 947 F.3d 837, 839 (7th Cir. 2020).

7. The background on the case was taken from *Pom Wonderful v. Purely Juice*, 2008 U.S. Dist. LEXIS 55426, *2–*11 (C.D. Cal. 2008).

8. Ibid., *31.

9. The information on the court's analysis of the case was taken from *Pom Wonderful*, 2008 U.S. Dist. LEXIS 55426, at *28–*31.

10. *Pom Wonderful v. Purely Juice*, 362 Fed. Appx. 577, 582 (9th Cir. 2009).

11. *Pom Wonderful*, 2008 U.S. Dist. LEXIS 55426 at *2–*4.

12. *Eli Lilly & Co. v. Arla Foods*, 893 F.3d 375, 383 n.3 (7th Cir. 2018) (noting that at least six Circuit Courts recognize false by necessary implication).

13. Rebecca Tushnet, "Running the Gamut from A to B: Federal Trademark and False Advertising Law," *University of Pennsylvania Law Review* 159 (2011): 1322.

14. *Time Warner Cable v. DIRECTV*, 497 F.3d 144, 158 (2d Cir. 2007).

15. Ibid.

16. The information regarding the Simpson commercial can be found at *Time Warner*, 497 F.3d at 149–50. The court's conclusion was taken from ibid., 154.

17. The information regarding the Shatner commercial can be found at *Time Warner*, 497 F.3d at 150.

18. Ibid., 154.

19. The information regarding the District Court's analysis can be found at *Time Warner*, 497 F.3d at 154.

20. The Second Circuit's analysis can be found at *Time Warner*, 497 F.3d at 158.

21. *United Industries Corp. v. Clorox Co.*, 140 F.3d 1175, 1182 (8th Cir. 1998).

22. *William H. Morris v. Group W*, 66 F.3d 255, 257 (9th Cir. 1995).

23. *United Industries*, 140 F.3d at 1180.

24. *Time Warner*, 497 F.3d at 153 (quoting *Schering Corp. v. Pfizer*, 189 F.3d 218, 229 (2d Cir. 1999)) (internal quotation marks omitted).

25. *Clorox Co. Puerto Rico v. Procter & Gamble Commercial Co.*, 228 F.3d 24, 36 (1st Cir. 2000).

26. Ibid., 33.

27. *Southland Sod Farms*, 108 F.3d at 1140.

28. *Prudential Insurance Co. v. Gibraltar Financial Corp.*, 694 F.2d 1150, 1156 (9th Cir. 1982).

29. *CKE Restaurant v. Jack in the Box*, 494 F. Supp. 2d 1139, 1141 (C.D. Cal. 2007).

30. The information regarding the commercials can be found at *CKE Restaurant*, 494 F. Supp. 2d at 1142.

31. "Burger Wars: Jack in the Box Sued over Ad," *Associated Press*, May 29, 2007, http://www.nbcnews.com/id/18894390/ns/business-us_business/t/burger-wars-jack-box-sued-over-ad/#.XhUWKutOnfY.

32. *CKE Restaurant*, 494 F. Supp. 2d at 1144.

33. Ibid.

34. *Johnson & Johnson-Merck Consumer Pharmaceuticals Co. v. Rhone-Poulenc Rorer Pharmaceuticals*, 19 F.3d 125, 134 n.14 (3d Cir. 1994).

35. *Novartis Consumer Health v. Johnson & Johnson-Merck Consumer Pharmaceuticals Co.*, 129 F. Supp. 2d 351, 367 (D. N.J. 2000).

36. Ibid. (quoting *Coca-Cola Co. v. Tropicana Prods.*, 538 F. Supp. 1091, 1096 (S.D.N.Y. 1982) (rev'd 690 F.2d 312 (2d Cir. 1982)).

37. The court's analysis of the survey can be found at *CKE Restaurant*, 494 F. Supp. 2d at 1144–45.

38. Ibid., 1145.

39. Richard J. Leighton, "Materiality and Puffing in Lanham Act False Advertising Cases: The Proofs, Presumptions, and Pretexts," *Trademark Reporter* 94 (2004): 587.

40. Ibid., 594–95.

41. Ibid., 595.

42. Ibid., 596–97.

43. Ibid., 597.

44. 15 U.S.C. § 1125(a)(1) (emphasis added).

45. See, e.g., *Balance Dynamics Corp. v. Schmitt Industries*, 204 F.3d 683, 690 (6th Cir. 2000); *Pizza Hut v. Papa John's International*, 227 F.3d 489, 497 (5th Cir. 2000).

46. *McNeil-PPC v. Pfizer*, 351 F. Supp. 2d 226, 247 (S.D.N.Y. 2005) (quoting *Johnson & Johnson v. Carter-Wallace*, 631 F.2d 186, 190 (2d Cir. 1980) (internal punctuation marks omitted)).

47. Ibid.

48. *Merck Eprova AG v. Gnosis S.p.A*, 760 F.3d 247, 259 (2d Cir 2014) (quoting *McNeilab v. American Home Products Corp.*, 848 F.2d 34, 38 (1988)) (emphasis added by 2d Cir.). In comparison, the Third Circuit held that there is no presumption of injury. *Ferring Pharmaceuticals v. Watson Pharmaceuticals*, 765 F.3d 205, 216 (3d 2014); and that plaintiffs must demonstrate that they are "likely to suffer irreparable harm if an injunction is not granted." Ibid., 217.

49. *Castrol v. Pennzoil Co.*, 987 F.2d 939, 949 (3d. Cir.1993).

50. 15 U.S.C. § 1125(a)(1).

51. *Pizza Hut v. Papa John's International*, 227 F.3d 489, 496 (5th Cir. 2000).

52. Ibid., 497.

53. *American Italian Pasta Co. v. New World Pasta Co.*, 371 F. 3d 387, 392 (8th Cir. 2004).

54. In re *Boston Beer Co.*, 198 F.3d 1370, 1372 (Fed. Cir. 1999).

55. Abhishek K. Gurnani and Ashish R. Talati, "The World's Most Trusted Article on Puffery: Non-Actionable Puffery or Misleading?" *Update*, November/December 2008, https://amintalati.com/wp-content/uploads/2016/09/2012_aba_panel3_the _worlds_most_trusted-authcheckdam.pdf.

56. *P&G Co. v. Kimberly-Clark, Corp.*, 569 F. Supp. 2d 796, 800 (E.D. Wis. 2008) (finding "natural fit" as a descriptor for diapers was based solely on consumer preference and thus could not be proven true or false).

57. *Saltzman v. Pella Corp.*, 2007 U.S. Dist. LEXIS 19650, *11–*12 (N.D. Ill. 2007) (finding that the defendant's reference to its window products as "durable," "manufactured to high quality standards," and "maintenance free" was mere puffery).

58. The court's analysis was taken from *Pizza Hut*, 227 F.3d at 498–99. The direct quotes can be found at ibid., 499.

59. The information in this paragraph was taken from *Pizza Hut*, 227 F.3d at 493.

60. See ibid., 501 for the court's conclusion.

CHAPTER 9

1. Floyd Abrams, *The Soul of the First Amendment* (New Haven, CT: Yale University Press, 2017), 53.

2. *New York Times v. Sullivan*, 376 U.S. 254, 257 (1964).

3. Anthony Lewis, *Make No Law* (New York: Random House, 1991), 13.

4. Robert D. Sack, "Book of the Times: New York Times v. Sullivan: A First Amendment Battle," *New York Times*, September 23, 1991, https://www.nytimes .com/1991/09/23/archives/books-of-the-times-times-v-sullivan-a-first-amendment -battle.html?searchResultPosition=1.

5. Lewis, *Make No Law*, 36.

6. Bruck Weber, "M. Roland Nachman, Lawyer in Times v. Sullivan Libel Case, Dies at 91," *New York Times*, December 4, 2015, https://www.nytimes.com /2015/12/05/us/m-roland-nachman-lawyer-in-times-v-sullivan-libel-case-dies-at-91 .html (internal quotation marks omitted).

7. The account of the trial was taken from Lewis, *Make No Law*, 28–29, 32–33.

8. The court's analysis was taken from *New York Times v. Sullivan*, 376 U.S. 254, 271–73 (1964).

9. *Sullivan*, 376 U.S. at 287.

10. *Clark v. Viacom International*, 617 Fed. Appx. 495, 501 (6th Cir. 2015).

11. Ibid.

12. *Martin v. Daily News L.P.*, 121 A.D.3d 90, 103 (N.Y. 2014).

13. *Haefner v. New York Media*, 82 A.D.3d 481, 482 (N.Y. 2011) (citing *Firth v State of New York*, 98 N.Y.2d 365, 371–72 (2002)).

14. Adeline A. Allen, "Twibel Retweeted: Twitter Libel and the Single Publication Rules," 15 J. High Tech. L. 63, 87 (2014).

15. *Yeager v. Bowlin*, 693 F.3d 1076, 1082 (9th Cir. 2012).

16. Ibid.

17. *Cianci v. New Times Publishing Co.*, 639 F.2d 54, 60–61 (2d Cir. 1980).

18. 47 U.S.C. § 230(c)(1).

19. 47 U.S.C. § 230(f)(3).

20. See, e.g., "Republication in the Internet Age," *Reporters Committee for Freedom of the Press*, https://www.rcfp.org/journals/news-media-and-law-summer-2014 /republication-internet-age/.

21. Hal Eisner, "People Online Twist the Real Story behind Photo of Woman Yelling at Boy," *Fox 11*, June 29, 2018, https://www.foxla.com/news/people -online-twist-the-real-story-behind-photo-of-woman-yelling-at-boy.

22. The case facts were taken from *La Liberte v. Reid*, 966 F.3d 79, 84–85 (2d. Cir. 2020).

23. The court's Section 230 analysis was taken from *La Liberte*, 966 F.3d at 89–90.

24. *McIntyre v. Ohio Elections Comm'n*, 514 U.S. 334, 342 (1995).

25. Adjustments may be made for public figures who are required to establish actual malice given that this standard is very difficult to show without the identity of the defendant. See *Doe v. Cahill*, 884 A.2d 451, 464 (Del. 2005).

26. The information on establishing a valid claim was taken from *Doe v. Cahill*, 884 A.2d 451, 463–64 (Del. 2005).

27. *Dendrite v. Doe*, 342 N.J. Super. 134, 141 (N.J. Super. Ct. App. Div. 2001).

28. *Cahill*, 884 A.2d at 461.

29. *Independent Newspapers v. Brodie*, 966 A.2d 432, 454 (Md. 2009); *Dendrite v. Doe*, 342 N.J. Super. 134, 142 (N.J. Super. Ct. App. Div. 2001).

30. In re *Anonymous Online Speakers*, 661 F.3d 1168, 1177 (9th Cir. 2011).

31. *Solers v. Doe*, 977 A.2d 941, 956 (D.C. 2009); *Cahill*, 884 A.2d at 461.

32. The information on the Cohen case was taken from *Matter of Cohen v. Google*, 25 Misc. 3d 945, 946–47, 950 (N.Y. Sup. Ct. 2009).

33. Dan Amira, "The Two Sides of Accused Model-Skank Liskula Cohen," *Intelligencer*, August 21, 2009, https://nymag.com/intelligencer/2009/08/the_two _sides_of_accused_model.html.

34. *Elias v. Rolling Stone*, 872 F.3d 97, 108 (2d Cir. 2017).

35. The case facts were taken from *Elias*, 872 F.3d at 102, 105-06.

36. Ibid., 107.

37. Ibid., 109.

38. Ibid., 110.

39. *Greene v. Paramount Pictures Corp.*, 138 F. Supp. 3d 226, 228–29 (E.D.N.Y. 2015).

40. Ibid., 230, 234.

41. Ibid., 229.

42. *Greene v. Paramount Pictures Corp.*, 340 F. Supp. 3d 161, 166 (E.D.N.Y. 2018).

43. Complaint and Jury Trial Demanded at 5-6, *Greene v. Paramount Pictures Corp.*, Case 2:14-cv-01044 (February 18, 2014).

44. *Greene*, 138 F. Supp. 3d at 229.

45. Ibid. (internal quotation marks omitted).

46. Ibid., 235.

47. See *Tamkin v. CBS Broadcasting*, 193 Cal. App. 4th 133, 147 (2011).

48. *Greene*, 138 F. Supp. 3d at 235 (citing *Springer v. Viking Press*, 90 A.D. 2d 315, 319 (N.Y. Sup. Ct. 1982)).

49. *Tamkin*, 193 Cal. App. 4th at 147 (citing *Smith v. Stewart*, 291 Ga. App. 86, 87–88 (2008)).

50. *Smith v. Stewart*, 291 Ga. App. 86, 92 (2008).

51. Ibid., 93.

52. *Greene v. Paramount Pictures Corp.*, 340 F. Supp. 3d 161, 166 (E.D.N.Y. 2018).

53. *Greene*, 138 F. Supp. 3d at 235.

54. Ibid.

55. *Greene*, 340 F. Supp. 3d at 171, n.6.

56. Information regarding the disclaimer was taken from *Greene*, 340 F. Supp. 3d at 172.

57. *Feriauto v. Hamsher*, 74 Cal. App. 4th 1394, 1404 (1999).

58. *Dilworth v. Dudley*, 75 F.3d 307, 310 (7th Cir. 1996).

59. *Feriauto*, 74 Cal. App. 4th at 1404 (citing *Milkovich v. Lorain Journal Co.*, 497 U.S. 1, 20 (1990)).

60. The case facts were taken from *Clifford v. Trump*, 339 F. Supp. 3d 915, 919 (C.D. Cal. 2018).

61. The information regarding Clifford's statement and the court's analysis was taken from *Clifford*, 339 F. Supp 3d at 926–27.

62. *McKee v. Laurion*, 825 N.W.2d 725, 733 (2013).

63. *Mathias v. Carpenter*, 402 Pa. Super. 358, 363 (1991).

64. Ibid.

65. *Ollman v. Evans*, 750 F.2d 970, 978–79 (D.C. Cir. 1984).

66. See ibid., 979.

67. See *Milkovich v. Lorain Journal Co.*, 497 U.S. 1, 19 (1991).

68. See ibid., 979–84 for an extended discussion of the four factors.

69. The case facts were taken from *Boulger v. Woods*, 917 F.3d 471, 474–75 (6th Cir. 2019).

70. Woods's argument and the court's analysis was taken from *Boulger*, 917 F.3d at 480, 482.

71. Ibid., 483.

72. *Nolan v. State of New York*, 158 A.D. 3d 186, 197 (1st Dept. N.Y. 2018).

73. Katie Moisse, "Allergic Girl Who Died At School Got Peanut From Another Child," *ABC News*, January 11, 2012, https://abcnews.go.com/Health/AllergiesFood/allergic-girl-died-school-peanut-child/story?id=15341841

74. The case facts were taken from *Pendleton v. Newsom*, 290 Va. 162, 166–70 (Va. 2015).

75. Ibid., 172.

76. The court's analysis was taken from *Pendleton*, 290 Va. at 173.

77. *Snyder v. Phelps*, 562 U.S. 443, 452–53 (2011).

78. *Philadelphia Newspapers v. Hepps*, 475 U.S. 767, 777 (1986).

79. *PETA v. Berosini*, 111 Nev. 615, 627–28 (1995).

80. *Lamb v. Rizzo*, 391 F.3d 1133, 1137–38 (10th Cir. 2004).

81. Ibid., 1137.

82. See David E. McCraw, *Truth in Our Times: Inside the Fight for Press Freedom in the Age of Alternative Facts* (New York: All Point Books, 2019), 258–62, 267.

83. See, e.g., McCraw, *Truth in Our Times*, 15–16.

84. See, e.g., Johnathan Peters, "'I Also Consider Myself a First Amendment Lawyer,'" *Virginia Sports and Entertainment Law Journal* 18 (2019): 122–23.

85. *Harte-Hanks v. Connaughton*, 491 U.S. 657, 666 (1989).

86. Ibid., 688.

87. Ibid.

88. *Biro v. Condé Nast*, 807 F.3d 541, 546 (2d. Cir. 2015).

89. *Eramo v. Rolling Stone*, 209 F. Supp. 3d 862, 871–72 (W.D. Va. 2016).

90. *Memphis Publishing v. Nichols*, 569 S.W. 2d 412, 418 (1978).

91. *Rosenblatt v. Baer*, 383 U.S. 75, 85 (1966).

92. *Eramo v. Rolling Stone*, 209 F. Supp. 3d at 869.

93. Ibid.

94. Complaint, *Eramo v. Rolling Stone*, No. CL15-210 (Va. Cir. Ct. City of Charlottesville, May 12, 2015) [hereinafter Eramo Complaint], https://www.court listener.com/recap/gov.uscourts.vawd.98554.14.1.pdf.

95. *Eramo*, 209 F. Supp. 3d at 869–71.

96. Ibid., 872–74.

97 See, e.g., T. Rees Shapiro, "Key Elements of Rolling Stone's U-Va. Gang Rape Allegations in Doubt," *Washington Post*, December 5, 2014, https://www.washingtonpost.com/local/education/u-va-fraternity-to-rebut-claims-of-gang-rape-in-rolling-stone/2014/12/05/5fa5f7d2-7c91-11e4-84d4-7c896b90abdc_story.html?itid=lk_inline_manual_5.

98. *Eramo*, 209 F. Supp. 3d at 874–75.

99. *Eramo v. Rolling Stone*, 2016 U.S. Dist. LEXIS 142185, *5 (W.D. Va. 2016).

100. Sheila Coronel et. al, "*Rolling Stone* and UVA: The Columbia Graduate School of Journalism: An Anatomy of a Journalistic Failure," *Rolling Stone*, April 5, 2015, https://www.rollingstone.com/culture/culture-news/rolling-stone-and-uva-the-columbia-university-graduate-school-of-journalism-report-44930/.

101. Ibid.; Sheila Coronel et. al, "How Columbia Journalism School Conducted this Investigation," *Columbia Journalism Review*, April 5, 2015, https://www.cjr.org/investigation/columbia_journalism_school_rolling_stone.php.

102. Coronel et al., "How Columbia Journalism School Conducted."

103. Coronel et al., "*Rolling Stone* and UVA."

104. Ibid.

105. Eramo Complaint.

106. Verdict, *Eramo v. Rolling Stone*, No. 3:15-CV-00023 (W.D. Va. Nov. 4, 2016) https://online.wsj.com/public/resources/documents/2016_1104_rollingstone_verdict.pdf.

107. Matthew Haag, "Rolling Stone Settles Lawsuit over Debunked Campus Rape Article," *New York Times*, April 11, 2017, https://www.nytimes.com/2017/04/11/business/media/rolling-stone-university-virginia-rape-story-settlement.html.

108. Bill Wyman, "5 Takeaways from the *Rolling Stone* Defamation Verdict," *Columbia Journalism Review*, November 29, 2016, https://www.cjr.org/analysis/rolling_stone_verdict_defamation_case.php.

109. See, e.g., Jeffrey Abramson, "Full Court Press: Drawing in Media Defenses for Libel and Privacy Cases," *Oregon Law Review* 96 (2017): 34; Kimberly Chow, "The Clash of Law and Ethics," *The News Media and the Law* (Spring 2015), https://www.rcfp.org/wp-content/uploads/2019/01/Spring_2015.pdf; Clay Calvert, "Media Mea Culpas and Journalistic Transparency: When News Outlets Publicly Investigate Their Reportage," paper presented at the annual conference for the Association of Education in Journalism and Mass Communication, Toronto, Canada, August 7–10, 2019.

110. *Shulman v. Group W. Productions*, 18 Cal. 4th 200, 211 (1998).

111. Ibid.

112. *PETA v. Berosini*, 111 Nev. 615 (1995).

113. *Shulman*, 18 Cal. 4th at 234.

114. Ibid., 237–38.

115. Restat. 2d of Torts, § 652D com. h.

116. *Catsouras v. Department of California Highway Patrol*, 181 Cal. App. 4th 856 (2010).

117. *Four Navy Seals & Jane Doe v. AP*, 413 F. Supp. 2d 1136 (2005).

118. *Catsouras*, 181 Cal. App. 4th at 905–06.

119. *Shulman*, 18 Cal. 4th at 229.

120. Ibid., 229–30.

Bibliography

Abrams, Floyd. *The Soul of the First Amendment*. New Haven: Yale University Press, 2017.

Abramson, Jeffrey. "Full Court Press: Drawing in Media Defenses for Libel and Privacy Cases." *Oregon Law Review* 96 (2017): 19–55.

ACLU. "ACLU of Maine Sues LePage Over Facebook Censorship." Aug. 8, 2017. https://www.aclu.org/news/aclu-maine-sues-lepage-over-facebook-censorship.

Allen, Adeline A. "Twibel Retweeted: Twitter Libel and the Single Publication Rules." *Journal of High Technology Law* 15 (2014): 63–96.

Amira, Dan. "The Two Sides of Accused Model-Skank Liskula Cohen." *Intelligencer*, Aug. 21, 2009. https://nymag.com/intelligencer/2009/08/the_two_sides_of_accused_model.html.

Apple Newsroom. "Apple Inc. and The Beatles' Apple Corps Ltd. Enter into New Agreement." February 5, 2007. http://www.apple.com/pr/library/2007/02/05apple.html.

Beerline, Jennifer Files. "Note: Anti-Dilution Law, New and Improved: The Trademark Dilution Revision Act of 2006." *Berkley Technology Law Journal* 23 (2008): 511–35.

Brassill, Gillian R., Giulia McDonnell Nieto del Rio, Billy Witz, and David Waldstein. "In Campaign Against Racism, Team Names Get New Scrutiny." *New York Times* (July 12, 2020). https://www.nytimes.com/2020/07/10/sports/football/washington-redskins-name-change-mascots.html.

Brenner, Lee S. and Allison S. Rohrer. "The De Minimis Doctrine: How Much Copying is Too Much?" *Communication Lawyer*, 24 (2006): 9–13.

Bunker, Matthew D. "Mired in Confusion: Nominative Fair Use in Trademark Law and Freedom of Expression." *Communication Law & Policy* 20 (spring 2015): 191–212.

Business Wire. "PRSA 'Devastated' that Supreme Court Fails to Clarify 'Free Speech' in Nike Case." June 26, 2003. https://www.businesswire.com/news/home/20030626005840/en/PRSA-Devastated-Supreme-Court-Fails-Clarify-Free.

Calvert, Clay. "Media Mea Culpas and Journalistic Transparency: When News Outlets Publicly Investigate Their Reportage." Paper presented at the annual conference for the Association of Education in Journalism and Mass Communication, Toronto, Canada, August 7–10, 2019.

Carlisle, Stephen. "DMCA 'Takedown' Notices: Why 'Takedown' should Become 'Take Down and Stay Down' and Why It's good for Everyone." *NOVA Southeastern University*, July 23, 2014. http://copyright.nova.edu/dmca-takedown-notices/.

CBS News. "Stalked." *48 Hours*. February 25, 2017. https://www.cbsnews.com/news/stalked-48-hours-investigates-pauley-perrette-fights-to-change-stalking-laws/.

Chokshi, Niraj. "Chris Farley's Family Settles With Bike Maker Over 'Fat Guy' Brand." *New York Times*, June 7, 2018. https://www.nytimes.com/2018/06/07/arts/chris-farley-wisconsin-bicycle-fat-guy.html?action=click&module=In%20Other%20News&pgtype=Homepage&action=click&module=Latest&pgtype=Homepage&login=email&auth=login-email.

Chow, Kimberly. "The Clash of Law and Ethics." *The News Media & the Law*, Spring 2015. https://www.rcfp.org/wp-content/uploads/2019/01/Spring_2015.pd.

Chung, Andrew. "F-words and T-shirts: U.S. Supreme Court weighs foul language trademarks." *Reuters* (Apr. 12, 2019). https://www.reuters.com/article/us-usa-court-profanity-idUSKCN1RO18W.

Coca-Cola Company. "The History of the Coca-Cola Contour Bottle." https://www.coca-colacompany.com/stories/the-story-of-the-coca-cola-bottle.

Coronel, Sheila, Steve Coll and Derek Kravitz. "How Columbia Journalism School conducted this investigation." *Columbia Journalism Review*, April 5, 2015. https://www.cjr.org/investigation/columbia_journalism_school_rolling_stone.php.

Coronel, Sheila, Steve Coll and Derek Kravitz. "Rolling Stone and UVA: The Columbia Graduate School of Journalism: An anatomy of a journalistic failure." *Rolling Stone*, April 5, 2015. https://www.rollingstone.com/culture/culture-news/rolling-stone-and-uva-the-columbia-university-graduate-school-of-journalism-report-44930/

Denniston, Lyle. "Useful or creative: A look at design protection." *SCOTUSblog*, May 2, 2016. http://www.scotusblog.com/2016/05/useful-or-creative-a-look-at-design-protection/.

Dogan, Stacey L. "Haelan Laboratories v. Topps Chewing Gum: Publicity as a Legal Right." In *Intellectual Property at the Edge: The Contested Contours of IP*, edited by Rochelle C. Dreyfuss and Jane C. Ginsburg, 17-38. Cambridge University Press, 2014.

Dogan, Stacey. "Stirring the Pot: A Response to Rothman's Right of Publicity." *Columbia Journal of Law and the Arts* 42 (2019): 321–29.

Dongre, Neal S. "The Right to Control the Use of Your Image and Likeness." *Gorman & Williams*, Nov. 22, 2010. https://www.gw-law.com/blog/news-publications.

Dresser, Michael. "Maryland, ACLU settle lawsuit over deleted comments on Gov. Hogan's Facebook page." *Baltimore Sun*, Apr. 2, 2018. http://www.baltimoresun.com/news/maryland/politics/bs-md-aclu-hogan-facebook-20180402-story.html.

Duff, Anderson. "4 Common Reasons for a Trademark Registration Refusal." *Revision Legal*, June 22, 2017. https://revisionlegal.com/ip/trademark-registration-refusal/.

Eisner, Hal. "People online twist the real story behind photo of woman yelling at boy." *Fox 11*, June 29, 2018. https://www.foxla.com/news/people-online-twist -the-real-story-behind-photo-of-woman-yelling-at-boy.

Findlaw. "Protection of Fictional Characters." July 3, 2017. https://corporate.findlaw .com/intellectual-property/protection-of-fictional-characters.html.

Finkelstein, Mark A., and Michell Stover. "Recent U.S. Case Law Rejects Requirement That Marks Must Be 'Identical' or 'Substantially Similar.'" *INTA Bulletin*, September 1, 2012. https://www.inta.org/INTABulletin/Pages/TrademarkDilution RecentUSCaseLawRejectsRequirementThatMarksMustBe%E2%80%9CIdentical %E2%80%9Dor%E2%80%9CSubstantiallySimilar%E2%80%9D.aspx.

Godoy-Dalmau, Gabriel, "Substantial Similarity: Kolus Got it Right," *Michigan Business & Entrepreneurial Law Review* 6 (2017): 241–42.

Grant, Daniel. "Free Speech vs. Infringement in Suit on Alabama Artwork." *New York Times*, January 30, 2012. https://www.nytimes.com/2012/01/31/sports /ncaafootball/artist-still-fighting-alabama-over-football-paintings.html.

Gurfinkel, David M. "The U.S. Trademark Registers: Supplemental vs. Principal." *The International Trademark Association Bulletin*, May 1, 2012. http://www .inta.org/INTABulletin/Pages/TheUSTrademarkRegistersSupplementalvsPrinci pal.aspx.

Gurnani, Abhishek K. and Ashish R. Talati. "The World's Most Trusted Article on Puffery: Non-Actionable Puffery or Misleading?" *Update*, November/December 2008. https://amintalati.com/wp-content/uploads/2016/09/2012_aba_panel3_the _worlds_most_trusted-authcheckdam.pdf.

Haag, Matthew. "Rolling Stone Settles Lawsuit Over Debunked Campus Rape Article." *New York Times*, April 11, 2017. https://www.nytimes.com/2017/04/11 /business/media/rolling-stone-university-virginia-rape-story-settlement.html.

Heath, Edward J., and John M. Tanski. "Drawing the Line Between Descriptive and Suggestive Trademarks." *Commercial & Business Litigation* 12 (Fall 2010). http://www.rc.com/upload/ARTICLE-Drawing-the-Line-Between-Descriptive -and-Suggestive-Trademarks-Heath-Fall-2010.pdf.

Hechinger, John. "Team-Color Bud Cans Leave Colleges Flat." *Wall Street Journal*, August 21, 2009. https://www.wsj.com/articles/SB125081310939148053.

Herrman, John, and Charlie Savage. "Trump's Blocking of Twitter Users Is Unconstitutional, Judge Says." *New York Times*, May 23, 2018. https://www .nytimes.com/2018/05/23/business/media/trump-twitter-block.html.

Inesi, Andrew. "A Theory of De Minimis and a Proposal for Its Application in Copyright." *Berkeley Technology Law Journal* 21 (2006): 945–95.

International Trademark Association. "A Guide to Proper Trademark Use." 2012. http://inta.org/Media/Documents/2012_TMUseMediaInternetPublishing.pdf.

Jacobs-Meadway, Roberta. "Providing Fame for Trademark Dilution Claims." *Lexis Practice Adviser Journal*, August 25, 2019. https://www.lexisnexis .com/lexis-practice-advisor/the-journal/b/lpa/posts/proving-fame-for -trademark-dilution-claims.

Johnson, Eric E. "Disentangling the Right of Publicity." *Northwestern University Law Review* 111 (2017): 891–943.

Kluft, David. "A Copyright Fable: Debunking The 'Seven-Second Rule.'" *Foley Hoag, LLP*, August 30, 2017. http://www.trademarkandcopyrightlawblog .com/2017/08/a-copyright-fable-debunking-the-seven-second-rule/.

Leighton, Richard J. "Materiality and Puffing in Lanham Act False Advertising Cases: The Proofs, Presumptions, and Pretext." *Trademark Reporter* 94 (2004): 585–633.

Lemley, Mark A. "The Modern Lanham Act and the Death of Common Sense." *Yale Law Journal* 108 (1999): 1687–1715.

Lemley, Mark A., and Mark McKenna. "Irrelevant Confusion." *Stanford Law Review* 62 (2010): 413–54.

Leval, Pierre N. "Nimmer Lecture: Fair Use Rescued." *UCLA Law Review* 44 (1997): 1449–65.

Leval, Pierre N. "Toward a Fair Use Standard." *Harvard Law Review* 103 (1990): 1105–36.

Lewis, Anthony. *Make No Law*. New York: Random House, 1991.

Lindig, Sarah. "How to Get a Hermès Birkin Bag: It's not as easy as dropping $20,000." *Harper's Bazaar*, August 26, 2018. https://www.harpersbazaar.com.au /fashion/how-to-get-an-hermes-birkin-bag-3326.

Lippman, Katherine. "The Beginning of the End: Preliminary Results of an Empirical Study of Copyright Substantial Similarity Opinions in the U.S. Circuit Courts." *Michigan State Law Review* (2013): 513–65.

Mann, Ronald. "Justices worry about 'killing knockoffs with copyright." *SCOTUSblog*, November 1, 2016. http://www.scotusblog.com/2016/11/argument -analysis-justices-worry-about-killing-knockoffs-with-copyright/.

McCraw, David E. *Truth in Our Times: Inside the Fight for Press Freedom in the Age of Alternative Facts.* New York: All Point Books, 2019.

Melvin, Sean. "Case Study of a Coffee War: Using the *Starbucks v. Charbucks* Dispute to Teach Trademark Dilution, Business Ethics, and the Value of Legal Acumen." *Journal of Legal Studies and Education* 29 (2012): 27–57.

Mon, Gonzalo E. "Don Henley Settles Right of Publicity Suit with Retailer." *Ad Law Access*, April 17, 2015. https://www.adlawaccess.com/2015/04/articles/don -henley-settles-right-of-publicity-suit-with-retailer/.

Papandrea, Mary-Rose. "Where Intellectual Property and Free Speech Collide." *Boston College Law Review* 50 (2009): 1307–14.

Peters, Johnathan. "'I also consider myself a First Amendment lawyer,'" *Virginia Sports & Entertainment Law Journal* 18 (2019): 109–26.

Progoff, Susan, and Alexandra J. Roberts. "The Art of Parody." *New York Law Journal*, January 20, 2009.

Rabban, David M. "The First Amendment in Its Forgotten Years." *Yale Law Journal* 90 (1981): 514–96.

Ransom, Rollin. "Nominative Fair Use For TMs: An Idea Whose Time Has Gone." *Law360*, June 16, 2015. https://www.sidley.com/-/media/publications/law360 nominative-fair-use-for-tmsan-idea-whose-time-has-gone.pdf.

Reporters Committee for Freedom of the Press. "Republication in the Internet age." https://www.rcfp.org/journals/news-media-and-law-summer-2014/republi cation-internet-age/.

Rivkin, Steve. "How Did Apple Computers Get Its Brand Name." *Branding Strategy Insider*, November 17, 2011. https://www.brandingstrategyinsider.com/2011/11 /how-did-apple-computer-get-its-brand-name.html#.XQKg9nspDq1.

Rothman, Jennifer E. *The Right of Publicity*. Cambridge: Harvard University Press, 2018.

Rothman's Road Map to the Right of Publicity. https://www.rightofpublicityroadmap .com/.

Sack, Robert D. "Book of the Times: New York Times v. Sullivan: A First Amendment Battle." *New York Times*, September 23, 1991. https://www.nytimes .com/1991/09/23/archives/books-of-the-times-times-v-sullivan-a-first -amendment-battle.html?searchResultPosition=1.

Samuelson, Pamela. "A Fresh Look at Tests for Nonliteral Copyright Infringement," *Northwestern University Law Review* 107 (2013): 1821–49.

Sariego, Jose. "High Court won't Take on Lenz DMCA Case—What Now?" *BilzinSumberg*, July 27, 2017. https://www.bilzin.com/we-think-big/insights /publications/2017/07/high-court-wont-take-on-lenz.

Schechter, Frank. "The Rational Basis of Trademark Protection." *Harvard Law Review* 40 (1927): 831.

Schlackman, Steve. "How to Submit a Copyright Takedown Notice." *Art Law Journal*, January 29, 2014. https://alj.artrepreneur.com/submit-takedown-notice/.

Shapira, Ian. "A brief history of the word 'redskin' and how it became a source of controversy." *Washington Post*, May 19, 2016. https://www.washingtonpost .com/local/a-brief-history-of-the-word-redskin-and-how-it-became-a-source-of -controversy/2016/05/19/062cd618-187f-11e6-9e16-2e5a123aac62_story.html.

Shapira, Ian., and Ann E. Marimow. "Washington Redskins win trademark fight over the team's name." *Washington Post*, June 29, 2017. https://www.washingtonpost .com/local/public-safety/2017/06/29/a26f52f0-5cf6-11e7-9fc6-c7ef4bc58d13 _story.html.

Shapiro, T. Rees. "Key elements of Rolling Stone's U-Va. Gang rape allegations in doubt." *Washington Post*, December 5, 2014. https://www.washingtonpost .com/local/education/u-va-fraternity-to-rebut-claims-of-gang-rape-in -rolling-stone/2014/12/05/5fa5f7d2-7c91-11e4-84d4-7c896b90abdc_story .html?itid=lk_inline_manual_5.

Simmons, Joshua L., and Miranda D. Means. "Split Personality: Constructing a Coherent Right of Publicity Statute." *Landside*, May 18, 2018. https://www .americanbar.org/groups/intellectual_property_law/publications/land slide/2017-18/may-june/split-personality/.

Sloan, Jason E. "An Overview of the Elements of a Copyright Infringement Cause of Action—Part II: Improper Appropriation." *American Bar Association*, August 27, 2013. https://www.americanbar.org/groups/young_lawyers/publications /the_101_201_practice_series/part_2_elements_of_a_copyright/.

Thomas, Lilsa M. "Creating and Protecting Rights in Personal Names." *INTA Bulletin* (July 15, 2011). http://www.inta.org/INTABulletin/Pages/CreatingandProtecting RightsinPersonalNames.aspx.

Treleven, Ed. "Chris Farley's family and Trek Bicycle settle lawsuit over Farley name." *Wisconsin State Journal*, June 7, 2018. https://madison.com/wsj/news/local/courts /chris-farley-s-family-and-trek-bicycle-settle-lawsuit-over/article_7ab33619-7627 -5090-a2c2-1b4cfef22d95.html.

Tushnet, Rebecca. "Make Me Walk, Make Me Talk, Do Whatever You Please: Barbie and Exceptions." In *Intellectual Property at the Edge: The Contested Contours of IP,* edited by Rochelle C. Dreyfuss and Jane C. Ginsburg, 405–440. Cambridge University Press, 2014.

Tushnet, Rebecca. "Running the Gamut from A to B: Federal Trademark and False Advertising Law." *University of Pennsylvania Law Review* 159 (2011): 1305–84.

U.S. Copyright Office. "Compendium of U.S. Copyright Office Practices." 2017. https://www.copyright.gov/comp3/docs/compendium.pdf.

U.S. Copyright Office. "Works Made for Hire." https://www.copyright.gov/circs /circ09.pdf.

U.S. Copyright Office. "Works Not Protected by Copyright." https://www.copyright. gov/circs/circ33.pdf.

United States Patent and Trademark Office. "Trademark Examination Guides." https:// www.uspto.gov/trademark/guides-and-manuals/trademark-examination-guides.

United States Patent and Trademark Office. "Trademark Manual of Examining Procedure." October 2018. https://tmep.uspto.gov/RDMS/TMEP/current.

Upcounsel. "Fanciful Trademark." https://www.upcounsel.com/fanciful-trademark.

Upcounsel. "Generic Trademark: Everything You Need to Know." https://www .upcounsel.com/generic-trademark.

Vick, Kevin L., and Jean-Paul Jassy. "Why a Federal Right of Publicity Statute is Necessary." *Communication Lawyer* 28 (August 2011): 14–19.

Volokh, Eugene. "Freedom of Speech and the Right of Publicity." *Houston Law Review* 40 (2003): 903–30.

Weber, Bruck. "M. Roland Nachman, Lawyer in Times v. Sullivan Libel Case, Dies at 91." *New York Times*, December 4, 2015. https://www.nytimes.com/2015/12/05 /us/m-roland-nachman-lawyer-in-times-v-sullivan-libel-case-dies-at-91.html

Werde, Bill. "Barbie's Manufacturer Is Ordered to Pay $1.8 Million in Legal Fees to Artist." *New York Times*, June 28, 2004. https://www.nytimes.com/2004/06/28/us /barbie-s-manufacturer-is-ordered-to-pay-1.8-million-in-legal-fees-to-artist.html.

Whitmore, Nancy J. "Facing the Fear: A Free Market Approach for Economic Expression." *Communication Law & Policy* 17 (2012): 21–65.

Wyman, Bill. "5 takeaways from the *Rolling Stone* defamation verdict." *Columbia Journalism Review*, November 29, 2016. https://www.cjr.org/analysis/rolling _stone_verdict_defamation_case.php.

Yen, Alfred C. "Eldred, the First Amendment, and Aggressive Copyright Claims." *Houston Law Review* 40 (2003): 673–95.

Zimmerman, Diane Leenheer. "Money as a Thumb on the Constitutional Scale." *Boston College Law Review* 50 (2009): 1503–24.

Index

About the Author

Nancy J. Whitmore is professor of journalism in the Eugene S. Pulliam School of Journalism and Creative Media at Butler University. She served as director of the school from 2008 to 2016. Her scholarly work focuses largely on First Amendment theory and includes published research on free speech issues and economic expression. Throughout her academic career, she has taught a variety of journalism and public relations courses and has extensive teaching experience in media law.